Deepa Iyer is a national figure in movements for racial and immigrant justice in America. Iyer is a senior fellow at the Center for Social Inclusion. She served as executive director of South Asian Americans Leading Together (SAALT) for a decade. She has also worked as an attorney at the Department of Justice's Civil Rights Division, the Asian Pacific American Legal Resource Center, and the Asian American Justice Center. Iyer was an activist-in-residence and an adjunct professor at the University of Maryland's Asian American Studies program. Iyer has been recognized for her activism by various groups, including the Asian American Legal Defense and Education Fund and Jews for Racial and Economic Justice. She regularly speaks and trains students, educators, and advocates about the issues in *We Too Sing America*.

www.deepaiyer.com

@dviyer

We Too Sing America

We Too Sing America

SOUTH ASIAN, ARAB, MUSLIM, AND SIKH IMMIGRANTS SHAPE OUR MULTIRACIAL FUTURE

Deepa Iyer

THE NEW PRESS

25 YEARS

NEW YORK
LONDON

Requests for permission to reproduce selections from this book
should be mailed to: Permissions Department, The New Press,
120 Wall Street, 31st floor, New York, NY 10005.

Excerpt from "I, Too" from *The Collected Poems of Langston Hughes*
by Langston Hughes, edited by Arnold Rampersad with David Roessel,
Associate Editor, copyright © 1994 by the Estate of Langston Hughes. Used by
permission of Alfred A. Knopf, an imprint of the Knopf Doubleday Publishing
Group, a division of Penguin Random House LLC. All rights reserved.

First published in the United States by The New Press, New York, 2015
This paperback edition published by The New Press, 2017
Distributed by Two Rivers Distribution

ISBN 978-1-62097-273-1 (pbk)
ISBN 978-1-62097-326-4 (e-book)
LIBRARY OF CONGRESS CATALOGING-IN-PUBLICATION DATA

Iyer, Deepa.
We too sing America : South Asian, Arab, Muslim,
and Sikh immigrants shape our multiracial future / Deepa Iyer.
pages   cm
Includes bibliographical references and index.
ISBN 978-1-62097-014-0 (hardback)
1. United States—Race relations—21st century. 2. Immigrants—United
States—Social conditions—21st century. 3. Hate crimes—United States—
History—21st century. 4. Racism—United States—History—
21st century. 5. Xenophobia—United States—History—21st century.
6. Islamophobia—United States—History—21st century.   I. Title.
E184.A1194 2015
305.80097309'05—dc23   2015020036

The New Press publishes books that promote and enrich public discussion and
understanding of the issues vital to our democracy and to a more equitable world.
These books are made possible by the enthusiasm of our readers; the support
of a committed group of donors, large and small; the collaboration of our many
partners in the independent media and the not-for-profit sector; booksellers, who
often hand-sell New Press books; librarians; and above all by our authors.

www.thenewpress.com

Composition by dix!

This book was set in Fairfield LH

Printed in the United States of America

*100 percent of royalties received will be invested
by the author to support leadership building and organizing
in Muslim, Arab, Sikh, and South Asian communities.*

For the next generation of storytellers and community builders

For Amma, my pillar of strength
For Ahilan, my little light
And in memory of Chellam Chandran

Contents

Preface to the Paperback Edition

Dear readers,

When I wrote *We Too Sing America: South Asian, Arab, Muslim, and Sikh Immigrants Shape Our Multiracial Future*, I expected and hoped that it would be a historic documentation of stories and experiences that are often unheard in the United States. I was mistaken. Instead, the book became a companion text to help many understand what was occurring in our nation in the span of a year, from November 2015, when we launched the book, to November 2016, when the presidential elections occurred.

At many of the community conversations and workshops I participated in on the *We Too Sing America* book tour, people raised concerns about the increased hostility and divisiveness that had emerged in the nation during the 2016 political season. Not surprisingly—given the history of policy and rhetoric in the decade and a half since the September 11 attacks described in this book—the communities that bore the brunt of this hatred and bigotry were Muslim or those perceived as Muslim.

In 2015 and 2016, reports of violence, school bullying, and profiling reached unprecedented rates, the likes of which community advocates had not seen since the days and weeks following

September 11, 2001. A few weeks after we marked the fifteen-year anniversary of 9/11, a Pakistani American first grader, Abdul Aziz, stepped off a school bus in Cary, North Carolina, with bruises that he claims were inflicted on him by other classmates who made fun of his name, punched and kicked him, and twisted his arm while saying "Muslim" over and over. This incident came on the heels of another that occurred in Richmond, California. Maan Singh Khalsa, a Sikh American, was driving home from work when two men assaulted him through his open car window. After yelling, "Cut his fucking hair," they allegedly pulled Khalsa's head through the window, cut a fistful of his hair with a knife, and hit him in the face.

These two disturbing events followed a summer of anguish for Muslim, South Asian, Arab, and Sikh communities. Almost every week during the summer of 2016, we heard news of vandalism to places of worship, reports of physical assaults, and stories of passengers being removed from airplanes. In late August, Nazma Khanam, a sixty-year-old Bangladeshi Muslim woman in the New York City community of Jamaica (Queens) was killed—just three weeks after a Bangladeshi imam and his assistant were murdered while walking in their Queens neighborhood after Friday prayers. In the middle of August, a Tulsa, Oklahoma, man with a history of making racial slurs about Arabs killed his neighbor, Khalid Jabara, a Christian Lebanese American.

In October 2016, just three weeks before the election, the Kansas U.S. Attorney's Office announced that three men had been actively conspiring to bomb an apartment complex and mosque in Garden City, Kansas, where 120 Somali Muslim refugees live and worship. The men, who were members of an anti-government, anti-immigrant, anti-Muslim group called the Crusaders, had planned to carry out their attacks on the day after the November election.

Of course, the political rhetoric during the election season contributed to the climate of fear and suspicion in America. President-elect Donald Trump routinely indicated his support for policies that would create a Muslim registration program, ban Muslims from entry, and form a deportation force. After the November 2016 election, communities of color, immigrants, Muslims, and LGBTQ people experienced a backlash. Organizations tracking hate violence and harassment reported an uptick in reported incidents including vandalism of churches and schools with swastikas and phrases such as "Make America White Again." Clearly, white nationalist groups had found an opening to mainstream their agenda through Mr. Trump's campaign and victory.

For many of us, the aftermath of the election felt like a second post-9/11 backlash. We experienced the bitter knowledge that some of the most devastating policies of the Obama administration—the regulatory framework of special registration, addressed in chapter 2, and the surveillance apparatus, addressed in chapter 3—could be further exploited by the incoming administration. We also recognized that the answer to the question "How did this happen?" could be traced back to the relative lack of national public outrage over the past fifteen years in response to state efforts to pass anti-Sharia laws and obstruct mosque construction and media narratives casting Muslims as terrorists.

Despite this alarming turn of events, what remains the same, and what continues to give me hope and solace, is the remarkable persistence of social change movements in America in working to make all of our lives better. In the wake of the November election, activists have been clear about building a resistance movement, one that is grounded in cross-movement solidarity. Many of the activists included in this book continue their struggles for justice and equity, whether through the Black Lives Matter movement, the organizing campaigns for immigrant and refugee rights, or within Muslim, Arab, Sikh, and South Asian communities. It is critical that we refuse to normalize efforts by elected leaders to use racist,

xenophobic, homophobic, and Islamophobic narratives and policies. We must remain centered in the histories of resistance that
our communities have demonstrated—from Ferguson to Standing
Rock.

Reverend Martin Luther King Jr. said at the 1963 March on
Washington that the country was "confronted with the fierce urgency of now" and that "there is such a thing as being too late." I
believe that we are facing a similar moment of urgency now. We
must all commit to being disruptors and bridge builders. There is
no time to waste.

Deepa Iyer

November 2016

Preface: My Point of Entry

At the age of twelve, I moved with my parents and brother to Louisville, Kentucky, from Kerala, India. Growing up in the South included periods of isolation and confusion during which I became keenly aware of what it meant to be different and how it felt not to belong to either side of the Black or White racial line. When I went to college, also in the South, I took every opportunity to celebrate my cultural background and to press for diversity efforts on campus. Still, I linked race mainly with notions of multiculturalism and inclusion and less with justice and equity. It was only in law school, while working at an immigration clinic, that I began to connect race more concretely with the concept of justice—or the absence of it. When I eventually found my way to Washington, D.C., in the late 1990s, I eagerly joined an emerging cadre of advocates who sought to place Asian Americans in the contemporary struggles for racial and economic justice in our country by supporting voting rights, affirmative action, and humane immigration policies. During the summer of 2001, I joined a burgeoning group of South Asian activists, lawyers, organizers, and service providers at a gathering called Desis Organizing in New York City. We felt as though we were on the cusp of broadening and deepening the movements for racial justice in America.

The events of 9/11 and its immediate aftermath would test our resolve. On 9/11, nineteen terrorists affiliated with Al Qaeda hijacked four airplanes and used them to destroy the World Trade Center in New York City and damage the Pentagon outside Washington, D.C., resulting in the deaths of more than three thousand people. At the time, I was working at the Civil Rights Division of the Department of Justice. I remember standing with my colleagues outside our evacuated office building on the streets of downtown Washington, feeling scared and confused. Later that day, I returned home to my apartment in Arlington, Virginia, located just a few miles from the Pentagon. As plumes of smoke wafted up into the night sky from the damaged Pentagon, I tried to comprehend what had occurred and to account for the whereabouts of friends in New York City and Washington. In the days that followed, I joined Americans around the country to grieve for the innocent lives that had so cruelly been cut short. I felt, as so many did, that everything had changed.

Almost immediately, a double grieving began. The days and weeks after 9/11 brought reports of backlash and incidents of reprisal. The targets included South Asians, Muslims, Arabs, Hindus, Sikhs, and anyone perceived to be from these communities. I passed the first six months after 9/11 in a blur of activity, collaborating with lawyers, organizers, and activists around the country who sought to address the tremendous needs that emerged seemingly overnight. I worked with colleagues at the Department of Justice to inform people of their civil rights in the face of discrimination and with a group of dedicated South Asians to shape a national community-based nonprofit organization called South Asian Americans Leading Together (SAALT).

A few years later, as the executive director of SAALT, I had the privilege of getting to know and work with many of the people who appear in these pages as we weathered one crisis moment after another, from those initial days after 9/11 to the Park51 community center controversy nine years later to the Oak Creek gurdwara massacre in 2012. We responded to the complex needs of community members experiencing unprecedented levels of violence, detentions and deportations, and racial and religious profiling. We pushed back on negative media coverage and political rhetoric that fueled Islamophobia and xenophobia. We built organizations that had not existed prior to 9/11 and began to develop deeper connections with Black and Latino groups.

The decade and a half since 9/11 has fundamentally altered South Asian, Arab, Muslim, and Sikh immigrant communities in the United States. Yet we continue to hear sanitized histories of post-9/11 America that all too often neglect their experiences. Young people, including many of my students at the University of Maryland— who were first or second graders when 9/11 occurred— have learned incomplete histories of this time period. This book contributes narratives, anecdotes, and analyses to provide a more comprehensive understanding of post-9/11 America.

It does not provide an all-encompassing representation of post-9/11 America, however. The book provides only a snapshot of the many government actions and incidents of discrimination and hate violence that have targeted community members over the past decade and a half. It also uses terminology that is still in the process of evolution. For example, the collective identities of "South Asian" or "Arab" used in this book do not adequately reflect the unique experiences of specific faith or national origin groups that may comprise those categories, such as Hindus or Christians. Additionally, there are issues outside the scope of what I address here— the experiences of Black Muslims and the impact of U.S. foreign policy toward South Asia and the Middle East on communities in America, for example—that warrant deeper research and analysis. I wrote this book keenly aware of these limitations, as well as with my own. I recognize that my life experiences—influenced by caste, class, language, and cis-gender privilege, to name only a few—differ in significant ways from those of the young people who are featured in this book. As such, my rendering of their stories is imperfect and inexact, and any shortcomings are mine alone.

What this book does posit is that our country has yet to fully confront the scope and effects of racial anxiety, Islamophobia, and xenophobia that have permeated our national narratives and policies in the years since 9/11. We must change this legal, cultural, and political climate of hostility and suspicion, especially as communities perceived as "others" change American cities, schools, and neighborhoods due to population increases and migration patterns. This book provides practices and ideas based on the experiences of young South Asian, Arab, Muslim, and Sikh communities that can alter the direction of post-9/11 America.

Meanwhile, the American racial landscape is undergoing a rapid and radical demographic transformation. South Asian, Arab, Muslim, and Sikh communities, along with Latino, Asian, and multiracial youth, are driving the changes that will within three decades lead to a time when people of color will be the majority population. As such, their bodies and lives are already becoming the sites where new battles of racism and xenophobia are waged. They are simultaneously perceived as the targets of racial anxiety—as well as potential members of the expanding category of "Whiteness." At stake is the preservation of "America" and the power to influence political, economic, and ideological conditions in our nation.

How must communities of color position themselves in order to shape a multiracial and equitable future for all Americans? How will new immigrants complicate and expand the Black or White racial binary? How will our individual and collective racial identities evolve as designated race categories no longer reflect our daily lives and interactions? Why must we expose and address the ongoing and systemic racism that creates unfair outcomes for people of color, even as the drumbeat of a postracial, color-blind, and multicultural nation gets louder? These are some of the many questions that await us in twenty-first-century America. This book provides ideas and recommendations for activists, educators, policy makers, diversity and inclusion professionals, and philanthropists who are committed to grappling with these questions in order to build multiracial and equitable classrooms, workplaces, and communities.

In my own personal journey, which has been markedly influenced by post-9/11 America, I have drawn tremendous strength from the resistance and audacity of people who reclaim and reshape what it means to be American day after day. They do this in the face of policies, rhetoric, and actions that marginalize, demonize, and criminalize them simply because of where they were born, the name they were given, their appearance, or the faith they follow. They are reshaping America with a strength and courage that calls to mind the spirit of Langston Hughes's poignant poem, "I, Too," written almost ninety years ago, in which he reminds us:

> *I, too, sing America.*
>
> *I am the darker brother.*
> *They send me to eat in the kitchen*
> *When company comes,*
> *But I laugh,*
> *And eat well,*
> *And grow strong.*

The brave and resilient young people in this book, and others like them, are building the America for us all, one in which the "others" not only belong but also thrive and guide us to a more humane, more equitable future.

Acknowledgments

My own beloved community anchors this book. My circle of supporters and mentors gave me the support to navigate the journey of writing about people and communities who are very dear
to me.

To my parents, Vasudeva and Padma Iyer, and my brother, Gopa:
your unconditional love is the source of my daily strength. Amma
and Appa, through your sacrifices and support, you have created
opportunities for me that I never imagined could be possible.

To Parag: your encouragement and generosity with time, ideas,
and space transformed this endeavor, like so many, from a mere
thought to a reality. You, along with Sushila and Lisa Khandhar,
have long been my cheerleaders.

To Ahilan, thank you for your patience with Mommy's long writing days. While this book didn't turn out to be the children's story
you wanted it to be, it holds a part of your own history.

This book is rooted in the experiences I had and the people I met
through my work at South Asian Americans Leading Together
(SAALT). I am deeply indebted to the staff and board members
who were my partners in building SAALT for a decade, and am in
awe of my colleagues at South Asian and Asian American organizations who are integral to our racial justice movements. While there

is not enough space to thank each of you here, this book stands as a tribute to you.

Several institutions and people supported me in different ways while I researched and wrote. To the Asian American Studies Program at the University of Maryland (in particular, Dr. Janelle Wong), the William Winter Institute for Racial Reconciliation (in particular, Dr. Susan Glisson and Dr. Jennifer Stollman), and Suman Raghunathan and the SAALT team: thank you for giving me the gifts of time, research, and soft landing places. I benefited greatly from workshopping many of the ideas in this book in classes, forums, and panel discussions. To my students at the University of Maryland: you motivated me to write the untold stories about post-9/11 America.

To Rinku Sen and Vijay Prashad, who regularly open doors for people like me to walk through: thank you for your guidance, mentorship, and faith in me. I promise to pay your generosity forward.

To Christina Modi: this book would not be what it is had it not been for your extraordinary research assistance. To Victoria Meaney: the hours of patient transcription, editing, and research you provided help to anchor the stories told here. To Janaki Kasawala, Jasmeet Sidhu, and Katie Sint: thank you for your research support. To Howard Shih: thank you for the data analysis in this book and for your tireless advocacy around data collection for Asian American communities. To Nadia Firozvi, Linda Sarsour, and Manpreet Teji: I am so grateful to you for taking the time to answer my unending questions about Arab, Muslim, and Sikh communities.

To Julie Enszer and Marc Favreau at The New Press: your personal and institutional commitment to nurturing and amplifying the voices of people like me is unsurpassed. Julie, your editorial support has tremendously improved this book from its initial iterations. I cannot thank you enough for your personal investment in its success. I am also indebted to the editorial support provided by

Sarah Fan and Ben Woodward at The New Press and copy editor
Mike O'Connor.

To scholars, thought leaders, and practitioners, including Glenn
Harris, Subhash Kateel, Soya Jung, Michael Omi, john a. pow-
ell, Eric Ward, and Dorian Warren: your input and feedback over
many conversations have been invaluable in developing the ideas
presented in this book.

A group of women has sustained me for decades as life guides,
karaoke and dance partners, and emotional touchstones (often simultaneously). I cherish you, Priya Murthy, Kathleen Ley, Vinnu
Deshetty, Radhika Chimata, Kirti Patel, Monica Cooley, Chaum-
toli Huq, Anouska Cheddie, Amanda Baran, Manar Waheed, Soya,
and Rinku. To Jayne Park, Peggy Nagae, Karen Narasaki, Angela
Oh, Urvashi Vaid, and Helen Zia: I am so grateful to you for paving
a path for women like me; I stand on your shoulders.

Finally, to the young activists I have had the privilege of getting to know and introduce to readers in this book: thank you for
your openness, and your trust in me to tell a part of your stories.
I know that others will become inspired, just as I have been, by the
paths that you are each forging to create and sustain our beloved
communities.

We Too Sing America

1

"Not Our American Dream": The Oak Creek Massacre and Hate Violence

It was early on a Sunday morning in August 2012, and Param-jit Kaur Saini was going about her morning routine. Her sons, twenty-year-old Kamal Singh Saini and eighteen-year-old Harpreet Singh Saini, wanted to sleep in a little longer, so Paramjit set out on her own to the local gurdwara, the Sikh Temple of Wisconsin. Paramjit was a familiar presence at the gurdwara, which had become a second home to her family and to many other Sikhs in Oak Creek, a small city located in the outskirts of Milwaukee. The gurdwara, built in 2007 on thirteen acres of land by Sikh immigrant families, sits on South Howell Street just a few miles from the Milwaukee airport and a short distance from a typical strip mall. On weekends, Sikh families gathered at the gurdwara to pray and connect with one another. The dining hall was filled with the sounds of people socializing and children laughing during *langar*, a free meal offered to anyone who came to the gurdwara. Kamal and Harpreet usually hung out with their friends and played football on Sundays at the gurdwara, while their mother helped in the kitchen and prayer hall.

But August 5, 2012, would not turn out to be a normal Sunday for Paramjit's family or for the Oak Creek community.

Soon after his mother had left the house, news reached Kamal that people inside the Sikh Temple of Wisconsin were in danger. Details were scarce, and, panic-stricken, Kamal rushed to the gurdwara to find that law enforcement vehicles had blocked off the driveway. Authorities asked Kamal to wait across the street in the parking lot of the Classic Lanes bowling alley, where he joined others also anxiously searching for information.

In the parking lot that day, Kamal met Mandeep Kaur, who would become a vital part of his support system in the months to come. The daughter of a convenience store worker and housewife, Mandeep was the first in her family to graduate from college. She worked as a business analyst at Johnson Controls in Milwaukee. Mandeep had recently begun to reengage with Sikhism, the world's fifth-largest religion, which has between 280,000 and 500,000 adherents residing in the United States alone.[1] On that Sunday morning, Mandeep had been on her way to the Oak Creek gurdwara to teach Punjabi language classes when she heard sirens and saw emergency vehicles heading in the same direction.

While waiting for information in the Classic Lanes parking lot together, Mandeep, Kamal, and others speculated about what might be happening inside the gurdwara. They wondered whether a dispute between community members had gone awry. Then Mandeep's close friend Kirandeep received a call from her father, who was inside the gurdwara. He whispered to her that he was hiding in the pantry of the kitchen because he had heard gunshots. He was one of around twenty-five people huddled, terrified, among bags of rice and fresh vegetables. Kirandeep's father told her not to come to the gurdwara under any circumstances.

As the day wore on, many of the people who had been inside were allowed to leave, and a fuller picture began to emerge about the rampage that had occurred inside the gurdwara that Sunday morning. Not seeing his mother and becoming increasingly anxious about her safety, Kamal left the parking lot. He called his friends, and together they went from hospital to hospital, hoping that Paramjit had been brought to one.

It would be a full eleven hours before authorities finally notified Kamal that his mother had been fatally shot inside the gurdwara. "When I first found out, I passed out," Kamal told me. "I woke up in an ambulance and immediately thought of my little brother. Telling him was the hardest thing I've ever done."

This wasn't the future that Paramjit had envisioned for her family when she and her two sons moved to America from India in 2004 to join her husband, who owned a number of gas stations in Wisconsin. It wasn't the life that Paramjit had planned to build when she mustered up the courage a few years later to begin working at BD Medical, a factory in a nearby town. "She used to be a housewife for a few years after we moved here because she had a problem with English," Kamal remembered. "But it's funny how she got the job because she had to do a phone interview. She was afraid they would call while we were in school and she wouldn't understand what they were saying. So it happened to be that the day she got the call, I was home. . . . She put it on speaker and they kept asking her questions and I kept translating for her." With Kamal's assistance, Paramjit passed the interview handily and started her job as an inspector at the medical factory, testing syringes to make sure that they did not have any cracks in them.

Paramjit's determination to care for her family is a point of deep pride for Kamal and Harpreet. Forty-five days after his mother was killed, Harpreet spoke about her in testimony before the U.S. Senate. He said, "My mother was a brilliant woman, a reasonable woman. Everyone knew she was smart, but she never had the chance to get a formal education. She couldn't. As a hard-working immigrant, she had to work long hours to feed her family, to get her sons educated, and help us achieve our American dreams. This was more important to her than anything else. . . . But now she is gone. Because of a man who hated her because she wasn't his

color? His religion? . . . She was an American. And this was not
our American Dream."[2]

Inside the Gurdwara: A Massacre

During the first twenty-four hours, news about what had transpired
inside the gurdwara trickled out. Around 10:20 a.m. on August 5,
forty-year-old Wade Michael Page, armed with a nine-millimeter
semiautomatic pistol, began his murderous rampage at the Oak
Creek gurdwara. In the gurdwara parking lot, Page shot and killed
forty-one-year-old Sita Singh, a father of four, and his brother,
forty-nine-year-old Ranjit Singh. After entering the building, Page
took aim first at Suveg Singh, an eighty-four-year-old grandfather
who usually sat in the lobby to greet people as they arrived at the
gurdwara.[3] He then shot and killed forty-one-year-old Paramjit Kaur
Saini inside the prayer hall before proceeding down a narrow hall-
way, where he shot thirty-nine-year-old Prakash Singh, an assistant
priest at the gurdwara whose wife and two children had arrived from
India just a month before to join him in Oak Creek. Page then shot
and killed sixty-five-year-old Satwant Singh Kaleka, the president of
the gurdwara and one of its founders. Page also severely wounded
sixty-five-year-old Punjab Singh, a visiting religious scholar who had
joined the gurdwara community just four days before. In the midst
of this shooting spree, several people were injured.

Page then entered the room where the kitchen and pantry were
located. He pursued people rushing toward an exit and found himself in the parking lot, where he faced Lieutenant Brian Murphy, an
officer with the Oak Creek Police Department. In the exchange of
gunshots that followed, twelve bullets entered Murphy's body. Sam
Lenda, a trained SWAT officer and marksman, shortly arrived to
provide backup.[4] The entire scene in the parking lot took place in just
six minutes, before Page fatally shot himself in the head.[5] Murphy,
who endured surgery on his neck, voice box, and hands, survived.

Later in the day, city officials revealed the names of the six vic-tims and the name of the perpetrator. For many, it was unclear in those early hours whether what had happened inside the gurdwara was another tragic incident of gun violence (the Aurora, Colorado, movie theater shooting had occurred less than a month earlier), a hate crime, or both.

Those of us working with South Asian, Arab, Muslim, and Sikh immigrant communities had little doubt about the nature of the tragedy. We believed it was a hate crime, another violent incident in the continuum of backlash targeting South Asians, Arabs, Muslims, and Sikhs since 9/11. At the time of the attack on the Oak Creek gurdwara, I was the executive director of South Asian Americans Leading Together (SAALT), a national advo-cacy organization. My first call upon hearing the news was to Amardeep Singh, whom I had met shortly after 9/11 when he and other volunteers formed the Sikh Coalition. "I'm already on my way there," Amardeep said when he answered my call. We talked about three immediate needs: ensuring that the families of the victims received the services they required, reframing the misleading media narrative, and alerting the Obama administra-tion and federal agencies. Amardeep asked me to reach out to government agencies and our partner organizations to reinforce these needs.

The media messaging in the hours after the tragedy was already flawed, an example of how mainstream media is ill-equipped to accurately cover South Asian, Arab, Muslim, and Sikh immigrant communities. Many news commentators wondered whether Wade Michael Page had actually intended to target Muslims and had mistakenly believed that Sikhs were Muslims. In the months after 9/11, some Sikhs and Hindus had relied on the message "We are not Muslims" as a reflexive response to shield themselves from the backlash targeting Muslims. Over the years, this reaction changed, as community members realized that perpetrators of hate violence did not distinguish among people who looked alike, and as a narrative of inclusion and unity developed in post-9/11 America.

Amardeep, Valarie Kaur, a Sikh American activist and filmmaker, and Jasjit Singh, executive director of the Sikh American Legal Defense and Education Fund, took to television and radio outlets and delivered this message. They placed the Oak Creek massacre in the larger context of the backlash that had affected many communities—Sikhs, Muslims, Arabs, and Hindus—since September 11, 2001. They observed that those intending to harm these communities did not see the distinctions between them, and that differentiating between them would not alter this reality. They reminded the media and the public that the message of "mistaken identity" may lead to the misguided conclusion that targeting Muslims was acceptable. Instead, they called upon Americans to stand united against hate violence in all its forms.

In addition to reframing the media narrative, advocates quickly connected with local, state, and federal government agencies. The federal government took over the criminal investigation while city officials worked with the families of the victims. Oak Creek's mayor, Steve Scaffidi, was at the center of the local response in Oak Creek. Scaffidi had assumed office just four months prior to the gurdwara massacre. He described the immediate aftermath to the tragedy as a crisis, 24/7. "We didn't have a full-time public information officer, so getting information out to the public and media was challenging. We had twenty-eight local, state, and federal agencies on the scene and involved. Coordinating among them was difficult. We knew that there were mental health and posttraumatic stress needs among the victims' families and other congregants, as well as with law enforcement and first responders. We also learned that many of the victims' families had complex immigration needs. Four of the victims were Indian citizens and had family members who wanted to be present for the funeral service."

A group of volunteer first responders, including Mandeep Kaur, stepped up to address many of these emerging needs. "In the beginning, we focused mainly on consoling the families and helping their relatives from India get here," Mandeep recalled. "Several of us cleaned the gurdwara to make sure that it was ready by the time the memorial service occurred a week later. And we focused on the children—some of them had been in the basement of the gurdwara when Page was shooting, and others had lost their parents."

Among the eleven children who lost their fathers or mothers in the massacre, five were in middle or high school at the time. Two of those children—Palmeet Kaur, twelve, and Prabhjot Singh, thirteen—had moved to Oak Creek from India only a month earlier to join their father, Prakash Singh.[6] Fourteen-year-old Gurvinder Singh had not seen his father, Ranjit Singh, since he was seven months old. He traveled from India only to see his father in a coffin.[7] Mandeep and other community members knew that these young children needed effective counseling and support to deal with the impact of the hate violence that had taken their parents from them.

Puni Kalra, a Sikh American clinical psychologist living in Denver, Colorado, perhaps understood this better than most people. Kalra had moved to Denver a few months before the Columbine High School shootings occurred in 1999 and had helped with trauma-response efforts there. She was also a first responder when the shooting at the movie theater in Aurora, Colorado, happened in 2012. Kalra's own background and training with trauma victims of gun violence made her an ideal person to marshal efforts to help the Oak Creek community. While her experiences with Columbine and Aurora survivors had prepared Kalra to respond to the situation in Oak Creek, her own background as a Sikh American who grew up attending a gurdwara in Palatine, Illinois, just an hour away from Oak Creek, was important as well. "Trauma is not new to me, but this is the first time it hit so close to home," she told me.

Kalra began to mobilize mental health providers around the

country to support the Oak Creek Sikh community. The members
of this network, called the Sikh Healing Collective, produced fact
sheets in English and Punjabi on a range of issues—posttraumatic
stress disorder, survivor guilt, insomnia, fear, bullying, and
harassment—and presented workshops at the Oak Creek gurdwara on weekends. Kalra and others involved with the Sikh Healing Collective knew that traditional interventions such as therapy
and counseling, as well as services provided by government agencies and nonprofits, might not resonate with the community due
to the reluctance among many South Asians to seek mental health
assistance, as well as cultural and linguistic barriers. For a year, the
Sikh Healing Collective worked with adult and youth groups in Oak
Creek to provide resources and support and to set up longer-term
assistance, all in culturally and linguistically appropriate ways.

Support for the Oak Creek community extended nationwide
as well. People organized vigils for the victims and contributed to
fund-raising campaigns to assist the families. Advocates drew attention to the increase in hate groups in the United States and
pressed for greater government intervention to stem the tide of violence that was spreading beyond Oak Creek. Several incidents of
violence occurred within weeks of the tragedy. Pigs' feet were left at
the planned site of the Al-Nur Islamic Center in Ontario, California.[8] A man used a high-velocity air rifle to shoot at a Chicago-area
mosque on August 12, 2012, and someone threw a homemade
bomb at a Muslim school in Lombard, Illinois.[9] Even as they
mourned and grieved for the victims of the Oak Creek massacre,
South Asian, Arab, Hindu, Muslim, and Sikh communities became
public targets of violence once again.

The Path to Oak Creek Began More Than a Century Ago

South Asian, Arab, Hindu, Muslim, and Sikh communities experienced unprecedented backlash after 9/11, but hate violence

targeting these communities has a much longer history. Arabs in particular faced high levels of suspicion, discrimination, and violence in the late 1970s and early 1990s when the Iran hostage crisis and the Persian Gulf War occurred.[10] The Oklahoma City bombing on April 19, 1995, when Timothy McVeigh detonated a truck bomb at the Alfred P. Murrah Federal Building, led to speculation that Arabs might have been behind this act of domestic terrorism. Similarly, racist and xenophobic attitudes and beliefs that devalue people of color and immigrants have motivated discrimination and violence against South Asians, including those who are Hindu, Muslim, or Sikh. South Asian communities have been targets of hate crimes from the Bellingham, Washington, riots in 1907 to the Dotbusters scare in the 1980s in New Jersey and street violence targeting immigrants in more recent decades.

The riots in Bellingham, which occurred in the early part of the twentieth century, are meaningful in understanding the roots of anti-Asian sentiment. At the time, all along the West Coast, Chinese, Korean, Filipino, Japanese, and Indian laborers were exploited for their labor but not welcomed as residents or as U.S. citizens. These racist attitudes, reinforced by laws such as the Chinese Exclusion Act and anti-naturalization policies, often took the form of actual violence. This is what occurred on September 4, 1907, in Bellingham, Washington, where five hundred White residents rounded up around two hundred South Asian migrant workers—most of them Sikhs and Hindus—and locked them in the basement of the city hall. They intended to drive out immigrant laborers who worked under contract in Bellingham's lumber mills. The city already boasted a chapter of the Japanese-Korean Exclusion League, which fostered hostility toward Japanese, Korean, and Chinese immigrant laborers. Chinese laborers could work and live in Bellingham only during salmon season; in this way, the city profited from their labor but denied them the right even to be present at any other time.[11]

Unsurprisingly, Bellingham's xenophobic reactions to South

Asian migrant labor reflected views institutionalized in laws and expressed in the media. The *Bellingham Herald*, for example, published an editorial the day after the riots that read, "The Hindu is not a good citizen. It would require centuries to assimilate him, and this country need not take the trouble. Our racial burdens are already heavy enough to bear."[12] That is, American society could not take in South Asian and other Asian immigrants because they were not only incapable of fitting in but also because they exacerbated existing racial dynamics, ostensibly between Whites and Blacks.

One hundred years later, the editors of the *Bellingham Herald* published an apology. In a September 2, 2007, editorial, they wrote, "It's time to apologize for the venomous racism, for the demeaning talk, for the refusal to defend human beings against a mob because of their skin tone and ethnicity. We apologize to the East Indian people in our community today, and to any right-thinking person who is disgusted by the actions this newspaper took in one of the darkest times in our community's history. We are disgusted too."[13]

As with this apology, as commendable as it is, change was slow to come. Racist policies that restricted the rights of South Asian and other Asian immigrants to migrate, naturalize, own property, or sponsor relatives did not fully change until well into the second half of the twentieth century. The civil rights struggles of Black communities in the 1950s and 1960s set the stage for legislation that removed many of these restrictions.[14] The second wave of Asian immigration after 1965 benefited both from relaxed immigration policies as well as the Civil Rights Act and the Voting Rights Act, which barred discrimination on the basis of race, national origin, or faith in the workplace, at hotels or restaurants, or in the voting booth.[15]

The South Asians who entered the United States after 1965 were markedly different from their earlier counterparts, who had been railroad workers, lumber mill laborers, and farmers. The preferences for skilled immigrants in the Immigration and Nationality Act of 1965 meant that a new set of professionals, including engineers, doctors, and professors, were entering the United States in large numbers.[16] However, class and educational privilege could not protect this second wave of South Asian immigrants from racism in the 1970s and 1980s. One well-known example involves a group called the Dotbusters who threatened violent action against Indian immigrants settling in Jersey City, New Jersey, in the late 1980s.[17] The Dotbusters believed that Indian immigrants were "taking over" their neighborhoods with their foreign customs and small businesses.[18] In a letter to the *Jersey Journal* during the summer of 1987, the Dotbusters claimed, "We will go to any extreme to get Indians to move out of Jersey City."[19]

This phenomenon of "move-out violence"—forcing new immigrant communities to leave through acts of harassment and physical violence—became common in Jersey City in the late 1980s. In September 1987, Navroze Mody, a manager at CitiCorp in Manhattan, died after being brutally beaten on a street corner in Hoboken by a group of people shouting, "Hindu, Hindu." A group of men beat and nearly killed Kaushal Saran, a thirty-year-old doctor, after he walked out of an office building in Jersey City Heights.[20]

Similar incidents of hate violence targeted South Asians around the nation in the 1990s, although they largely occurred under the public's radar. According to hate crime audits published by Asian Americans Advancing Justice, South Asians were reporting the highest numbers of hate crimes among all Asian ethnic groups, with forty-one and fifty-two incidents in 1998 and 1999, respectively.[21] The victim of one of the more highly publicized hate crimes of the 1990s was twenty-year-old Rishi Maharaj. On September 20, 1998, Rishi was walking with his cousins in a residential neighborhood in South Ozone Park, Queens, when three men wielding baseball bats followed him and beat him. In the police report, witnesses claim that the three attackers yelled, "You fucking little Indian piece of shit. . . . This is never going to be a neighborhood until you leave."[22] Rishi, who was born and raised in New York

City, is the youngest in an Indo-Trinidadian family that has been in the United States for generations. He knew no country other than America.

Rishi underwent several surgeries to recover from his injuries, including the placement of two steel plates in his mouth to hold his jaw in place.[23] He became the object of media and public attention, and even though he did not want to be a spokesperson against hate violence, he continued to position the attack in the context of a broader movement for racial justice. Rishi's story soon became a clarion call for the eventual passage of a hate crimes law in New York in 2000.[24]

That same year, I joined Rishi's family at the trial of Nuno Martins, Luis Amorim, and Peter DiMarco, the three men who had attacked him.[25] Martins was sentenced to eight years in jail after being convicted of assault in the first degree, assault in the third degree, and two counts of aggravated harassment, while Amorim and DiMarco were acquitted of all charges.[26] Rishi's mental, physical, and legal ordeal had touched me deeply. His story confirmed that American citizenship, an American accent, and an American childhood could not shield South Asians from hate violence.

About a year later, Rishi became part of a documentary produced by SAALT titled *Raising Our Voices: South Asian Americans Address Hate* that highlighted the experiences of South Asian survivors of hate violence. Along with the production team led by Aashish Kumar and Aabha Adhiya, I traveled to different parts of the country to document the experiences of South Asians who had endured violence simply because of their actual or perceived race, national origin, or faith. Rishi's story provided the arc for the documentary.

One of the incidents covered in SAALT's film is the April 28, 2000, shooting rampage on the outskirts of Pittsburgh, Pennsylvania, by Richard Baumhammers, who operated a website that called for the end of non-White immigration, which he claimed had been "disastrous for Americans of European ancestry."[27] Baumhammers killed five people and paralyzed one in the shooting spree.[28] His victims included a list of people targeted for their non-European ethnicities or faiths: sixty-three-year-old Anita "Nicki" Gordon, his Jewish neighbor; Thao Pham, a twenty-seven-year-old Vietnamese American; Ji-ye Sun, a thirty-four-year-old Chinese American restaurant manager at the Ya Fei Chinese restaurant; Garry Lee, a twenty-two-year-old Black man exercising at a karate school; and Anil Thakur, a thirty-one-year-old customer at India Grocers.[29]

While at India Grocers, Baumhammers also shot twenty-five-year-old Sandip Patel, who had been working at the store.[30] Sandip, who had come to the United States just a few months before the shooting, had been an active member of the local Hindu Jain temple. While he survived the attack, he was paralyzed from the neck down and required constant care.[31] Sandip died in 2007 at just thirty-two years old.[32] Meanwhile, Baumhammers was charged with and convicted for a range of crimes, including ethnic intimidation. He received the death penalty.

The common strands of racial anxiety, bigotry, and anti-immigrant sentiment run through many of the incidents of hate violence endured by South Asians for more than a hundred years in the United States. Often these incidents were coupled with or reinforced by negative media portrayals and discriminatory laws and policies. But nothing could have prepared the community for what occurred after 9/11.

American Backlash

Within days after 9/11, the media reported accounts of people being pulled off trains, profiled at airports, and even chased down city streets. SAALT found 645 reported incidents of discrimination and violence in the span of just the first week following 9/11. These occurred against people of South Asian, Arab, and Muslim backgrounds and often at places of worship such as mosques, temples, and gurdwaras.[33]

On September 15, 2001, the first fatal 9/11-related hate crime happened.[34] Balbir Singh Sodhi, a Chevron gas station owner in Mesa, Arizona, was killed by Frank Roque, who then went on to shoot at a Lebanese American–owned service station and at the home of a family of Afghan descent.[35] On the same day, in Texas, Mark Stroman, dubbed the "9/11 revenge killer," killed Waqar Hasan, a forty-six-year-old Pakistani father of four daughters, inside a Dallas grocery store. Stroman also shot and killed Vasudev Patel, a married father of two from India, at Patel's gas station.[36] A few days later, Stroman shot Rais Bhuiyan, a Bangladeshi immigrant, at a convenience store. Bhuiyan suffered facial injuries and damage to his vision, but he later publicly forgave Stroman and even attempted to stop his execution in Texas.[37]

Tensions around the nation were high as people of all races and faiths struggled to understand what was happening. On September 17, 2001, President George W. Bush visited the Islamic Center of Washington, D.C., and advised, "Those who feel like they can intimidate our fellow citizens to take out their anger don't represent the best of America."[38] Civil rights and interfaith leaders around the country echoed President Bush's message.

In Washington, D.C., I joined a diverse group of leaders including Wade Henderson with the Leadership Conference on Civil and Human Rights, Karen Narasaki with Asian Americans Advancing Justice, and Jim Zogby with the Arab American Institute at a press conference at the Japanese American Memorial to Patriotism During World War II. Standing in front of the memorial walls etched with the names of internment camps such as Amache, Gila River, and Heart Mountain, we called for unity and solidarity. We reminded our country not to repeat the mistakes made during the World War II internment of Japanese Americans by targeting certain communities in the name of national security or patriotism. In that space, filled with people representing the diversity of our country, I felt a strong sense of hope. Perhaps the tide could be reversed.

Sadly, this would not be the case. In addition to hate violence, misleading and inflammatory media coverage that frequently associated Sikhs and Muslims with terrorists began to fuel animosity toward these communities.[39] This trend began the day after 9/11 with the false arrest of a Sikh American, Sher Singh, who wears a long beard, a *kirpan* (a ceremonial sword or dagger), and a turban, all revered articles of the Sikh faith. Singh had been traveling on an Amtrak train to Boston when law enforcement agents aiming rifles at him placed him under arrest at the Providence station. Soon after, national media outlets, including the Associated Press, CNN, and Fox News, broadcast images of Singh's arrest. After Singh was released a few hours later, those same national media outlets neglected to report that he had not been charged with any crimes.[40] Instead, the public was left with unexplained pictures of a bearded and turbaned brown man suspected of being a terrorist and apprehended by law enforcement authorities. These images of bearded and turbaned brown men as terrorists have become seared into our collective national imagination.

In the weeks and months after 9/11, government agencies and community activists began to take emergency measures to respond to the rash of hate violence; vandalism at gurdwaras, mosques, and temples; and workplace bias occurring around the country. At the U.S. Department of Justice (DOJ), Joseph Zogby, Alia Malek, and I helped to create and staff a new federal effort called the Initiative to Combat Post-9/11 Discriminatory Backlash.[41] We worked with a cadre of dedicated attorneys within the DOJ's Civil Rights Division to engage in outreach to affected communities and investigate complaints of discrimination. In the months after 9/11, we received complaints from people alleging discrimination at workplaces, schools, and airports. Yet we quickly realized that existing civil rights laws could not cover all the ways in which South Asians, Arabs, Muslims, and Sikhs experienced discrimination in the wake of 9/11. At the time, in order for the federal hate crimes law to apply, a victim had to be engaging in a federally protected activity (such as voting) when he or she was attacked in order for the law to apply. For people like Balbir Singh Sodhi, shot while at his gas station, federal laws provided little recourse, if any at all. Additionally, people experiencing religious profiling at airports could not pursue legal remedies. There were also no tracking mechanisms to adequately account for or assess the breadth and scope of post-9/11 bias.

As reports of discrimination dramatically increased at the workplace, the Equal Employment Opportunity Commission (EEOC), a federal agency that investigates employment discrimination complaints, began to uniquely track and report complaints related to 9/11 bias. Since 9/11, the EEOC has brought legal charges against many employers who failed to hire or promote South Asians, Arabs, Muslims, and Sikhs or who fostered a hostile environment in the workplace. In fact, the EEOC reported a 250 percent increase in complaints of religious discrimination involving Muslims immediately after 9/11. Between 9/11 and March 2012, the EEOC reported receiving 1,040 charges filed by South Asians, Arabs, Muslims, and Sikhs related to workplace discrimination.[42]

Complaints of discrimination at the workplace continued to persist in the years after 9/11. For example, in July 2009 the EEOC filed a lawsuit against the Sahara Hotel and Casino for retaliating against an Egyptian employee who reported being harassed at work by supervisors and co-workers with comments such as "Go back to Egypt." They also called him "Bin Laden" and "sand n——r." The Sahara settled the case for $100,000 in 2010.[43]

More recently, in 2013, the EEOC filed charges against Abercrombie & Fitch for not hiring Samantha Elauf, a Muslim teenager who wore a hijab (a headscarf worn by some Muslim women), despite being recommended for hire by an interviewer. Abercrombie claimed that the hijab did not fit its look policy, which barred caps from being worn and called for an "East Coast collegiate style," and that Elauf never made a specific request for religious accommodation. The case went through several appeals and was argued before the U.S. Supreme Court, who ruled in favor of Elauf and the EEOC in June 2015. In the 8–1 ruling (with Justice Clarence Thomas as the sole dissenter), Justice Antonin Scalia noted that it is not necessary to make a specific request for religious accommodation in order to seek relief under laws that prevent discrimination in the workplace. Faith advocates welcomed the decision wholeheartedly.[44]

Since 9/11, educational institutions also have come under scrutiny for discriminatory actions. In 2014, the Department of Justice reached a settlement agreement with DeKalb County, Georgia, related to allegations of the harassment of a Sikh student on the basis of his nationality and religion. The agreement requires the county to address and prevent this kind of harassment and provide training for students and school staff, including teachers, counselors, bus drivers, and administrators, about Sikh, South Asian, Muslim, and Arab communities.[45]

Meanwhile, the number of reported hate crimes has also continued to climb. According to the FBI Hate Crimes Report, 27.2 percent of reported hate crimes in 2001 that were motivated by religious bias were classified as "anti-Islamic." This represented a 1,600 percent increase from the previous year and likely included violence against Sikhs, Hindus, and Arabs as well.[46] This record-high number of "anti-Islamic" crimes dropped to just under 11 percent over the next two years, but then rose to 13 percent in 2004.[47] After dipping to 7.7 percent in 2008, the rate climbed to 9.3 percent in 2009, and eventually to 14.2 percent in 2013.[48] Advocates believe that these ebbs and flows in hate violence often happen in relation to the annual 9/11 anniversary, a spike in anti-Muslim rhetoric in political or media spheres, or destabilizing events taking place in South Asia or the Middle East.

Incidents of hate violence have not been limited to Muslims and Sikhs. At the end of 2012, a forty-six-year-old Indian Hindu man named Sunando Sen was shoved onto the path of an oncoming train at a subway stop in New York City. According to authorities, Erika Menendez, the woman held in custody for pushing Sen, said, "I pushed a Muslim off the train tracks because I hate Hindus and Muslims ever since 2001 when they put down the twin towers."[49] Sen died as a result of his injuries. In May 2015, Menendez received a sentence of twenty-four years in prison.[50]

On the tenth anniversary of 9/11, the DOJ released a report that revealed that hate violence toward people and property (primarily places of worship) had not abated. In the first six years after 9/11, the DOJ investigated more than eight hundred incidences of violence, threats of violence, or arson perpetrated against South Asian, Arab, Hindu, Muslim, and Sikh communities and those perceived to be part of those groups. Between 2001 and 2011, the DOJ prosecuted fifty defendants in thirty-seven different cases.[51] By the time the Oak Creek gurdwara tragedy occurred, the list of names of those killed or hurt since 9/11 had already grown too long.

"An Act of Terrorism, an Act of Hate"

I arrived in Oak Creek five days after the massacre occurred to pay my respects at the memorial for the six victims of the tragedy. As I approached Oak Creek High School, the site of the memorial service, I could see hundreds of people waiting in line outside. People of all races and faiths had gathered in the quintessential American space—a high school gymnasium—to mourn the six Sikh immigrants who had lost their lives to hate violence in America's heartland. The gym echoed with the spontaneous call-and-response of

"Bole So Nihal, Sat Sri Akaal" (a traditional shout of triumph and victory) from the Sikhs in the audience.

As the memorial program began, we were asked to pay our respects to the victims by lining up to view the caskets. I tried to prepare myself for looking into the faces of the six innocent people who had lost their lives, but I was even more shaken as I realized that next to each casket stood their children and loved ones. What do you say to comfort a child who has lost a parent in an act of hate?

Next to Satwant Singh Kaleka's casket stood his two adult sons, Amardeep and Pardeep, who would become leading national voices in efforts to end gun and hate violence. Flanking Ranjit Singh's casket was his fourteen-year-old son, Gurvinder Singh. Next to Paramjit Kaur's casket stood Kamal and Harpreet. I murmured the only words of comfort and reassurance that I could muster. *Our community will stand by you.* I believed them fully in my heart, but I also knew that they could provide little solace at this time. As I returned to my seat, I saw Jasjit Singh and Amardeep Singh, two Sikh American leaders who had become a visible presence in Oak Creek since the tragedy. Our embraces spoke volumes. How could this have happened again? How can our community bear it? What more could have been done after 9/11 to prevent this massacre from occurring? We would ask ourselves these questions for months afterward.

The memorial service proceeded with a number of speeches from community leaders and elected officials. Among them was attorney general Eric Holder, who said, "For our nation's law enforcement community, our resolve to prevent acts of terrorism and combat crimes motivated by hatred has never been stronger. And that is precisely what happened here: an act of terrorism; an act of hatred; a crime that is anathema to the founding principles of our nation and to who we are as a people." Holder also rightly placed the tragedy on the long continuum of hate violence that Sikh communities had endured since 9/11: "Unfortunately, for the Sikh community, this sort of violence has become all too common in recent years. In the recent past, too many Sikhs have been targeted and victimized simply because of who they are, how they look, and what they believe."[52]

The public backlash that Sikhs, along with Muslims, Hindus, South Asians, and Arabs, have experienced since September 11, 2001, had indeed become "all too common." But it did not happen in a vacuum. As subsequent chapters show, this violence was reinforced by racist, anti-Muslim, and xenophobic political rhetoric, by media narratives that stereotype and dehumanize South Asians, Arabs, Muslims, and Sikhs, and by the government's own policies and practices that targeted and profiled these same communities in the name of national security.

The Culture and Climate of Hate Violence

Hate violence affects everyone in America. A hate crime affects not only the person being targeted but the entire community to which that person belongs. Acts of hate violence can disrupt and affect even those who do not belong the community being directly targeted, as we witnessed in Oak Creek, Wisconsin, where non-Sikhs also experienced fear and anxiety in the wake of the massacre. It is important, then, for us to mount multisector approaches to address the epidemic of hate violence in our nation.

Annual reports from the Federal Bureau of Investigation (FBI) and the Bureau of Justice Statistics (BJS) provide a snapshot of the landscape of hate crimes against a person (including assaults and homicides) or property (including vandalism to places of worship or cross-burnings). The BJS reports that the percentage of hate crimes involving violence increased from 78 percent in 2004 to 90 percent in 2011 and 2012.[53] The grounds for hate crimes have remained steady in recent years. The FBI's 2013 report finds that 48.5 percent of the 5,922 single-bias hate crime incidents that year were motivated by racial bias, followed by 20.8 percent on the basis of sexual orientation, 17.4 percent by religious bias, 11.1 percent by ethnicity, 1.4 percent by disability, 0.3 percent on the basis of gender bias, and 0.5 percent on the basis of gender identity.[54] Areas of concern for advocates include the increase in "anti-Islamic" crimes since 9/11 detailed earlier in this chapter, as well as the rise in reported hate crimes targeting transgender women of color.[55]

Given the culture of underreporting hate crimes, the numbers might be much higher than we believe. Immigrants, people of color, women, and members of lesbian, gay, bisexual, and transgender communities in particular are likely to underreport hate crimes for many reasons including distrust of police, lack of proficiency with English, a personal sense of shame for enduring an attack, or undocumented status. For South Asian, Arab, Muslim, and Sikh immigrants especially, reporting can present even greater obstacles. Many community members feel uncomfortable reporting crimes to a local FBI office or police department when some of these same law enforcement agencies are also responsible for conducting surveillance on their activities. They also fear that providing any information to law enforcement, including a hate crimes complaint, could lead to a national security or immigration-related investigation of their and others' families.

New mechanisms for tracking hate crimes may lead to increased reporting. Prior to 2013, the FBI did not track hate crimes against Sikhs, Hindus, or Arabs. Hate crimes against these communities were instead filed under various categories such as "anti-Islamic," "anti-Asian," or "other."[56] The impact of the need for specific hate crimes data was articulated by Harpreet Singh Saini, Kamal's younger brother, on September 19, 2012, at a hearing before the U.S. Senate Committee on the Judiciary organized by Senator Dick Durbin (D-IL) and his chief counsel, Joseph Zogby, who had been one of the leading Civil Rights Division attorneys to address the backlash in the immediate aftermath of 9/11. In his testimony, Harpreet said, "Senators, I came here today to ask the government to give my mother the dignity of being a statistic. The FBI does not track hate crimes against Sikhs. My mother and those shot that day will not even count on a federal form. We cannot solve a problem we refuse to recognize."[57]

Due to the advocacy of the Oak Creek community and organizations around the country, this practice has changed. Near the one-year anniversary of the Oak Creek gurdwara massacre, the Department of Justice announced that the FBI would begin to track hate crimes against Sikhs, Hindus, and Arabs for the first time.[58] The new policy went into effect on January 1, 2015. In February 2015, the FBI released a revised law enforcement training manual that includes scenarios to help law enforcement distinguish between crimes against Arabs, Sikhs, and Hindus.[59]

Governmental tracking and monitoring of hate crimes incidents must continue. In addition, state and federal prosecutors must bring hate crime charges and prosecutions in order to send clear messages to the general public that as a society we will not tolerate hate violence. State antibias and anti-hate-crime laws, as well as federal laws such as the 2009 Matthew Shepard and James Byrd, Jr., Hate Crimes Prevention Act (HCPA), have become important tools for law enforcement agencies to address hate violence through the criminal justice system. HCPA provides federal penalties for many types of violent acts committed because of actual or perceived race, color, religion, national origin, gender, disability, sexual orientation, or gender identity. The law also provides more entry points for federal law enforcement agencies such as the FBI to investigate these crimes.[60]

Prior to the passage of the HCPA, prosecutors were hamstrung by the "federally protected activity" requirement that had to be met in order to bring hate crime charges. HCPA removed this requirement, allowing federal investigators greater leeway. However, the standard of proof to show actual or circumstantial bias on the part of the perpetrator remains high. Federal prosecutors are often

unable to bring hate crime charges in a wide range of cases—
such as the shooting of Trayvon Martin by George Zimmerman in
2012—because of this high standard of proof. Attorney General
Holder has indicated that the standards of proof in federal hate
crime cases need to be "adjusted . . . [in order] to make the federal
government a better backstop."[61]

At the same time, it is important to keep in mind that hate
crimes laws and prosecutions provide victims and the communities
to which they belong with limited satisfaction. A hate crime charge
may increase the sentencing time for a perpetrator, but this form of
retributive punishment wielded by an inequitable and ineffective
criminal justice system cannot address or eliminate bigotry and hatred overall. That is why we must deal with the root causes that lead
to hate violence. These include racist and xenophobic attitudes and
beliefs that we hold about one another, which are often reinforced
by governmental policies, political rhetoric, and media narratives.
For example, the brand of post-9/11 racism targeting South Asian,
Arab, Hindu, Muslim, and Sikh communities includes individual
attitudes of bias and acts of discrimination such as hate violence
or a hostile workplace. It also consists of policies implemented by
government actors, such as national security and immigration laws,
that result in the systemic mistreatment of these communities.
Adding to this individual and systemic racism is xenophobia, which
includes a set of negative attitudes and policies about and toward
immigrants, questioning their utility, contributions, and humanity. Racism and xenophobia can lead to various consequences from
"microaggressions" such as slights and insults we direct toward one
another based on our implicit biases to policies and systems that
disadvantage minorities, as compared to Whites.

In the course of addressing the root causes of hate violence, one
arena that deserves greater attention is the rise in right-wing groups,
a trend that is likely to continue as the country's racial demographics
rapidly shift. By 2043, America will become a "majority-minority"

nation for the first time in its history with the majority of the population comprised of people of color.[62] These demographic changes will reverberate through our nation's cultural, political, legal, and media spaces and generate a variety of responses. This new landscape is likely to give rise to racial anxiety about the perceived loss of an imagined "American" culture threatened by an immigrant influx and the growing power of people of color.

As a result, racist and xenophobic beliefs and attitudes could become even more prominently held and articulated. In fact, racial anxiety is already influencing the goals of many organized hate groups in the United States, including the ones that Wade Michael Page, the Oak Creek domestic terrorist, joined.

I spoke with Mark Potok, senior fellow at the Southern Poverty Law Center (SPLC) and editor of the Center's quarterly *Intelligence Report*, to understand the goals of these hate groups. Potok noted that the mix of groups that exist in the United States today include anti-immigrant, antigay, and anti-Muslim groups, as well as antigovernment "patriot" groups.[63] Many are reacting to what they perceive as fundamental changes in America, including the election of an African American man as president, the events of 9/11, and the influx of immigrants into the country.[64] Many of the organized radical right groups believe that the true nature of an American nation of White Christians is being threatened. According to the SPLC, the types and numbers of organized hate groups rose through much of the first decade of the 2000s. In 2001, the SPLC tracked 676 hate groups.[65] This number grew to 926 in 2008, the year President Barack Obama was elected.[66] It climbed to 1,002 in 2010 and 1,007 in 2012.[67] In 2013 and 2014, the numbers of hate groups declined to 939 and 784, respectively.[68]

Most right-wing hate groups agitate around the existence and perceived influence of people of color, certain faith communities, and immigrants in America. Patriot groups, for example, believe that the federal government has secret plans to impose martial law on the United States in order to force the country into a so-cialistic one-world government known as the New World Order.[69] Anti-Muslim hate groups are a relatively new phenomenon in the United States, many of them forming in the wake of 9/11. These organizations and their spokespersons foment fears about the per-ceived influence of Islam in America. Anti-immigrant groups use one of two theories to support their racist propaganda: that there is a secret plan for Mexico to reclaim the U.S. Southwest or that the American, Canadian, and Mexican governments are creating an alliance similar to that of the European Union.[70]

In addition, neo-Nazi and racist skinhead groups, including the Aryan Terror Brigade, the National Socialist Movement (NSM), and Hammerskin Nation, continue to recruit members. The NSM website, for example, includes language denouncing "all non-White immigration" and demanding that "all non-Whites currently resid-ing in America be required to leave the nation forthwith and return to their land of origin: peacefully or by force."[71] These groups spew rhetoric that is steeped in the belief that only Whites should have access to the benefits, rights, and institutions of the United States because they are superior to other races.

Wade Michael Page was drawn to the beliefs of White suprem-acist groups. In 1995, when Page was serving in the U.S. Army in his early twenties, he was stationed at Fort Bragg, near Fayetteville, North Carolina, where a group of White supremacist soldiers flew Nazi flags and listened to music that endorsed the murders of Afri-can Americans and Jews.[72] The National Alliance, a neo-Nazi group that believed in White supremacist and White separatist ideologies, even recruited soldiers at the base.[73] Page began his deeper involve-ment in the White supremacist movement through White power music. He played music with groups such as 13 Knots (for the num-ber of knots in a noose), Definite Hate, Celtic Warrior, and Blue Eyed Devils, among others.[74] He eventually became an active mem-ber of a skinhead group called the Northern Hammerskins.[75] By the time Page barged into the Oak Creek gurdwara in August 2012, he had developed deep roots in extremist ideology and loyalty to groups that supported the notions that non-Whites and immigrants were inferior people who corrupted the true nature of American society.

"Lone wolves" like Page who are heavily influenced by White supremacist hate groups are becoming more commonplace, according to Potok at the SPLC.[76] In addition, hate group propaganda is beginning to influence mainstream political discourse as well as policies that concern the rights of immigrants and race and faith groups. "Radical right groups talking about immigrants taking our jobs and Muslims imposing Sharia law and recruiting jihadists has a lot of public appeal," Potok said. "And keep in mind that this is moving into [the] American political mainstream." Jill Garvey, the executive director of the Center for New Community, an organization that tracks and analyzes far-right movements, agrees. "As our demographics change, White supremacist and extremist groups will continue to exist, but they will package their ideology differently," she explained. According to Garvey, these groups might not use racist language explicitly, but their membership will be all White, and they will support anti-Muslim, anti-immigrant policies.

One intervention that policy makers can make to address hate violence is to allocate greater resources and attention toward combating these right-wing domestic hate groups. The federal government appears to be fully aware of the threat of right-wing extremism in our country. In April 2009, a Department of Homeland Security (DHS) report titled "Rightwing Extremism: Current Economic and Political Climate Fueling Resurgence in Radicalization and Recruitment" was leaked to the media. The report warned law enforcement agencies about the increase in "rightwing extremist activity." It also specifically identified hate groups and White power militias that were dissatisfied with the election of President Obama, the economic recession, and immigration.[77] The report found that "white supremacist lone wolves pose the most significant domestic terrorist threat because of their low profile and autonomy."[78]

Despite the DHS report's findings, the Obama administration's policies to counter violent extremism—which surely includes hate violence and right-wing hate groups—seem instead to be focused elsewhere: on the threat of radicalization in Muslim communities. The White House has defined violent extremists as "individuals who support or commit ideologically-motivated violence to further political goals." Notwithstanding this broad characterization, the Obama administration has targeted its efforts toward what it believes to be the "preeminent terrorist threat to our country"— namely, Al Qaeda and affiliated groups or adherents.[79] The administration's "countering violent extremism" program has been roundly criticized for its lack of attention to right-wing hate groups as well as for its emphasis on Muslim communities, which furthers anti-Muslim suspicion in the nation.[80]

Our government must utilize a broader definition of violent extremism and put in place strategies and tools to address its various manifestations effectively. In addition to the "lone wolf" phenomenon, the presence of right-wing groups like the Ku Klux Klan has become more insidious around the country. In the midst of the protests in Ferguson, Missouri, in August 2014, after Michael Brown was shot and killed by a white police officer, the Traditionalist American Knights of the Ku Klux Klan passed out flyers in St. Louis County calling attention to "the terrorists masquerading as 'peaceful protestors'" and threatening "lethal force."[81] The New Empire Knights of the Ku Klux Klan also threatened to come to Ferguson to protect White businesses during protests.[82] The Ku Klux Klan's xenophobic attitudes were also on full display in July 2014 when the Imperial Wizard of the Loyal White Knights responded to the surge of children migrating across the U.S.-Mexico border that summer by saying, "If we can't turn them back, I think if we pop a couple of them off and leave their corpses laying at

the border maybe they'll see we're serious about stopping immigration."[83] Outrageous public remarks and actions such as these
place communities of color and immigrants in danger around the
country—and demand federal oversight and monitoring.

The epidemic of hate violence specifically affecting South
Asian, Arab, Muslim, and Sikh communities also deserves unique
attention from government agencies given its scope, impact, and
frequency. A similar precedent exists with the National Church
Arson Task Force (NCATF), which President Bill Clinton put
in place in 1996.[84] The NCATF was a coordinated government
response to bombings, attempted bombings, and arson against
houses of worship in African American communities in the South.
Through prosecutions, coordinated government involvement, and
consistently strong messages from the president and high-ranking
officials, the NCATF reduced arsons by 53 percent between 1996
and 1999 and opened 945 investigations between 1995 and 2000.[85]

Post-9/11 hate violence requires a similar aggressive response
from the government to ensure that South Asian, Arab, Muslim, Sikh, and Hindu communities are not living in fear. In the
wake of the Oak Creek tragedy, SAALT and many national organizations proposed that the Obama administration create a federal interagency task force on post-9/11 hate violence similar to
the NCATF.[86] In November 2014, the Department of Justice announced the establishment of an Interagency Initiative on Hate
Crimes task force that "will promote cross-agency collaboration
and will address prevention of violent hate crimes, as well as effective responses to hate crimes."[87]

Perhaps such a task force could be useful in preventing deaths
like that of fifteen-year-old Abdisamad Sheikh-Hussein in Kansas
City, Missouri, in December 2014 by a man driving an SUV as
he left the Somali Center of Kansas City. Sheikh-Hussein's legs
were nearly severed in the incident, and he died from his injuries.
The Kansas chapter of the Council on American-Islamic Relations

noted that the Muslim community in Kansas City had received threats for months before the incident and that the car allegedly involved in the hit-and-run incident had been observed months earlier with an anti-Islamic message written on a rear window.[88]

Given the likelihood that incidents of hate violence will continue around the nation, it is important that we are adequately prepared. Without systemic solutions and practices that challenge and change the culture and climate of hostility toward Muslim, Arab, Hindu, Sikh, and South Asian communities, efforts to counter hate violence through only legal solutions will not stick. Both the public and private sectors must be ready to address the immediate medical, linguistic, psychological, and immigration needs of victims of hate violence and their families. Government agencies must develop rapid-response teams with appropriately trained personnel who can serve as first responders in the event of an act of hate violence. Educators must be prepared to have discussions with students about the collective impact of hate violence on a community and to provide support for young people who have witnessed trauma or lost loved ones to tragedy. Elected officials must quickly condemn hate violence in public settings, as Mayor Scaffidi did in Oak Creek, and emphasize that the broader community is standing with those directly affected.

In addition, state and local legislators can introduce legislation to develop government and community rapid-response mechanisms, monitor hate groups, and hold formal sessions to hear directly from community members and leaders about the scope of hate violence. Politicians must abide by a code of civility and hold one another accountable for racist and xenophobic rhetoric. Philanthropic stakeholders can invest in the efforts of community-based organizations that are often at the front lines of responding to the heightened sense of alarm that their constituents experience.

Fostering a climate based on mutual understanding and respect of the multiracial communities we are fast becoming in America will take vigilance from each of us. It starts with a better understanding of one another's stories, histories, and experiences, and with the intention of finding common threads and identifying one another's humanity. It includes civic, faith, education, and business leaders, working in partnership with artists and cultural bridge builders who can create spaces and opportunities that allow people to be in deep and honest dialogue with one another.

That is precisely what is happening in Oak Creek.

Lessons from Oak Creek

I have visited the Oak Creek community several times since the 2012 tragedy. During my most recent trip, in 2014, I spoke with a number of young people between the ages of twenty and thirty-three, who consider themselves a part of the Sikh and South Asian communities. They discussed their own healing processes and their hopes for Oak Creek.

Kanwardeep Singh, who lost his uncle in the massacre at the gurdwara, said, "I think of my day of birth and August 5, 2012, as the two most important days of my life." After the tragedy, Singh began to grow his hair and wear a turban to proclaim, publicly and visibly, his Sikh faith. "I don't shy away from conversations about my faith," he said. "I have random conversations with people about who I am on purpose, while I'm at the gas station or walking down the street." Kanwardeep feels a sense of personal purpose to let people know who he is because "it is important to learn the stories of others and find a sense of common humanity." According to Mandeep Kaur, many young people in the community have responded similarly in the wake of the tragedy. "Young people will wear their turbans more now and keep their hair," she said. "Because they want to educate, to show people who we really are."

Another shift that is occurring within the Sikh community in Oak Creek is the desire of young people to become more visible and influential in civic and political institutions. Historically the gurdwara's leadership had focused on addressing immediate internal needs and challenges and fostering a climate of support for newcomers. This is a common approach that many immigrant groups take in the United States. The creation of a safe community space and the emphasis on building infrastructure and networks are sequential steps in the process of any immigrant group's civic and political maturation. Now, catalyzed by the tragedy in Oak Creek, Sikh youth leaders are ready to take the next step and become more involved and engaged in the broader community.

"We have to get out of the walls of the gurdwara," said Rahul Dubey, who is active with various civic organizations in Milwaukee. "We have to be out there and let people know who we are, and we have to take on positions of power, too." Rahul makes it a point to regularly attend events coordinated by interfaith and LGBTQ groups and by communities of color. Similarly, Mandeep became a member of One Milwaukee, which recruits emerging leaders from diverse communities. "We make presentations together. We are connected to the political leadership. Milwaukee is a very segregated city, and it's important to make the effort and get to know people from different backgrounds," Mandeep said.

Many young Sikhs mentioned that the segregated neighborhoods and schools of Milwaukee and surrounding areas have contributed to a range of systemic problems, including the lack of understanding among communities of color. They want to find ways to break through the systemic barriers and internal racism that divide communities from one another. For example, Navi Gill, a twenty-year-old student at the University of Wisconsin–Milwaukee, was concerned that many South Asians in the Milwaukee area are disconnected from Black communities. "The liquor stores located in the north side of Milwaukee, where Black people live, are owned mainly by our own people," Gill noted. "And even though we do business there, we keep African Americans at a distance. Why? We have to change this." As the Oak Creek community continues to heal, the prospect of building stronger bridges with other communities of color remains a priority for young people in particular.

After the tragedy, Mayor Scaffidi also realized the need for the various communities in Oak Creek to come together. He partnered with the Interfaith Conference of Greater Milwaukee to hold dinner dialogues at the homes of local residents to bring people of different religious backgrounds together. Through structured questions, participants learn more about one another's faiths, community histories, and experiences living in the area, while having a meal together. The city of Oak Creek has also worked with Not in Our Town, an organization that utilizes films and discussion tools to empower localities and schools to foster mutual respect and a spirit of inclusion. Not in Our Town produced the film *Waking in Oak Creek: Working Together for Safe, Inclusive Communities*, which has been shown to law enforcement and community groups and on campuses throughout the nation.

Marking the anniversaries of the tragedy has also become a significant part of the healing and bridge-building process. For the past two years, young people have organized a 6K run/walk—one kilometer for each of the six killed in the gurdwara—in the spirit of Chardi Kala, a Sikh concept that means finding optimism in oneself in the face of adversity. On the first anniversary of the tragedy, more than six hundred people from diverse backgrounds and faiths participated. The organizers placed the tragedy in Oak Creek in the continuum of other gun-related shootings around the country by providing pictures of people killed in Aurora, Colorado, and Newtown, Connecticut, to participants to carry on the 6K run/walk. Robbie Parker, who lost his daughter in the massacre of twenty schoolchildren and six adults at Sandy Hook Elementary School in Newtown, just four months after the Oak Creek tragedy, attended the anniversary events with his family. In a moving speech, he connected Newtown's experiences of loss, pain, and psychological trauma with those of the Oak Creek community.

The process of individual and community healing continues in Oak Creek. It was reflected in young Palmeet's face when she sat next to me during *langar* one Saturday afternoon in the spring of 2014 and told me in a tentative voice about her summer plans. Palmeet finds community and love in the same place where her father lost his life in an act of hate. During my visit, I also heard about the long road to healing from the family of Punjab Singh, who was severely wounded during the massacre. He remains in a coma at a nearby care facility where his son, who traveled to Wisconsin from India after the tragedy, sits vigil over him.

The grief of losing his mother is palpable on Kamal's face and shoulders. He carries it with him. But his personal tragedy has also opened him to feeling deeply for others who share similar losses. When we met last, he told me about his profound sadness upon hearing about the gun massacre at Sandy Hook Elementary School. In response, Kamal decided to connect personally and directly with the community in Newtown. He told me, "After the Sandy Hook shooting, I think I relived that day [August 5, 2012, the date of the Oak Creek tragedy]. When I woke up, my phone was already blowing up with calls from friends and family, because they wanted to know my take on it. A few weeks later, we put together a banner, 'Sikh Temple of Wisconsin and Oak Creek Stands with You.' So I talked to my friends, and we flew to New York and then drove to Connecticut to deliver the banner. Right when we got off the highway, there was a tent. We went there first, and there were thousands of teddy bears and a huge bunch of posters, flowers, and memorabilia for the kids, the police officers, the teachers. I cried for about twenty minutes because I thought it was so powerful. We took the banner inside, but the lady that was in charge there, she recognized me and saw me crying. I told her who I was, and she couldn't believe we came all the way from Oak Creek. It was the most amazing thing I've ever done."

2

Journeys in a Racial State

America is a racial state. We are the inheritors of systems and institutions that enable the denial of basic human rights to indigenous
and Black and Brown communities, from colonization to slavery,
from Jim Crow segregation to the Japanese American internment.
The post-9/11 treatment of South Asian, Arab, and Muslim communities by the U.S. government continues this shameful legacy.

In the years after 9/11, the state took on several functions and
roles, many of which operated in direct contradiction to one another. Federal government agencies conducted outreach and en-
forced civil rights laws that protected South Asian, Arab, Muslim,
and Sikh communities against discrimination and hate violence on
the basis of race, national origin, or religion. Simultaneously, other
parts of the federal government implemented domestic policies that
essentially treated South Asian, Arab, and Muslim immigrants as
the "other." The state viewed members of these particular communities as potential threats who were worthy of suspicion. Through
national security and immigration policies, the state targeted individuals from Middle Eastern, North African, and South Asian
countries, as well as those who practice Islam, for purposes of investigation, scrutiny, detention, and deportation. While this book
focuses exclusively on the state's domestic policies and practices,

it is important to keep in mind that America's rendition and torture policies, its treatment of detainees in Guantánamo, and its wartime and intelligence operations in South Asia and the Middle East all have significant consequences for South Asian, Arab, and Muslim communities in the United States as well.

In effect, after 9/11, the state became both a champion for defending the civil rights of South Asians, Arabs, and Muslims *and* the enforcer of harmful policies that led to the surveillance and detentions of thousands of immigrants from these communities. These conflicting roles have been confusing and harmful, because for many community members the state is one entity, seamless and interconnected. As a result, many government agencies have faced tremendous challenges in building trust and partnerships with South Asian, Arab, and Muslim communities and the organizations that represent them. The state's actions have served only to reinforce public perceptions and media narratives that members of these communities are "others" who should be viewed with suspicion and whose rights, presence, and lives are essentially disposable.

Despite the vast architecture of detrimental policies enacted after 9/11, many flew under the radar of the media and the general public. The most well-known piece of post-9/11 legislation is the USA PATRIOT Act (Uniting and Strengthening America by Providing Appropriate Tools Required to Intercept and Obstruct Terrorism Act), which passed in Congress with little debate and was signed into law by President George W. Bush on October 26, 2001.[1] The Patriot Act drew upon legal precedents to deter terrorism set by the far-reaching Antiterrorism and Effective Death Penalty Act (AEDPA), enacted by Congress in 1996.[2] AEDPA broadened the definition of "national security" justifications, allowed the use of secret evidence against noncitizens suspected of supporting terrorist groups even if they did not personally engage in criminal activities, and made it a felony to provide material support to terrorist organizations even if assistance was directed toward lawful activities.[3]

The Patriot Act took AEDPA several steps further. It increased the federal government's powers to conduct searches, surveillance, and detentions with little oversight or governance. Some of the most criticized aspects of the Patriot Act include the ability of government officials to conduct searches and seizures without meeting the constitutional standard of probable cause if they suspect terrorist activity. This extended the government's authority to access records being held by third parties, including libraries and universities. The law also broadened the grounds for detaining and excluding nonimmigrants suspected of having ties to terrorist organizations.[4] The extent to which the constitutional and privacy rights of Americans have been compromised through the application of the Patriot Act is still unclear. Between 2001 and 2014, Congress has reauthorized and amended the Patriot Act five times. In 2015, various provisions of the Patriot Act expired, including the bulk collection of phone records by the National Security Agency and the use of roving wiretaps by law enforcement authorities.[5]

The Patriot Act's passage in 2001 also set the stage for an overhaul and reorganization of the federal government. In November 2002, Congress enacted the Homeland Security Act, which brought more than twenty federal agencies under the purview of the U.S Department of Homeland Security (DHS).[6] The new agency's primary mission was to focus explicitly on terrorist response, both in terms of preventing attacks and preparing the country to confront future threats of terrorism.[7] Several agencies fell under the ambit of DHS, including the Transportation Security Administration, the Federal Emergency Management Agency, and a set of immigration agencies including Immigration and Customs Enforcement, the U.S. Citizenship and Immigration Services, and Customs and Border Protection.[8]

Components of the DOJ and the DHS implemented many of

the policies that targeted South Asian, Arab, and Muslim immigrants for ties to terrorist activities in the immediate aftermath of 9/11. The key tool in the government's arsenal became immigration law. Given that many South Asians, Arabs, and Muslims were noncitizens, the government relied upon the immigration enforcement system to target these communities. This practice of blending national security and immigration policies has resulted in an unprecedented level of detentions and deportations of South Asian, Muslim, and Arab immigrants in the decade and a half since 9/11.

Within ten days after the terrorist attacks, for example, the DOJ issued an interim rule that gave federal law enforcement agents the ability to detain noncitizens for forty-eight hours or longer without charging them if the state could show that "an emergency or other extraordinary circumstance" existed.[9] Armed with this expanded authority, government authorities arrested and detained 738 noncitizens between September 11, 2001, and August 2002.[10] Those taken away became known as "The Disappeared," because they literally vanished from their streets, homes, and small businesses. In addition, the government held more than six hundred secret immigration hearings were held pursuant to a memorandum by chief immigration judge Michael Creppy. The media, family members, and the public at large were barred from knowing the charges, evidence, or outcomes of these cases, many of which involved South Asian, Muslim, and Arab immigrant men.[11] The government justified these tactics of arresting people from particular communities without charging them or conducting secret hearings with the use of one blanket phrase: "national security reasons."[12]

It is still unclear which criteria the government used to determine whether individuals rose to the level of being national security threats. In many circumstances, Federal Bureau of Investigation agents and local police officers identified and detained individuals based *not* on evidence of their potential ties to terrorism or actual criminal behavior but on unconfirmed tips from the public or chance encounters. For example, on November 25, 2001, a resident in Torrington, Connecticut, informed police that he had heard two "Arabs" talking about anthrax. Police officers followed the two men (who were actually Pakistani) suspected of having had this conversation. When the two men reached a gas station, they were summarily arrested. Agents also arrested Ayazuddin Sheerazi, an Indian businessman who worked at the gas station, and another man from Pakistan who just happened to be at the gas station at the same time. The police did not offer any explanation for why they were arrested. Sheerazi was detained for eighteen days before being released on bond; meanwhile, the Torrington caller failed a voluntary polygraph test regarding the tip.[13] This incident is but one example of the government's use of inaccurate and unconfirmed information to detain community members and its failure to consider more measured alternatives or the civil rights repercussions on the people subjected to such enforcement actions.

In addition to forcibly detaining individuals from South Asian, Muslim, and Arab communities, often without cause, the DOJ also conducted "voluntary" interviews of more than three thousand nonimmigrant men from countries where Al Qaeda may have been in operation between September 11 and November 9, 2001. Despite the supposed voluntary nature of these interviews, some of the men questioned were arrested for violating immigration laws, including staying past the expiration dates of their visas or working without legal authorization.[14] For these men, a voluntary government program turned into a serious investigative process with the risk of deportation.

Another policy, the Absconder Apprehension Initiative, implemented in January 2002, sought to locate more than three hundred thousand people with court orders of deportation already against them.[15] As Asa Hutchinson, undersecretary for border and transportation security, explained before a congressional committee in

2003, the initiative was "aimed at aggressively tracking, apprehending, and removing aliens who have violated U.S. immigration law, been ordered deported, then fled before the order could be carried out." According to Hutchinson, the first phase of this initiative targeted "some 5,900 aliens from countries where Al Qaeda is known to operate or recruit."[16] While the policy at first glance seemed like a race-neutral enforcement measure to locate *all* individuals who had run afoul of immigration laws, the actual implementation focused only on people from Middle Eastern, Arab, and South Asian countries.

Some have argued that the federal government had the right to scrutinize individuals from Muslim-majority countries or those who practice Islam, given the origins and faith of the 9/11 terrorists. They also argue that the government had the authority to remove individuals who are not authorized to be legally present in the United States if law enforcement personnel become aware of such situations during the course of a national security investigation. But the outcome of deportation should not be the default when the intent and application of national security policies are premised on unlawful profiling of individuals on the basis of race, religion, or national origin and without consideration of factors such as family ties and economic contributions to America. The selective enforcement of national security and immigration policies deprived South Asian, Arab, and Muslim immigrants of their rights to equal protection under the law and presumed their guilt by association.

Perhaps the most harmful state policy implemented in the wake of 9/11 is the National Security Entry-Exit Registration System (NSEERS). On August 12, 2002, the Department of Justice published a final rule in the *Federal Register* that set forth registration requirements for nonimmigrants (individuals in the United States temporarily, such as students, visitors, and temporary workers) entering the United States from certain countries. Under the rule,

nonimmigrant males sixteen years and older from specific countries had to report to immigration authorities upon arrival; thirty
days after arrival; every twelve months after arrival; upon events
such as a change of address, employment, or school; and upon de-
parture from the United States.[17] Individuals who did not comply
with NSEERS were placed into a database that could be shared
with local law enforcement and were at risk of being apprehended
at a later point.[18]

While the program may seem like an important mechanism
to monitor who enters the United States, NSEERS was actually
applied to nonimmigrants from only twenty-five countries: Af-
ghanistan, Algeria, Bahrain, Bangladesh, Egypt, Eritrea, Indone-
sia, Iran, Iraq, Jordan, Kuwait, Lebanon, Libya, Morocco, North
Korea, Oman, Pakistan, Qatar, Saudi Arabia, Somalia, Sudan,
Syria, Tunisia, the United Arab Emirates, and Yemen.[19] Most of
these countries are located in the Middle East, North Africa, or
South Asia; almost all have majority-Muslim or significant Muslim
populations.

The *Federal Register* final rule revealed the reasons why the
federal government implemented NSEERS: "Recent terrorist incidents have underscored the need to broaden the special registration requirements for nonimmigrant aliens . . . whose presence in
the United States requires closer monitoring, to require that they
provide specific information at regular intervals to ensure their
compliance with the terms of their visas and admission, and to
ensure that they depart the United States at the end of their authorized stay."[20] In other words, the federal government deemed
the NSEERS program necessary to ensure the country's national
security. In instituting NSEERS, the state exposed two dangerous
assumptions: (1) it presumed that people of particular nationalities
or faiths were more likely to have ties to terrorism or knowledge
of terrorist activities, and (2) it affirmed its authority to subject
entire swaths of particular faith and national origin communities

to "special" requirements without any evidence of individual criminality or even potential wrongdoing.

Around the country, lawyers and activists sprung into motion to denounce NSEERS. Many community members expressed dread and alarm when the first round of special registration began at the end of 2002. Misinformation spread, heightened by the fact that, at first, the government did not engage in its own outreach or provide in-language notices of the registration requirements beyond publishing them in the *Federal Register*, a federal publication not easily accessible to the public, much less by immigrants who are not proficient in English. As a result, many were not aware of special registration requirements, and no one could be sure of what would occur during the registration process.

As soon as the first round of registration began, reports of differential treatment from region to region emerged, with some striking examples of mistreatment and improper interrogation. In December 2002, the immigration office in Los Angeles allegedly arrested up to seven hundred individuals who had come to comply with the requirement, casting doubt on the program's purported data-gathering motives.[21] In addition, the information sought by the government seemed suspicious and disconnected from the publicly stated goals of NSEERS. Many of the men who complied with NSEERS nationwide reported that immigration authorities asked them for their financial records, their travel histories to Middle Eastern and South Asian countries, and their connections with political or religious organizations, including which mosques they frequented.[22] Still others were unfairly detained and harassed by immigration enforcement officers.[23] Legal challenges to NSEERS did not succeed, as federal courts have consistently found that the United States acted within its constitutional authority in implementing a program aimed at preserving national security.[24]

NSEERS took a significant toll on South Asian, Muslim, and Arab communities at many levels. At the time, I worked at the

Asian Pacific American Legal Resource Center (APALRC), a local, community-based organization that connected low-income Asian Americans with legal services. We coordinated a legal clinic in 2003 at the Muslim Community Center in Silver Spring, Maryland, to address NSEERS requirements. During the clinic, many community members expressed confusion and anxiety. One after the other, green card holders, U.S. citizens, refugees, undocumented immigrants, and students of Pakistani, Bangladeshi, and Indian descent described the fears that had permeated their families and communities since 9/11, as well as their increasing feelings of marginalization and exclusion in America.

After the legal clinic, a Pakistani family approached me. Clinic lawyers had just informed the father that he fell under the NSEERS guidelines. He understood that because he was undocumented, it was likely that he could be put into deportation proceedings if he complied with NSEERS. Yet not registering meant that he might be subjected to fines and eventual deportation. "Can anything be done at all?" his wife asked me pleadingly. Her husband was the sole breadwinner for the family, and his deportation would mean that her family would be separated and that their children's futures would be permanently altered. I had no answers for her. There were no words to explain the injustice behind policies that targeted her family simply because of their nationality and faith, and there were no meaningful alternatives to offer.

We now know that nearly 83,000 men complied with the NSEERS program, and that more than 13,000 of them were placed in deportation proceedings. Thirty-five percent of those who were deported as a result of NSEERS were of Pakistani descent.[25] Given these high numbers, advocates believe that the government automatically placed individuals in detention if any immigration irregularities were found without utilizing discretion and weighing various factors, such as family ties in the United States.

Behind the numbers of those deported are broken families and broken homes. Small businesses holding the hopes of Pakistani and Bangladeshi families in thoroughfares like Coney Island Avenue in Brooklyn had to close their doors. Dreams of college or work were deferred or discarded altogether. Brothers, fathers, husbands, and sons were separated from their sisters, children, wives, and mothers. Deported men struggled to make new lives in countries they had left in search of their American dreams. At the same time, those they were separated from had to make impossible decisions about whether to return to their country of origin and join a deported son, father, brother, or husband or rebuild lives in Queens, Chicago, and Fremont. We have yet to fully grapple with the financial and psychological toll on families split apart by NSEERS.

Meanwhile, the federal government has not revealed whether information of any importance to the nation's security was gathered during NSEERS. In 2011, the government announced the removal of the countries listed under NSEERS because it had identified more effective ways to gather information about foreign nationals in the United States.[26] The Obama administration acknowledged that NSEERS "does not provide any increase in security" and the DHS Office of Inspector General called for the full termination of the program.[27] Advocates continue to press the DHS to provide a reprieve for those who did not comply with NSEERS as well as immigration benefits to those who registered and were indiscriminately placed in deportation proceedings.

The Practice of Profiling

NSEERS is an example of profiling, a discriminatory policy and practice often undertaken by the government to identify criminal activity. Profiling is a law enforcement strategy grounded in the assumption that people with particular characteristics (including race, national origin, religious affiliation, accent, immigration status, gender, gender identity, or sexual orientation) are more likely to commit certain criminal acts. When law enforcement authorities utilize profiling, they assume that someone will engage in criminal behavior based on her or his group status rather than on specific individual actions that actually evince criminality. Racial profiling has been utilized in law enforcement initiatives such as the War on Crime and the War on Drugs to target Blacks and Latinos as perpetrators of street crimes or drug-related offenses. Profiling has also been a factor in routine law enforcement activities such as stop-and-frisks and traffic stops that disproportionately affect Black and Latino males. Many of the same tools, mechanisms, and narratives that underpin the War on Crime and the War on Drugs have been utilized in the targeting of South Asian, Muslim, and Arab communities in the War on Terror.

Prior to 9/11, support had slowly been building in the courts, Congress, and the federal government toward ending the use of profiling in law enforcement activities because of its ineffectiveness in identifying criminal activity and the mistrust it engenders between communities and those who are sworn to serve and protect them.[28] In *United States v. Montero-Camargo* (2000), the U.S. Court of Appeals for the Ninth Circuit held that while Border Patrol agents had reasonable suspicion under the Fourth Amendment to stop defendants near the U.S.-Mexico border, their practices did not reflect our constitutional values. The court noted that "stops based on race or ethnic appearance send the underlying message to all our citizens that those who are not white are judged by the color of their skin alone."[29] The drumbeat to eliminate profiling practices soon extended to Congress, where Representative John Conyers Jr. (D-MI) and Senator Russell Feingold (D-WI) introduced the End Racial Profiling Act on June 6, 2001.[30]

Just three months later, the 9/11 attacks changed the landscape altogether. Law enforcement and government agencies began to overtly engage in profiling through programs such as NSEERS.

Airport profiling became commonplace. Muslim and Sikh travelers who wear hijabs or turbans were subjected to secondary screenings for no reason other than their appearance. South Asian, Muslim, and Arab travelers also faced routine targeting at border checkpoints by Customs and Border Protection agents who searched their electronic equipment and detained them without cause.[31] In addition, the government placed individuals—many with South Asian, Arab, or Muslim names—on "no-fly lists," preventing them from visiting or reuniting with their loved ones or performing job duties that require airplane travel.[32] In 2014, a federal court called into question the constitutionality of these lists in part because of the government's failure to notify people about the reasons for not being able to fly.[33] This decision prompted the government to implement a process for notifying individuals of the reasons for their placement on the no-fly list, but whether the information provided is sufficient is up for debate.[34]

Despite the utilization of profiling as a post-9/11 strategy in airport travel and national security investigations, the Bush administration released guidance in 2003 that limited the use of profiling in many law enforcement activities. Relying in part on the language in the *Montero-Camargo* case, the 2003 guidance from the Department of Justice claimed: "Racial profiling in law enforcement is not merely wrong, but also ineffective. Race-based assumptions in law enforcement perpetuate negative racial stereotypes that are harmful to our rich and diverse democracy, and materially impair our efforts to maintain a fair and just society."[35]

The 2003 DOJ guidance prohibited law enforcement actors from profiling individuals on the basis of race or ethnicity, but it did not ban profiling on the basis of national origin or religion. But it also created a gaping exception by allowing law enforcement actors to use profiling in national security investigations, airport screening, and border security activities. Relying on 9/11 as the reason for this loophole, the 2003 DOJ guidance stated:

Since the terrorist attacks on September 11, 2001, the President has emphasized that federal law enforcement personnel must use every legitimate tool to prevent future attacks, protect our Nation's borders, and deter those who would cause devastating harm to our Nation and its people. . . . Given the incalculably high stakes involved in such investigations, however, Federal law enforcement officers who are protecting national security or preventing catastrophic events (as well as airport security screeners) may consider race, ethnicity, or other relevant factors to the extent permitted by our laws and the Constitution.[36]

In effect, the 2003 guidance allowed federal law enforcement agencies and officers to utilize profiling in matters involving national security. Absent language that outlined the criteria for identifying a national security threat, the 2003 guidance presumptively sanctioned wide-scale profiling of South Asian, Arab, Muslim, and Sikh communities by law enforcement agencies.

Many of the policies that began under the Bush administration, including surveillance and data-gathering by the FBI, have continued well into the Obama administration. While the Obama administration responded to community pressure to revise the Bush guidance on racial profiling, it ultimately fell short of remedying its gaps. In 2014, the Obama administration banned the use of profiling based on race, ethnicity, gender, national origin, religion, sexual orientation, or gender identity by federal law enforcement in routine activities, including traffic stops.[37] The expansion of the list of prohibited factors to include sexual orientation, gender identity, and religion is a significant improvement. However, the profiling ban does not apply to particular activities of specific agencies, including data-gathering activities of the Federal Bureau of Investigation, border and port-of-entry enforcement by Customs and Border Protection, and airport security by the Transportation

Security Administration.[38] The 2014 guidance explicitly carves out an exception for the demographic mapping of particular racial and ethnic groups by the FBI, noting the following example:

> An FBI field office attempts to map out the features of the city within its area of responsibility in order to gain a better understanding of potential liaison contacts and outreach opportunities. In doing so, the office acquires information from public sources regarding population demographics, including concentrations of ethnic groups. This activity is permissible if it is undertaken pursuant to an authorized intelligence or investigative purpose.[39]

Given these exemptions in the 2014 guidance, federal agents from certain agencies will have the leeway to stop, interrogate, gather intelligence about, detain, and search people on the basis of factors such as race, religion, or national origin. Who are the communities that will most likely be affected by this incomplete ban on profiling? Sikhs, Muslims, South Asians, and Arab Americans are one segment. We already know that many members of these communities face routine profiling at airports, and that the FBI maps their neighborhoods, restaurants, mosques, and student associations for the purposes of data-gathering and surveillance.[40] Another group of people who are likely to be affected includes immigrants, mainly Latinos, who are stopped at borders and immigration checkpoints.[41]

The approach taken by the Obama administration's 2014 federal guidance is nothing short of a serious setback in advancing toward what is a universal goal: protecting the basic civil rights of all people. Instead, the guidance creates a group of individuals who will have a different set of rights than others, resulting in a sort of second-class citizenship for some. And, it practically ensures that targeted communities will continue to engage with law enforcement agents, state or federal, with trepidation and fear.[42]

In the coming years, it will be important for South Asian, Arab, Muslim, and Sikh communities and broader civil rights and racial justice organizations to collaborate effectively in advocating for amendments to the 2014 guidance. Racial justice organizations must stand alongside South Asian, Arab, Muslim, and Sikh communities to demand that the Department of Justice address the deficiencies and loopholes in the guidance. Additionally, local legislators should introduce anti-profiling bills that ban the practice by state and local law enforcement actors who are not covered under the federal guidance.

The Role of Political Rhetoric

For nearly a decade and a half, national security and immigration policies have had harmful effects on South Asian, Arab, and Muslim communities. The government's actions have reinforced public hostility toward community members and set dangerous precedents in terms of policies that sanction profiling on the basis of national origin or faith. In addition to these government actions and laws, some elected and public officials have engaged in a pattern of political rhetoric that has contributed to the climate of hostility and suspicion against South Asians, Arabs, Muslims, and Sikhs.

A 2010 report by South Asian Americans Leading Together (SAALT) points to examples of xenophobic and racist political rhetoric from political leaders. For example, in 2001 Congressman John Cooksey (R-LA) said, "If I see someone [who] comes in that's got a diaper on his head and a fan belt wrapped around the diaper on his head, that guy needs to be pulled over."[43] Cooksey soon apologized for his racist remarks.[44] In 2005, Representative Mark Kirk (R-IL), later elected as a U.S. senator, made statements sanctioning discrimination of individuals who come from the Middle

East. "I'm OK with discrimination against young Arab males from terrorist-producing states. I'm OK with that. I think that when we look at the threat that's out there, young men between, say, the ages of 18 and 25 from a couple of countries, I believe a certain amount of intense scrutiny should be placed on them."[45] These kinds of statements created an environment that effectively fueled and condoned public acts of harassment, discrimination, and violence against South Asians, Arabs, Muslims, and Sikhs.

Unfortunately, incendiary political rhetoric shows no sign of abatement. In March 2011, Representative Peter King (R-NY), the then chairman of the Committee on Homeland Security in the U.S. House of Representatives, held hearings on the extent of radicalization in the American Muslim community.[46] In response, a broad array of organizations opposed the hearings, claiming that they targeted religious minorities and increased anti-Muslim sentiment in the country. Still, xenophobic political rhetoric has continued. A 2014 SAALT report documented statements from former U.S. congressman Joe Walsh (R-IL), who said, "When it comes to our immigration, we need to begin profiling who our enemy is in this war: young Muslim men."[47] Divisive rhetoric also came from local officials, such as Deborah Pauly, a Republican member of the city council of Villa Park, California, who said—at a protest outside a Muslim charity event—"What's going on over there right now . . . that is pure, unadulterated evil. I know quite a few Marines who will be very happy to help these terrorists to an early meeting in paradise."[48]

During a time when many communities feel under attack and suspicion, our elected officials must foster a climate of respect and understanding and abide by zero-tolerance policies for offensive rhetoric. Policy makers must hold one another accountable for racist and xenophobic statements that fuel hostility and negative perceptions.

Citizenship and Belonging in Post-9/11 America

U.S. citizens and lawful permanent residents, commonly known as "green card holders," also experienced the impact of post-9/11 profiling and discrimination. The government policy called the Controlled Application Review and Resolution Program (CARRP) affected citizens-in-waiting or those eligible for naturalization in particular. Under CARRP, the U.S. Citizenship and Immigration Service (USCIS) subjected certain lawful permanent residents who had applied for naturalization to differential treatment simply because of their country of origin. USCIS identified or labeled naturalization applicants as "national security concerns" if an individual had traveled to or paid remittances to family members living in a country that has known terrorist activities, made a lawful donation to a charity that was accused of supporting terrorist organizations, or was found on a terrorist watchlist. Not surprisingly, CARRP disproportionately affected South Asian and Arab lawful permanent residents seeking to be naturalized. The naturalization adjudication process became a process that lasted years for some community members.

Those who hold U.S. citizenship—either by birth or by naturalization—have been negatively affected in the post-9/11 climate as well. The privileges and guarantees of citizenship become meaningless for South Asians, Arabs, and Muslims because of state policies and public actions against members of their communities who are immigrants. Legal scholar Neil Gotanda calls this process citizenship nullification.[49] Asian Americans in particular face the prospect of citizenship nullification because of the pervasive perception that they are "perpetual foreigners" who are unable to assimilate or integrate and who are disloyal to the United States, regardless of their American citizenship. These perceptions were at the core of anti-immigrant policies that targeted Asian immigrants in the early twentieth century and Executive Order 9066, which authorized the internment of Japanese Americans during World War II.

Citizenship nullification has occurred in the post-9/11 climate as well. American citizens of South Asian, Arab, Muslim, Sikh, and Hindu backgrounds realized that the legal privileges of citizenship did not exempt them from discrimination or targeting, either by the public or by the state. Citizenship status has few, if any, visible identifiers. Therefore, all those who "look" like they could be Muslim or from a South Asian, North African, or Middle Eastern nation—regardless of their citizenship—became potential targets in post-9/11 America.

Many activists and scholars have compared post-9/11 profiling practices to wartime policies that the government implemented during World War II when nearly 120,000 individuals of Japanese descent—two-thirds of whom were American-born citizens—were forced into internment camps because of their presumed disloyalty to the United States.[50] The U.S. Supreme Court upheld the executive order that led to the internment, stating that the "exclusion of those of Japanese origin was deemed necessary because of the presence of an unascertained number of disloyal members of the group."[51] For this unjust policy and decision, the Supreme Court, Congress, and the executive branch have made considerable apologies.[52] As recently as 2011, the then acting solicitor general of the United States Neal Katyal declared a "Confession of Error" in decisions made by his office to justify the internment of Japanese Americans. Katyal noted that the solicitor general did not disclose important information that discredited allegations of Japanese disloyalty when the U.S. Supreme Court considered cases that challenged the internment.[53]

Unfortunately, in the post-9/11 climate, many of our policy makers and government officials seem to have forgotten the immeasurable harm visited upon constitutional principles and on the Japanese American community more than half a century earlier.

Post-9/11 policies and the narratives used to justify them bear an eerie resemblance to those implemented during World War II. Their ultimate ineffectiveness, selective enforcement, and relatively tenuous relationship to—or success in—fighting terrorism generate the inquiry: are these policies, in effect, ways to purge America of its "undesirable" immigrants? Given the ongoing harmful impact of the post-9/11 policies on South Asian, Arab, and Muslim immigrant communities, the answer to this question is yes.

Changing Course

The United States has run afoul of both constitutional and international human rights standards in the post-9/11 environment. In 2008, the United Nation's Committee on the Elimination of Racial Discrimination (CERD) articulated its concerns with post-9/11 practices when it noted: "Despite the measures adopted at the federal and state levels to combat racial profiling . . . such practice continues to be widespread. In particular, the Committee is deeply concerned about the increase in racial profiling against Arabs, Muslims and South Asians in the wake of the 11 September 2001 attack, as well as about the development of the National Entry and Exit Registration System (NSEERS) for nationals of 25 countries, all located in the Middle East, South Asia or North Africa."[54]

Given the valid criticism from legal scholars, advocates, and international human rights bodies, the United States must take critical steps to roll back the harmful impact of post-9/11 practices. These include amending the 2014 anti-profiling guidance to close the loopholes and exemptions; ending ineffective programs to counter violent extremism that focus exclusively on Muslim communities; and ceasing federal surveillance, mapping, and information-gathering programs. The government must also analyze and share publicly the outcomes of many of the policies and programs described in this chapter, from NSEERS to CARRP. This information should include the extent to which national security goals were reached as well as the numbers and nationalities of people placed in detention and deportation proceedings as a result of post-9/11 national security investigations.

Especially as our nation's demographics change, it is vital that the state assess carefully the impact of its policies and positions on communities of color and immigrants. The state cannot both welcome immigrants and enforce the civil rights of people of color while simultaneously engaging in practices that justify wholesale profiling of these same communities. Instead, the state must hold itself to the highest civil and human rights standards at all times, especially during times of significant national turmoil. Otherwise, we risk losing our nation's core values and compromising the ideals that draw so many immigrants to America.

While it might seem impossible in today's climate, advocates should press the state to begin a process of documenting post-9/11 civil and human rights violations and considering apologies and reparations. In so doing, we can draw upon the lessons from the Japanese American redress movement, which used a variety of strategies—including a public commission that documented the impact of the internment, financial reparations, the passage of civil rights legislation (the Civil Liberties Act of 1985), and a formal apology by Congress and the president. The Japanese American Citizens League and Japanese American advocates worked with the Anti-Defamation League, the Leadership Conference on Civil Rights, and the American Civil Liberties Union to secure these goals.[55]

Similarly, Congress should establish a commission to document the lived realities and experiences of South Asian, Arab, Muslim, and Sikh communities in the post-9/11 environment through public hearings around the country. The commission should provide a

set of recommendations for action by federal government agencies
and Congress. In time, perhaps the U.S. government will offer con-
fessions of error in denying equal protection under the law in the
wake of 9/11 similar to those that were made upon review of activities taken during the internment of Japanese Americans during
World War II. As Professor Eric Yamamoto has observed in relation to the Japanese American redress movement, "Reparations, if
thoughtfully conceived, offered and administered, can be transformative. They can help change material conditions of group life and
send political messages about societal commitment to principles of
equality."[56]

In seeking governmental apologies and redress for post-9/11 violations, South Asian, Arab, and Muslim communities must be fully
engaged in and supportive of similar efforts on behalf of African
American, Native Hawaiian, and indigenous communities. On this
point, Yamamoto's reflections on the legacy of the Japanese American redress movement are apt. He asks of Japanese Americans,
"Would we draw upon the lessons of the reparations movement and
work to end all forms of societal oppression, or would we close up
shop because we got ours?"[57] The liberation and legacy of South
Asian, Arab, Muslim, and Sikh immigrants must go well beyond
this notion of being satisfied with "getting ours." Instead, as subsequent chapters of this book show, they are inextricably linked to
racial justice movements for all communities of color in the United
States.

3

Surveillance Nation

Faiza Ali vividly remembers the summer of 2010. In May of that year, a community board representing Lower Manhattan backed the construction of a fifteen-story building on Park Place, two blocks from the World Trade Center site. The Cordoba Initiative, founded by Imam Feisal Abdul Rauf, planned to construct a building there that would hold a prayer space, library, and cultural center. But the community center, which would come to be known as Park51, swiftly garnered opposition because of its proximity to the site of the 9/11 attacks and its inclusion of a Muslim prayer space. Some families who had lost loved ones on 9/11, as well as conservative politicians and media commentators, claimed that the construction of Park51 amounted to building a mosque, thus defiling the hallowed ground of the site where the World Trade Center had stood.[1] On the other hand, proponents of Park51—including city officials such as mayor Michael Bloomberg, some families of 9/11 victims, and many Jewish and Christian organizations—pointed to the range of enriching services that the center would offer to all New Yorkers, the First Amendment rights of Muslims to construct prayer spaces, and the fact that pubs, fast food restaurants, and even a "gentlemen's club" (all of which could be perceived as unrefined establishments) existed just three blocks from the site of the World Trade Center.[2]

Throughout the summer of 2010, people and institutions voiced their opinions about Park51. A Quinnipiac University poll concluded that most of New York City's likely voters opposed the construction of Park51 near the World Trade Center site.[3] The Anti-Defamation League, a national organization that advocates against anti-Semitism and bigotry, announced in July 2010 that an alternative space for Park51 should be found, saying that the controversy surrounding it was "counterproductive to the healing process."[4] Some political and public figures also used the Park51 controversy as a way to inflame tensions and draw attention to their own platforms. Between June and September 2010, South Asian Americans Leading Together (SAALT) documented twenty-three remarks from political figures about Park51, some of whom called the construction "insensitive" and invoked fears of "territorial conquest" by Muslims. For example, in August 2010, Ron McNeil, a Republican candidate for a congressional seat in Florida, said about Park51: "I'm totally against it. If I had my way it'd be pretty much over my dead body to build a mosque there. The Muslims will have that place to gloat about for years if they get their way and it was the Muslim religion that caused the problems we had on 911."[5] In September 2010, Renee Ellmers, a Republican running for a congressional seat in North Carolina, released a television ad stating, "After the Muslims conquered Jerusalem, and Cordoba, and Constantinople they built victory mosques. And, now, they want to build a mosque by Ground Zero."[6] These statements further fueled the public outrage against Park51 by characterizing the community center as a mosque and by demonizing the entire religion of Islam.

Hateful actions against South Asian, Arab, Muslim, and Sikh community members echoed this divisive political rhetoric. In August 2010, a passenger in the cab of Ahmed Sharif, a Bangladeshi taxi driver in New York City, asked Sharif if he was Muslim and then began to demean Islam. The passenger yelled, "This is the checkpoint," and then forced a folding knife through the open window of the cab's partition to slash Sharif's throat. Sharif needed fifteen stitches to close a six-inch wound at his throat.[7] Across the country, in Washington State, a Sikh convenience store clerk was punched after being called "Al Qaeda."[8] In August and September of 2010, mosques in Phoenix, Arizona; Hudson, New York; Arlington, Texas; and Madera, California, to name a few, reported incidents of vandalism.[9] Burnings of the Quran were planned in Florida and actually occurred in other parts of the United States, including outside a Muslim community center in Chicago and mosques in San Francisco and East Lansing, Michigan.[10] In September 2010, a man burned a copy of the Quran outside the proposed Park51 site in Lower Manhattan.[11]

President Obama stepped into the national debate over Park51 in August 2010, when he remarked during a White House Iftar (the meal at which Muslims break fast during the holy month of Ramadan) that "Muslims have the same right to practice their religion as everyone else in this country. And that includes the right to build a place of worship and a community center on private property in Lower Manhattan, in accordance with local laws and ordinances. This is America."[12] While President Obama subsequently backtracked from his strong support of Park51 by noting that he was not commenting on the "wisdom" of constructing a mosque there, supporters of Park51 and Muslim organizations and allies appreciated his attempts to quell the national furor.[13]

Community organizations in New York City and around the country worked double time to address the Park51 controversy. Twenty-five-year-old Faiza Ali and her colleagues at the Council on Islamic Relations of New York (CAIR-NY) put in eighty-hour weeks to push back against the negative framing around the Park51 community center and to buttress their alliances with other organizations in the city. Each night, they combed through fax after fax filled with bigoted language directed at CAIR-NY and Muslims. "It would be things like 'You pigs, you swine, no mosque on sacred land, Ground

Zero is sacred land.' It kept coming in and we kept putting it away,"
Faiza recalled. "I feel like I became numb to it after a while."

Faiza, a Pakistani American Muslim born and raised in Brooklyn, had become accustomed to stares, questions, and even harassment after 9/11, but she had not directly experienced the level of
vitriolic bigotry that emerged during the Park51 summer. "I used
to go to school downtown and had always walked by Ground Zero
without feeling uncomfortable. But I didn't feel safe doing that
during the Park51 summer. I was walking by there one day and
there was a guy near the site reading passages from the Quran,
tearing the pages out, and burning them. When he saw me, he
started to videotape me. It was too much." But Faiza's commitment
to her community could not be easily deterred. She traces it to her
childhood and specifically to her parents.

"I call my mom the original organizer," Faiza told me. In the late
1980s, as many of Faiza's relatives from Pakistan arrived in New
York City, Faiza's home in Midwood functioned as a gateway apartment to help family members acclimate to their new lives. Many
of Faiza's family members, including her parents, had experience
working in the textile industry in Pakistan, and they found work
at a nearby knitting factory in Brooklyn when they first arrived.
Faiza's mother used an industrial-size sewing machine that she
stored in the family's apartment to make garments for sale. As the
years passed, Faiza's mother regularly hosted meetings with friends
and family in their home to build support for a mosque to be established on Coney Island Avenue.

When the knitting factory that employed Faiza's father and other
family members relocated to New Jersey, Mr. Ali started a new
job as an elevator operator, one that he held for decades. He also
joined the local union. Faiza often accompanied her father to pay
his union dues or to participate in a rally. "In some way, I feel like
organizing was always there and around me," she remembered.

A series of personal experiences right before and after 9/11 solidified Faiza's path of organizing and activism. During the summer of 2001, she decided to start wearing a hijab. Then, a few weeks prior to the terrorist attacks, her father passed away. Faiza and her family were in mourning when 9/11 occurred. Her mother, hearing stories of harassment of Muslims and those perceived to be Muslims, kept Faiza and her two younger siblings at home from school during the week after the attacks. Faiza recalled, "My mom said we would stay home until she figured it out, and I remember thinking, 'What are you going to figure out? What do you mean?'"

Faiza began to understand the scope of her mother's fears a few days later when she and her younger sister, Asma, were targets of violence and harassment. Wearing their hijabs, Faiza and Asma had gone out for the first time since 9/11 to a nearby Rite Aid store to buy milk. Faiza was browsing through a magazine in the checkout line when her sister suddenly grabbed her shoulder. "I turn around and my sister was almost in tears. She was telling me that this woman just came and hit her," Faiza remembered. "As Asma is talking to me, the woman comes back and starts screaming, and everything that my mom was afraid of happening to other people was happening to us. This woman said, 'You did this' and pointed at us. I didn't know what to say . . . I wanted to say that, no, we didn't do this, and also my sister's best friend's father has been missing since 9/11 and we don't know where he is."

Amid her swirling emotions, Faiza understood immediately that she and her sister were being targeted because of their visible Muslim presence. She also observed that no one else in the store said anything to stop the physical and verbal assault that she and Asma endured. "There were people who were in front of us in line, behind us in line, there was the cashier, there was a security guard that was peeking over, and no one said anything. There were people in the store who knew us and knew our family. I was raised in that neighborhood. No one said anything." Although Faiza and Asma didn't tell their mother about the incident until years later, it became a turning point in Faiza's life. "I never ever want to be someone who witnesses something that doesn't make me feel good—and doesn't do something about it," she said.

This basic value of speaking up against injustice has grounded Faiza's activism and organizing work. As a college student at Pace University, Faiza became involved with anti–Iraq War protests and the Muslim Student Association. She also volunteered with CAIR-NY and was hired on as a full-time staffer upon graduation. At CAIR-NY, Faiza worked on a range of issues, but none more taxing than the Park51 dispute during the summer of 2010. "I was exhausted," she recalled. "I remember coming home and just feeling overwhelmed all the time." Faiza left CAIR-NY shortly after the controversy subsided.

By the end of the summer of 2010, a New York City commission decided that the Park51 construction could move forward.[14] Perhaps due to the public backlash against the site, developers have changed their vision for it over the years, with the most recent plans involving the construction of a museum that provides community programs about Islam and its arts and culture.[15] Even though the Park51 controversy had died down, the damage was done. Targeting South Asian, Arab, and Muslim immigrants became acceptable in the eyes of the public, lawmakers, media, and law enforcement. With Park51 behind them, New York City advocates prepared for their next campaign: accountability from the New York Police Department.

Reforming the NYPD

In 2012, Linda Sarsour, a Palestinian American Muslim and the executive director of the Arab American Association of New York

(AAANY), recruited Faiza to become a community organizer. Faiza and Linda made a formidable pair of activists in New York City. Both are fiercely committed to issues of racial justice, and their different styles complemented one another. While Linda is publicly visible and outspoken, Faiza is more of a reflective, behind-the-scenes activist who considers all points of view. "When Faiza does speak," Linda noted, "it's clear that she's thought through all the various pieces—and everyone listens."

One of Faiza's key responsibilities at AAANY included working with the Muslim American Civil Liberties Coalition for Truth and Justice (MACLC), a coalition of faith leaders, organizers, attorneys, and groups. Their focus became the New York Police Department (NYPD), which had engaged in surveillance of South Asian, Arab, and Muslim communities for years as part of its counterterrorism efforts.

The NYPD's own report *Radicalization in the West: The Homegrown Threat* provided a window into the agency's tactics. The report, made available in 2007, identified "radicalization incubators," or venues where Muslims were likely to become radicalized by engaging in or listening to extremist rhetoric. These venues included mosques, cafés, cab driver hangouts, prisons, student associations, nonprofit organizations, hookah bars, butcher shops, and bookstores. According to the NYPD, seemingly anyplace that Muslims frequented could be a potential venue for radicalization.[16] "It didn't come as a surprise to us when the report came out," Faiza said. "We all knew that the NYPD had been spying on Muslim communities in the city for years."

MACLC and other advocacy organizations pointed out that the strategies outlined in the report alienated Muslim communities and stirred prejudice and suspicion. They also warned that the report could pave the way for law enforcement activities in New York City and elsewhere that targeted Muslim communities. During the summer of 2009, the NYPD included a weak "statement of clarification" in the report to emphasize that its findings were not intended as prescriptive policy for law enforcement.[17]

This after-the-fact acknowledgment by the NYPD did little to abate public concerns about the agency's surveillance activities. In August 2011, the Associated Press (AP) published a Pulitzer Prize–winning series of articles that detailed the mapping and spying operations of the NYPD's Demographics Unit (later renamed the Zone Assessments Unit) on Muslim communities in New York City and even in parts of New Jersey.[18] Apparently, the NYPD's Demographics Unit had designated twenty-eight "ancestries of interest," including African (e.g., Somalian), Eastern European (e.g., Chechen), South Asian (e.g., Indian, Pakistani, Bangladeshi), Middle Eastern (e.g., Egyptian and Bahraini), as well as Guyanese and "American Black Muslim."[19] The categories sounded much like the countries of interest identified by the federal government in programs such as the National Security Entry-Exit Registration System (NSEERS) in the wake of 9/11.

According to the AP's investigative reports, NYPD undercover officers routinely visited "hot spots," including restaurants, bookstores, hookah bars, and butcher shops, to keep track of activities there. The NYPD also used informants called "mosque crawlers" who attended prayer services where they could gather intelligence.[20] In a few instances, the NYPD even monitored meetings and online content of Muslim student associations established on college campuses.[21]

The book *Enemies Within: Inside the NYPD's Secret Spying Unit and bin Laden's Final Plot Against America*, written by AP reporters Matt Apuzzo and Adam Goldman, revealed additional information about the NYPD's surveillance activities.[22] *Enemies Within* referred to a document called the "Sports Venue Report," written by the Demographics Unit of the NYPD for police use. The report included a map of parks where South Asian and Arab community members gathered to *play* sports as well as detailed information and pictures about places where they congregated to *watch* sports. For example, the report included a picture of a barbershop in Brooklyn and provided the ethnicity of its owner. It noted that Egyptians, Palestinians, Syrians, Moroccans, Algerians, and Lebanese congregated at the barbershop to view soccer games. The report provided similar information about South Asian restaurants, including a picture of the Flamingo Cricket and Social Club in Jamaica, Queens, whose owner is Guyanese and caters to Bangladeshi, Pakistani, and Indian customers.[23]

Why did the Demographics Unit expend taxpayer funds, time, and resources to gather information about where South Asians and Arab Americans played cricket or watched soccer matches? The answer is clear: the NYPD believed that South Asian, Arab, and Muslim communities were suspicious enough to be spied upon even as they engaged in the most mundane, lawful, innocent, and ordinary of activities. Indeed, the NYPD had been engaged for years in a systemic practice of racial and religious profiling in the name of national security and counterterrorism, and with no oversight.

In 2012, a group of New Jersey plaintiffs, including students at Rutgers University, a coalition of New Jersey mosques, and the owners of a grade school for Muslim girls, brought the first legal challenge against the NYPD for spying on Muslim communities.[24] The U.S. District Court for the District of New Jersey dismissed the case against the NYPD.[25] Two nonprofit organizations, Muslim Advocates and the Center for Constitutional Rights, are appealing this decision before the U.S. Court of Appeals for the Third Circuit.[26]

The profiling of South Asian, Muslim, and Arab communities is not limited to local law enforcement agencies like the NYPD. Since 9/11, the practice of targeting these communities has spread to local, state, and federal law enforcement agencies throughout the nation, often in coordinated fashion. Take the example of the FBI's Joint Terrorism Task Forces (JTTFs), which exist in 104 cities around the country, with seventy-one established since 9/11. JTTFs include approximately four thousand members from five hundred state and local agencies and fifty-five federal agencies designated to be the "nation's front line on terrorism." JTTFs work closely with a national network of fusion centers, which receive, analyze, and share intelligence information.[27] These fusion centers assess terrorism threats, including those gleaned from "suspicious activity reporting" by the public, called SAR (more commonly known as "See Something, Say Something") reports.[28] Civil liberties organizations have identified a range of concerns related to the JTTFs and fusion centers, from their infringement of privacy rights to their use of racial and religious profiling in investigating innocent members of the public.[29]

For example, Asian Americans Advancing Justice–Asian Law Caucus in San Francisco has identified a pattern of racial and religious profiling in many of the activities undertaken by California's six fusion centers.[30] Yaman Salahi, a staff attorney at the Asian Americans Advancing Justice–Asian Law Caucus, explained that SAR reports targeting South Asian, Muslim, and Arab communities are often based on flimsy information. He described the situation of a Middle Eastern physician in the Lodi area who was investigated in 2010 by the federal government just because of a complaint that he was "unfriendly." In addition, men and women of Middle Eastern descent taking photos of various landmarks have also been investigated.[31] Salahi believes that the only reason these lawful and ordinary activities triggered an investigation or a visit by law enforcement is because the subjects were South Asian, Muslim, or Arab.

Partly in response to JTTF and fusion center activity in California, the Coalition for a Safe San Francisco (made up of the Asian Americans Advancing Justice–Asian Law Caucus; other civil rights groups; and Arab, Muslim, and South Asian organizations) advocated for the enactment of the Safe San Francisco Civil

Rights Ordinance.[32] The ordinance, signed into law in May 2012 by Mayor Ed Lee, requires that JTTFs adhere to local civil rights standards, that any future agreements between the San Francisco Police Department (SFPD) and the FBI about JTTF activities be open for public comment, and that annual reports be provided about the SFPD's work with the JTTF.[33] While it will take time to assess whether the JTTF's activities conform with the Safe San Francisco Civil Rights Ordinance, the imposition of civil rights standards and public oversight is an important step to bring accountability to law enforcement practices.

From New York to California, South Asian, Muslim, and Arab communities have lived under institutional surveillance by their own government. Linda Sarsour of AAANY explained that these actions have waged "psychological warfare" on Muslims by criminalizing normal everyday activities such as eating, praying, expressing one's opinions, and attending meetings on college campuses. Most Americans take for granted the ability to worship freely, attend public demonstrations, and meet friends at their favorite restaurants to watch a sports game. But for Muslim, Arab, and South Asian community members, these routine actions have potentially dangerous consequences. As a result, many community members—from imams composing sermons to college students organizing political discussions on campuses—have had to censor their activities to avoid arousing suspicion. This self-censorship leads to a myriad of emotional repercussions, from isolation to fear to a sense of not belonging in America.

In August 2013, the psychological warfare that Linda described came even closer to home. The AP reported that several community-based organizations—including AAANY, where Linda and Faiza worked—had been labeled by the NYPD as "terrorist enterprises."[34] Apparently, the NYPD had sought to infiltrate AAANY—a social service organization that provides English as a Second Language classes and job training, among its activities—by attempting to place an informant on their board of directors. Linda wrote in September 2013, "While [the] news about NYPD spying was nothing new to me—it's an issue I have been working on for the last few years—this time, it was different. This time I felt hurt. I felt broken. When I saw AAANY's name on that document, it became even more personal."[35]

The political had become personal in more ways than one.

Who's Watching the NYPD?

By the summer of 2013, the rallying cry to hold the NYPD accountable for its practices of profiling had become ubiquitous. Decades of work to address police violence and brutality had led to the evolution of a multisector, multiracial coalition called Communities United for Police Reform (CPR), which included South Asian, Arab, and Muslim organizations.

According to Joo-Hyun Kang, CPR's director, the roots of the police accountability movement in New York City can be traced to the mid-1990s when a multiracial alliance called the Coalition Against Police Brutality (CAPB) was formed to address police violence. At the time, this coalition included the Audre Lorde Project, a center for organizing lesbian, gay, bisexual, two-spirit, trans, and gender-nonconforming people of color around social and economic justice; CAAAV–Organizing Asian Communities, which organizes poor and working-class Asian immigrant and refugee communities; the Justice Committee, which works with Latino communities to build a movement against police violence; and the Malcolm X Grassroots Movement, which builds networks of Black organizers and activists to defend basic human rights. The inclusion of Asian, Latino, and LGBTQ communities expanded the base of CAPB and drew attention to how non-Black communities also experienced the impact of discriminatory police activities.

In 1999, Amadou Diallo, an unarmed twenty-two-year-old West

African immigrant, was killed by four NYPD police officers who fired forty-one shots at him while he was entering his apartment building in the Bronx.[36] CABP mobilized into action and organized forty-one days of action and civil disobedience. One of the groups that joined this effort was Desis Rising Up and Moving (DRUM), a Queens-based organization whose members include low-income and undocumented South Asian immigrants. DRUM helped make the critical connections between South Asians experiencing abuses at the hands of immigration enforcement agencies and Black communities facing police profiling and violence.

By 9/11, the movement to end police brutality had gained public traction in New York City. But according to Joo-Hyun Kang, the events of 9/11 and the subsequent ramping up of law enforcement for national security activities hampered significant progress. "After 9/11, our work got pushed back, because it wasn't possible to have a real voice around criticizing law enforcement," Kang explained. With the guidance of the late Richie Perez from the National Congress for Puerto Rican Rights, CAPB worked with the Center for Constitutional Rights to bring a lawsuit against the City of New York in 1999 challenging its unjust stop-and-frisk policy. In settling the litigation in 2003, the NYPD agreed to disband its Street Crimes Unit, which was responsible for racially profiling people of color.[37] This settlement helped pave the way for the successful outcome in the 2013 litigation of *Floyd v. City of New York*. In that case, a federal judge held the NYPD liable for a pattern and practice of racial profiling and unconstitutional stop-and-frisks that disproportionately affected African Americans and Latinos.[38]

The momentum to end police profiling helped CPR coalesce around three primary goals: "We wanted to reduce the NYPD's discriminatory actions, to lift up community voices, and to work within and across communities to reshape the public dialogue about the role of law enforcement," explained Djibril Toure of the Malcolm X Grassroots Movement. From the start, CPR's strategy included bringing diverse groups that had endured profiling and targeting by the NYPD to the table. These groups included the homeless; lesbian, gay, bisexual, and transgender communities; and immigrant workers represented by unions. As news of NYPD surveillance of Muslim communities emerged, CPR's members came to understand the importance of including South Asian, Muslim, and Arab organizations in their broad-based coalition as well. "We let the Arab, Muslim, South Asian groups take the lead on issues related to oversight of the NYPD because they were the ones who were infiltrated," Toure said.

Linda and Faiza of AAANY and Fahd Ahmed and Monami Maulik of DRUM became the most visible organizers and representatives of South Asian, Muslim, and Arab communities in CPR's coalition. They reviewed and suggested inclusive language for the proposed legislation, engaged their own membership to take part in CPR rallies, attended meetings and media events, and deepened relationships with other coalition partners. Faiza and Linda were present at many CPR events, even when issues affecting South Asian, Muslim, or Arab communities were not addressed. "I've been to many Mother's Day rallies to stand behind and with African American mothers who have lost their children," Linda explained. "It's important—because no one expects it—to be a presence, to make it clear to the public that an Arab Muslim woman, mother, and New Yorker cares about these issues too."

In February 2012, Jumaane Williams and Brad Lander, two New York City Council members, introduced a package of legislation known as the Community Safety Act (CSA).[39] One bill bans profiling and discrimination by the NYPD and expands the bases of prohibited discrimination to include actual or perceived color, creed, age, alienage or citizenship status, gender, sexual orientation, disability, and housing status in addition to race, ethnicity, religion, and national origin. It also provides individuals who experience profiling or discrimination with a private right of action to bring legal claims against the NYPD.[40] Another bill, which reflected the concerns about surveillance in particular, establishes oversight of the NYPD's operations, policies, programs, and practices by the commissioner of the New York City Department of Investigation.[41]

The New York City Council passed the CSA in June 2013, but Mayor Bloomberg vetoed it the following month.[42] CPR immediately mounted an advocacy and grassroots campaign to convince the council to override the veto. On August 22, 2013, at around 2:20 a.m., the council overrode the mayor's veto to cheers from advocates who had gathered in the chamber.[43] The CSA took effect on January 1, 2014.[44]

Another victory occurred in April 2014, when Mayor Bill de Blasio's administration announced that the NYPD would be disbanding its controversial Demographics Unit, which had engaged in systemic spying on community members.[45] Yet it is unclear whether the functions of the Demographics Unit have been entirely eliminated or whether they have simply been moved into other sections within the NYPD.

CPR's efforts to pass the Community Safety Act reflect some best practices around creating compelling and universal narratives while leveraging the strengths of different organizations and diverse constituencies. The enactment of the CSA is the result of multiracial solidarity building that strategically sought support from various sectors, including labor unions; LGBTQ communities; and Black, Latino, Asian, and Muslim groups.

An element of successful multiracial coalition building revolved around the use of racial justice language. The coalition placed issues like surveillance—which in the post-9/11 environment primarily affect South Asians, Arabs, and Muslims—within the broader racial justice framework, rather than relegating them to a national security context. Members of the coalition also deferred to South Asian, Arab, and Muslim advocates to determine the bill's language related to government oversight. Another best practice involves the work of local, grassroots South Asian, Muslim, and Arab groups to mobilize a base of supporters for public actions and press conferences. South Asian, Muslim, and Arab communities successfully made connections between the profiling and surveillance they experience and broader law enforcement activities that have historically targeted Black and Brown communities.

Kang and Toure believe that without this type of multisector and grassroots alliance building, the Community Safety Act might not have become law. "We were able to tell the story that profiling affected *all* New Yorkers," Kang emphasized. "This wasn't just about one community. We were able to tell a joint story which was not only about stop-and-frisk or broken windows that affects Black and Latino communities but also about surveillance and profiling of Muslims as well." The relationships formed during the fight to pass the CSA are being nurtured to support future coalition efforts in New York City, especially in light of the current movement for Black lives and police accountability.

For Faiza Ali, the passage of the CSA is a significant victory for all New Yorkers, including her own community. Working on the legislation in coalition with Black, Latino, Asian, and LGBTQ communities stoked her curiosity in how government agencies can effectively support emerging immigrant and faith communities in New York City. In line with these burgeoning interests, Faiza accepted a position as community liaison with the New York City Council's Speaker's Office over the summer of 2014. In her new position with the city, Faiza continues to interact with Linda Sarsour and other community leaders on issues of public safety and police accountability. As the movement for Black lives, discussed later in this book, took center stage in New York City, Faiza would again find herself in the thick of an issue that was deeply meaningful to her and her community.

4

Islamophobia in the Bible Belt

On June 4, 2013, twenty-two-year-old Drost Kokoye drove from her home in Nashville to Manchester, Tennessee, with three other Muslim activists, Remziya Suleyman, Mohamed Shukri, and Zulfat Suara to attend a community forum organized by the American Muslim Advisory Council (AMAC). Drost and her colleagues were deeply involved with grassroots efforts to address the wave of anti-immigrant, anti-refugee, and anti-Muslim sentiment that had taken hold in parts of Tennessee since 2010. Drost and Remziya worked for an American Muslim grassroots organization called the American Center for Outreach, and Mohamed and Zulfat were affiliated with AMAC.

On their drive, the four activists discussed the distinct possibility of encountering protests at the Manchester community forum. In fact, just a few weeks earlier, Barry West, the commissioner of Coffee County, where Manchester is located, had posted on Facebook a picture of a white man in a cowboy hat pointing a gun. West called the post "How to Wink at a Muslim." When asked about the picture, West responded: "I'm prejudiced against anyone who's trying to tear down this country, Muslims, Mexicans, anybody . . . If you come into this country illegally or harm us or take away benefits, I'm against it."[1] West's remarks made his opinions on who is the "us" and who is the "other" in Tennessee quite clear.

West's comments did not occur in a vacuum, however. Over the previous three years, parts of middle Tennessee had become a breeding ground for Islamophobia and anti-immigrant rhetoric. That is why AMAC had organized the community forum in Manchester. The forum, open to all residents, provided an opportunity for Muslim leaders to share basic information about Islam and American Muslims and to hear about civil rights protections from representatives of the U.S. Attorney's Office.

While Drost, Remziya, Mohamed, and Zulfat were prepared to face opposition from anti-Muslim spokespersons and organizations at the forum, they had no idea about the extent of it until they arrived. "We didn't expect it to be four hundred people," Drost remembered. "Outside the location, there was a sort of pep rally going on. Pam Geller had been speaking to the crowd, riling people up." Geller is a prominent figure who promotes Islamophobia in the United States. She is the co-founder of groups such as the American Freedom Defense Initiative and Stop Islamization of America, which have been listed on the Southern Poverty Law Center's map of hate groups.[2]

Geller often frames her messages of intolerance of Muslims by claiming that she has a right to free speech. While this appeals to one aspect of core American values, Geller's incendiary rhetoric diminishes our equally cherished ideals of religious freedom, respect, and plurality. At the "pep rally" outside the Manchester forum, for example, Geller fueled fears of Muslim radicalization and encouraged the crowd to speak out against the "most brutal and oppressive ideology on the planet."[3] The crowd responded with cheers and applause.

When the forum started, nearly five hundred people packed the room. It turned out that many had been brought in from other parts of Tennessee or the South. Drost and her colleagues sat in the first row. One of the Muslim speakers, Sabina Mohyuddin, provided a basic overview of Islam with information about the long history of Muslims in the United States and the community's beliefs in prayer, charity, and peace. But she was interrupted consistently from the audience with racial and religious slurs.

"We hadn't seen anything like this before," Drost recalled. "Even when U.S. attorney Bill Killian began his remarks about civil rights, the audience wouldn't let him speak. They shouted and booed him. They had no respect." When Zak Mohyuddin, a Bangladeshi American who had resided in Coffee County for twenty-five years, addressed the crowd, people shouted, "Speak English!" and "Go home!" Drost was most shocked by the crowd's response to seeing pictures of mosques that had been firebombed and vandalized in recent years in different parts of Tennessee. "When the crowd saw these pictures, they actually applauded and cheered," Drost said. "They believed that these incidents were positive ones, that they should actually happen in our state."

As the forum proceeded, Drost began to feel increasingly un-comfortable and unsafe in her front-row seat. At one point, a woman sitting behind her spat at Drost and muttered anti-Muslim slurs. During the question-and-answer portion of the forum, when Drost rose to pass out index cards to the audience, a man shouted, "Watch out, she might blow up!" The crowd laughed in response.

These experiences at the Manchester forum motivated Drost and her colleagues to redouble their efforts to address intolerance and bigotry in their home state. But they also knew that they faced an uphill battle in parts of Tennessee, where socially conservative policies and beliefs continue to wield influence, even as immigrant communities are reshaping the state's racial landscape.

The demographic changes in Tennessee are striking. One in sixteen Tennesseans is either Latino or Asian, and they wield increasing economic and political power in the state. In 2012, the purchasing power of Latinos and Asians was $6.1 billion and $4.8 billion, respectively. In addition, the children of immigrants in Tennessee are poised to become a strong electoral bloc in decades to come. According to the Urban Institute, 89 percent of children in Asian families and 87 percent of children in Latino families were U.S. citizens in 2009, meaning that they are on their way to becoming voters.[4]

The city of Nashville has witnessed the most dramatic demographic changes in Tennessee. Between 2000 and 2012, the city's foreign-born population grew 86 percent, compared with an 11 percent increase in the native-born population.[5] In 2012, Nashville had the fastest-growing immigrant population of any city in America, as increasing numbers of Burmese, Kurdish, Somali, and Sudanese immigrants and refugees began to call it home.[6] They followed in the footsteps of Chinese, Indian, and Latino communities who had moved to the city in earlier decades. On Nolensville Pike, which has become an immigrant hub, a building called Casa Azafrán stands as a testament to these diverse communities. It houses organizations such as the American Center for Outreach, the Tennessee Immigrant and Refugee Rights Coalition, and Conexión Américas, all of whom work with the booming immigrant and refugee populations in the Nashville metropolitan area.

Drost and her family are part of this wave of newcomers who have made Nashville their home. Originally from Kurdistan, the Kokoye family arrived in the United States in 1997 as refugees escaping political persecution in Iraq. Drost explained that U.S. military forces had recruited her parents to assist with efforts to overthrow the Iraqi government, an experience not uncommon for many Kurds. When the Iraqi government discovered that Drost's father was assisting the American government, the family knew that their lives were in danger. U.S. forces quickly moved them out of the area. Drost and her family first traveled to refugee camps in

Turkey. There they were approved for refugee status by the U.S. government for demonstrating that if they were to return to Iraq, they feared persecution due to their religion, nationality, or political opinion. They traveled next to Guam and then were finally resettled in Phoenix, Arizona. As refugees, Drost's family received medical and cash assistance from the federal government for a limited period of time to help them settle into their new country.

After ten months in Phoenix, Drost's parents decided to move to Nashville, which had become home to the largest Kurdish population in the United States. An estimated eleven thousand to thirteen thousand Kurds live there.[7] On Nashville's south side, in an area near Nolensville Pike and Elysian Fields Road, sit Kurdish bakery shops, a food market, and a mosque called the Salahadeen Center of Nashville. But the wider community did not easily accept Kurdish refugees. Drost remembered that her adolescent and teenage years were marked with outsider status as a refugee. "In Iraq, we were seen as helpful allies to the United States, but once you [were] here, people saw you as a charity case needlessly receiving federal money and wondered why you were here in the first place," she told me.

After 9/11, Drost realized that she was being treated as a "double other"—a refugee and a Muslim. "It went from us being refugees getting free handouts to us now being a danger to the community. At this point, we became the threat. We became the ones that people run away from all of a sudden." Growing up as a refugee and a Muslim in post-9/11 America can be a difficult experience altogether, but navigating those identities in the U.S. South presented unique challenges for Drost. "You never escape the Bible Belt, even in any social setting," she said. "So, for our community and the kids, it's balancing that and not feeling ashamed or guilty about your faith and identity. When all you see is the news condemning what you believe, you start to want to run away from it as well." But Drost did just the opposite. Along with other activists and community leaders, she directly responded to the wave of anti-Muslim sentiment spreading throughout parts of Tennessee.

In February 2008, Eric Ian Baker and two others vandalized and burned down the Islamic Center in Columbia, Tennessee, using Molotov cocktail explosion devices. They also painted swastikas and the phrase "White Power" on the mosque.[8] In 2010, the Al-Farooq Islamic Center, attended mainly by Somalis in Nashville, was vandalized with the words "Muslims Go Home."[9] When area mosques came together to create a rapid-response team to address the growing incidents of vandalism and property destruction, Drost became involved as well.

In the fall of 2010, Drost enrolled as a sophomore at Middle Tennessee State University in Murfreesboro. She would soon become part of local efforts to address one of the most publicized anti-mosque campaigns and examples of religious bigotry in the history of our nation.

"The Perfect Fertile Ground"

On a balmy July afternoon in 2014, I drove from Nashville to Murfreesboro to meet with Abdou Kattih, Dr. Saleh Sbenaty, and Dr. Ossama Bahloul at the Islamic Center of Murfreesboro, located about forty miles outside Nashville. Demographically, Murfreesboro is predominantly white (75.6 percent) with a sizable African American population (15.2 percent) and smaller Asian and Latino communities (3.4 percent and 5.9 percent, respectively).[10] As I neared Murfreesboro, suburban streets, strip malls, and vacant stretches of land dotted the landscape. The Islamic Center, with its striking green dome and minarets, stood out prominently from its location on Veals Road.

Abdou Kattih warmly greeted me at the Islamic Center's front doors and took me on a tour. In addition to a large prayer hall, the center includes a library, a kitchen, and play areas for young children. Kattih told me that prior to the property being purchased Muslim families used to gather at an office building for prayer. As the population of Muslims grew in Murfreesboro and surrounding areas, community members raised funds to purchase land for construction of the Islamic Center. The center draws a diverse group of congregants, including Syrians, African Americans, Pakistanis, and Moroccans; many are students enrolled at Middle Tennessee State University.

Kattih, a pharmacy manager at Walgreens, has lived in Murfreesboro with his wife and four children for nine years. They settled in Murfreesboro because of its small size and proximity to Nashville. "It is a nice place to raise a family without the bustle of a large city," Kattih told me. And while he and his family had experienced some incidents of discrimination immediately after 9/11, Kattih said that these paled in comparison to the backlash that occurred in response to the construction of the Islamic Center.

That opposition began in January 2010, when vandals spray-painted the words "Not Welcome" on a sign erected on the vacant lot where the mosque would be built.[11] "After the first sign was vandalized, we put up another. Someone drove a truck through that one," Kattih remembered.

The backlash was not limited to incidents of vandalism. During a public hearing held by the Rutherford County Regional Planning Commission on June 17, 2010, more than six hundred people, mainly White residents of Murfreesboro, gathered to express their anger about the commission's decision to approve the construction of the Islamic Center.[12] They claimed that the commission had not provided sufficient advance notice to the public. Yet their complaints and objections seemed to be less grounded in the lack of process and more reflective of Islamophobia, racism, and anti-immigrant sentiment.

For example, during the public comment period of the hearing, one resident warned that "some of the things that [the Islamic Center] had on their website . . . [were] 'to establish Arabic as a second language in our schools.' America is a target for the jihadi Muslims to invade, kill, and come to power, and to take America by force. To enslave us as infidels." Others believed that the Murfreesboro mosque would become a training ground for radicals and jihadists. One man said, "The Islamist [sic] is not a religion like Baptist, Church of Christ, Methodist. It's a political way of life and . . . I'm afraid we are going to end up with another training camp here in Rutherford County."[13] These narratives about Muslims changing the culture of Tennessee through the introduction of different languages and customs echoed the growing anxiety that many residents felt about the demographic changes in the state.

In that vein, some community members made statements about an immigrant and Muslim "takeover." One resident warned, "We've opened up our hearts to these people [Muslims], and they have taken it and stabbed us in the back with it. . . . We have got to wake up. . . . We have to got to take this country back." Another person claimed that the construction of the Islamic Center would lead to the imposition of Islamic law: "Islam is a system of government. Islam is a system of justice. The purpose and the desire of Islam is to enforce Sharia law on to every non-Islamic country."[14] Many of the speakers added the disclaimer that they were not being bigoted in expressing their concerns, although their comments clearly evince racial and religious prejudice.

The anti-Muslim and anti-immigrant sentiment that permeated the June 2010 hearing in Murfreesboro echoed what was occurring around the country, particularly in New York City, where the Park51 community center controversy had begun to take shape. The characterization of Islam as a political ideology—rather than a faith like Christianity, Judaism, or even Hinduism—further deepened the fears of many Tennessee residents. The identification of "foreign" elements—languages, Sharia law, customs—triggered racial anxiety in many who were worried that their home state would lose its unique character as Muslim immigrants settled there.

Not surprisingly, some state public officials seized on the opportunity to inflame these viewpoints. Lou Ann Zelenik, a Republican running for a 2010 congressional bid and former Rutherford County Planning Commission member, issued a statement through her campaign that read:

> Let there be no mistake. Lou Ann stands with everyone who is opposed to the idea of an Islamic training center being built in our community. This "Islamic Center" is not part of a religious movement; it is a political movement designed to fracture the moral and political foundation of middle Tennessee. . . . Until the American Muslim community find it in their hearts to separate themselves from their evil, radical counterparts, to condemn those who want to destroy our civilization and will fight against them, we are not obligated to open our society to any of them.[15]

Zelenik's statements politicized and legitimized unfounded concerns and fears that Muslims wanted to eliminate Western civilization.

Lieutenant governor of Tennessee Ron Ramsey, at the time running for a contested gubernatorial seat, echoed similar sentiments when asked about the Islamic Center construction, saying, "I'm all about freedom of religion. . . . But you cross the line when they start trying to bring Sharia law into the United States. . . . You could even argue whether being a Muslim is actually a religion or is it a nationality, way of life or cult, whatever you want to call it."[16] Remarks such as these by political figures fostered a climate in which members of the public felt that they could voice similar sentiments.

The positioning of Islam as a political system instead of as a religion—by political leaders, no less—and the portrayal of Muslims as ungrateful immigrants who seek to corrupt the "American" way of life have become common narratives, especially since 9/11. Anti-Muslim spokespersons and organizations fuel Islamophobia. A small but well-resourced and influential group of organizations, philanthropic entities, and spokespersons is chiefly responsible for the Islamophobia industry in the United States. According to a report titled *Fear, Inc.*, published by the Center for American Progress, five key spokespersons and a group of seven foundations have provided more than $40 million to various entities for the development and dissemination of misleading propaganda about Islam and the American Muslim community.[17] The recipients of these funds include David Yerushalmi, the author of anti-Sharia laws that have been introduced in many states; Robert Spencer, the director of Jihad Watch; and the Clarion Fund, which produces alarmist films about Islam, including *Honor Diaries*, which many criticized for its depictions of Muslim women.[18] The members of the Islamophobia industry regularly appear on conservative radio and television shows, take out bus and subway advertisements denouncing Islam, and ally with political leaders and groups to tack on anti-Muslim messages to political platforms. Their primary goal is to present harmful images and ideas to Americans about Muslims and Islam in order to divide communities.

Around the time of the Islamic Center's construction, many of the groups and spokespersons fomenting Islamophobia focused their attention on Tennessee. Groups such as ACT! for America and the Center for the Study of Political Islam invested heavily in Tennessee.[19] For example, they experimented with legislation and media campaigns against mosque construction and Sharia law in order to identify the most effective methods to build public momentum. Anti-Muslim spokespersons such as Pamela Geller and Frank Gaffney visited Tennessee and made speeches that roiled fear and anxiety around the growth of Muslim communities and the threat of Islam.[20] Many of the community members and residents who spoke at the hearing in Murfreesboro in opposition to the Islamic Center's construction used language from Geller and Gaffney. A shared vocabulary of Islamophobia—the bigotry against, demonization of, and "othering" of Islam and Muslims—had emerged in parts of Tennessee as well as around the country as a whole.

The scope and virulence of the backlash in middle Tennessee shocked members of the Muslim community. "We had never heard any of it before. It was so painful for us," Dr. Saleh Sbenaty told me. An immigrant from Syria, Sbenaty is a professor of engineering technology at Middle Tennessee State University. He has lived in Murfreesboro with his family for more than two decades and had never experienced anything like the backlash to the Islamic Center's construction. "They went so far as to target, attack our children in schools," he said. "Our children were called terrorists in their schools. Many of us who were leaders in the community received threatening messages and phone calls. It lasted about two years."

Even though the opposition to the mosque had extended to the personal lives of community members, their response was measured. The emphasis was on openness and collaboration. Representatives of the Islamic Center held open houses and picnics for the Murfreesboro community at large. Dr. Ossama Bahloul, who had moved to Murfreesboro in 2008 to become the imam of the Islamic Center, is proud of how the Muslim community faced the backlash. "We made it clear that we were part of Murfreesboro and that there is no conflict between being a good American and a good Muslim," he said.

A progressive coalition of people and organizations supported the Muslim community in Murfreesboro. For the two years that the mosque faced opposition, Muslim community leaders worked with concerned residents and organizations to host open houses and picnics to promote understanding and build community alliances. Civil rights groups such as the NAACP, peace groups such as Coexist, and immigrant rights groups such as the Tennessee Immigrant and Refugee Rights Coalition organized and participated in rallies and vigils.[21]

Still, the road to the construction of the Islamic Center, despite its approval by the Rutherford County Regional Planning Commission, was a long one. It involved litigation, federal intervention, community mobilization, and public pressure. In September 2010, Kevin Fisher, James Estes, Henry Golczynski, and Lisa Moore filed a lawsuit against the Rutherford County Regional Planning Commission.[22] The lawsuit included language that made the perceived Muslim threat very clear. The complaint noted that the plaintiffs "have been and will be irreparably harmed by the risk of terrorism generated by proselytizing for Islam and inciting the practices of Sharia law."[23]

As mosque construction began, the lawsuit wound its way through the Tennessee state courts. In July 2012, the U.S. Department of Justice filed an injunction against Rutherford County claiming that the county's refusal to issue a certificate of occupancy to the Islamic Center violated the Religious Land Use and Institutionalized Persons Act of 2000, which prohibits religious discrimination and provides legal protections against unjustified burdens on the exercise of one's religion.[24] A federal court agreed with the DOJ and ordered the county to provide a certificate of occupancy. A few weeks later, in July 2012, the Islamic Center opened in time for the Muslim holy season of Ramadan.[25] The original plaintiffs sought to appeal their case to the U.S. Supreme Court, which decided not to review it. After a grueling two-year ordeal, the Islamic Center and its allies had prevailed.

Looking back on the period between 2010 and 2012, community leaders and activists believe that it is important to understand the broad scope and significance of the campaign against the Islamic Center. "Murfreesboro became a 'test case' to put Islam on trial," Dr. Sbenaty explained. "We became the perfect fertile ground for a well-financed, well-organized campaign." This campaign was the result of a coalition that included conservative political leaders associated with the Tea Party, organizations with far-right, anti-immigrant policy aims, and national anti-Muslim groups. They united to mount legislative and cultural battles against immigrants, refugees, and Muslim communities in Tennessee, ones that could be replicated in other parts of the nation.

States like Tennessee with new immigrant communities are vulnerable to these sorts of attacks. Jill Garvey, the executive director of the Center for New Community (CNC), a nonprofit organization that conducts analysis and research on far-right movements, explained that anti-Muslim backlash has become a way of testing out anti-immigrant views and policies to see how the public responds. "Muslim communities have become the easiest targets of anti-immigrant groups who believe that they can rely on Islamophobia to trigger negative public attitudes towards all immigrants in general," Garvey said. CNC's research finds that the anti-immigrant organizations and Islamophobia networks often work closely together in order to advance a restrictive legislative strategy at a statewide level and to create divisive debates about American values.[26] "There is a long-term benefit that [these far-right movements] see in terms of continuing the mainstream racialization of Islam," Garvey said.

This has certainly been the case in parts of Tennessee. Eben Cathey, advocacy director of the Tennessee Immigrant and Refugee Rights Coalition (TIRRC), explained that anti-Muslim and anti-immigrant sentiment often go hand in hand in parts of Tennessee. "There is a Bermuda Triangle of anti-immigrant backlash and Islamophobia," Cathey said. "It stretches from Murfreesboro to Shelbyville to Manchester." Indeed, these three areas have seen significant demographic changes over the past decade, including the settlement of Somali Muslims in Shelbyville, many of whom work at a Tyson Foods plant, and the consistent influx of immigrant students matriculating at Middle Tennessee State in Murfreesboro.[27]

The dual-pronged attack on immigrants who were Muslims did not escape the attention of immigrant rights advocates at TIRRC. "We started to notice that the same anti-immigrant legislators started to target the Muslim community. Many of them were conservative Republicans, and some had run on Tea Party platforms," explained Stephanie Teatro, co–executive director of TIRRC. A sampling of anti-immigrant, anti-Muslim legislation at the state and municipal levels includes an English-only ordinance that was passed by the Nashville Metro Council in 2007 (but vetoed by Mayor Bill Purcell);[28] a 2011 anti-Sharia bill that made following foreign law, including the Islamic code, a felony punishable by fifteen years in jail (which passed, but without specific mention of Islam);[29] and an anti-refugee bill (defeated in April 2013).[30] Even though these laws did not pass as introduced, their mere existence fostered divisive debates and created a climate of suspicion and fear about immigrants, refugees, and Muslim communities in Tennessee.

Community groups organized efforts to defeat many of these bills, including the anti-Sharia law that was introduced in the Tennessee State Senate. This law stoked the unfounded fears of many residents over the imposition of Sharia law—a code of moral guidance for Muslims primarily related to religious observances—in the American justice system.[31] While there is no precedent for the imposition of Sharia law over U.S. law, anti-Muslim organizations and spokespersons regularly use its perceived dominance to fuel hysteria and fear about Muslims in general.

Tennessee is not alone in considering anti-Sharia laws. By February 2011, legislators around the nation had introduced anti-Sharia laws in thirty-three states. While the proponents of anti-Sharia legislation claimed that they were merely banning or limiting the application of foreign law in American courts, their rhetoric made it clear that they were taking aim at Islam and American Muslim communities. In seven states—Arizona, Kansas, Louisiana, North Carolina, Oklahoma, South Dakota, and Tennessee—these anti-Sharia laws passed.[32] While the law that Tennessee eventually passed does not have explicit references to Islam or Muslims due to the work of immigrant and community-based activists, its proponents saw the public campaign behind it as a victory by exposing the perceived threats of Sharia and Islam.[33]

In various states around the country, the copy-and-paste pattern of mosque opposition combined with anti-Sharia and anti-immigrant legislation indicates that similar groups are working together. In the years leading up to 2012, the Pew Research Center found a total of fifty-three controversies over mosques in California, Connecticut, Georgia, Florida, Illinois, Kentucky, Maine, Maryland, Massachusetts, Michigan, Minnesota, Mississippi, New Jersey, New York, Ohio, Oklahoma, Pennsylvania, Tennessee, Texas, Virginia, and Wisconsin.[34] The federal government has opened twenty-eight matters (eighteen since 2010) under the Religious Land Use and Institutionalized Persons Act of 2000.[35] Mounted by far-right conservatives and the Islamophobia network, the campaigns against mosque construction, anti-immigrant rhetoric, and anti-Sharia laws together represent concerted and coordinated efforts intended to stoke fear among Americans about losing their culture, communities, and power.

Communities United Against Islamophobia

In Tennessee, young Muslim activists such as Drost Kokoye, Mohamed Shukri, and Remziya Suleyman responded to the attacks on their communities by creating grassroots organizations. "Muslims were being affected in a unique way, and it was important that our communities represented our interests," Drost explained. By 2010, three organizations became particularly active in Tennessee: the

American Center for Outreach (ACO), the American Muslim Advisory Council (AMAC), and Our Muslim Neighbor.

Remziya Suleyman, a Kurdish American refugee who was a key figure in establishing the American Center for Outreach, served as the organization's policy director. "The community was ready for a proactive approach," Suleyman said. "We knew that things wouldn't just go away unless we were more politically and civically engaged." ACO, established in 2011, is a 501(c)(4) organization that has coordinated voter registration efforts at mosques, developed candidate scorecards to provide information about the positions of those running for elected office, and held forums with candidates responding to questions from Muslim community members about their stances on immigration and civil rights issues. Political education and empowerment of Muslims in Tennessee has become an important strategy to identify public officials who will support affirmative policies that welcome immigrants and refugees.

Another tactic that Muslim organizations use is to convey information to government officials about Muslim communities in Tennessee. The American Muslim Advisory Council (AMAC), led by a twenty-eight-year-old Somali refugee, Mohamed Shukri, educates government officials about the Muslim community and works to build trust between Muslims and public agencies. Mohamed's own life experiences have shaped his political views around the importance of community engagement. His family fled Somalia and lived in Kenya as refugees for nine years before coming to the United States in the late 1990s. Growing up in the South, Mohamed began to realize that Muslims, especially those who are Black, confront multiple layers of bias. He witnessed this firsthand as an advocate in Tennessee with the Somali Muslim immigrant community in Shelbyville. "A lot of Somali immigrants had moved to the Shelbyville area to work at the Tyson Foods factory there. But they faced a lot of discrimination," he said. "You had the county newspaper writing bad things every day [about] how we were going to take over."

AMAC's work has evolved in response to the community's experiences, with a particular emphasis on state government agencies and officials. AMAC members frequently provide "Islam 101" presentations to convey basic information about Islam and the contributions and histories of Muslims in Tennessee. AMAC also brings communities and government representatives together for forums.

Abdou Kattih and Dr. Saleh Sbenaty of the Islamic Center of Murfreesboro are convinced that these new civic organizations and emerging young leaders can play critical roles in preventing and addressing future tensions and concerns in Tennessee. Islamophobes "failed legally, they failed through violent action. They're now going to move to long-term planning like eliminating any reference of Islam in public school textbooks or preventing Muslims from running from public office," Kattih surmised. Indeed, a public school textbook campaign has been gaining momentum thanks to a Tennessee-based group called Proclaiming Justice to the Nations, which has mounted a nationwide campaign to remove anti-Semitic and anti-Christian references in K–12 textbooks and curricula.[36] Again, while the purpose seems far-reaching, the rhetoric has focused exclusively on Islam.[37]

The growth of grassroots civic and political organizations shaped by Muslim, South Asian, and Arab community members is a critical strategy in the long-term efforts to address anti-immigrant and anti-Muslim sentiment and policies in Tennessee and other parts of the South. Centralizing these organizations and their constituents in multiracial coalitions can lead to a broader base of support and involvement by immigrants and communities of color in racial justice campaigns. Far-right movements are working with one another to foster division within communities and to test out legislative strategies, as they have attempted to do in Tennessee.

A 2014 study by the Institute for Public Understanding (ISPU) titled "Manufacturing Bigotry: A State-by-State Legislative Effort to Pushback Against 2050 by Targeting Muslims and Other Minorities" bears this out. The ISPU analyzed state legislation between 2011 and 2013 that dealt with issues such as restrictions on reproductive rights, bans on same-sex marriage, restrictions on the right to work, anti-immigrant proposals, voter identification requirements, and anti-Sharia legislation. The study found that in some states pieces of legislation restricting rights in multiple contexts were introduced. Particularly with anti-Sharia legislation, the study found that 80 percent of the 102 anti-Sharia bills proposed were co-sponsored by an overlap legislator who had sponsored or co-sponsored a restrictive law in one of the other arenas examined in the report. The ISPU study found that often legislators introducing anti-laws also proposed or sponsored bills restricting the right to vote or the right to work.[38]

It is critical to be vigilant about these local and statewide efforts around the country. Even more important, we must build multi-issue and multiracial coalitions to advance affirmative legislation and to be ready to push back against policies that restrict the hard-won civil rights of people of color, immigrants, women, and LGBTQ communities. No longer can we afford to work in silos or only on one issue. As we develop these state and local multiracial and multi-issue coalitions, we must also centralize the communities who are being singled out for bigotry.

Beyond the development of civic organizations that advance the interests of the community, political representation can help change negative perceptions. In 2014, Zak Mohyuddin, the Bangladeshi American who was involved with the Manchester County forum, ran for a seat on the Coffee County Commission against incumbent commissioner Mark Kelly. Mohyuddin is a twenty-five-year resident of the area who moved to Tennessee with his family in

1975. He became more involved civically when the anti-mosque backlash started in Tennessee.

"There is a fear about Muslims coming in and imposing their views on everyone," Mohyuddin explained. "Politicians recognize and respond to that fear. It increases their visibility. And when those things work together, they form this negative narrative about us." Mohyuddin's opponent, Mark Kelly, seemed to have taken this strategy to heart. In a letter to constituents asking for their vote, Kelly wrote, "My opponent has expressed his beliefs publicly that the United States is not a Christian nation; that the American flag should be removed from public buildings because it is a symbol of tyranny and oppression; that public prayer should be banned because it insults non-Christians; and that the Bible should be removed from public places."[39] Mohyuddin dismissed these allegations as lies and misinformation intended to stoke fear and suspicion in voters.

Although Mohyuddin lost the race, he hopes to run for political office again. "I find that it is an excellent way to change the ideas of what a candidate looks like and sounds like in this part of the country," he told me. "I'm not Black or White. I have an accent. I'm an immigrant in Tennessee who has lived here for decades. It's a good way for people to get to see who you are, even if you seem different, because at the same time, you're talking about issues important to everyone." In March 2014, Mohyuddin was elected vice chair of the Coffee County Democratic Party.

In December 2014, President Obama traveled to Nashville. He visited Casa Azafrán to build support for his executive actions on immigration relief for segments of the undocumented immigrant population. Prior to President Obama's arrival, Mohamed Shukri of AMAC and Paul Galloway of ACO penned an open letter to the president in which they informed him about the anti-Muslim sentiment in Tennessee. They wrote, "President Obama, we implore you to address anti-Muslim hate in your remarks on immigration. We believe that xenophobes, who spew anti-Muslim rhetoric, do so to the detriment of all immigrant communities and ultimately all Americans. . . . You can help us call them on their bluff."[40] In this way, organizations such as AMAC and ACO are highlighting issues affecting Muslim communities in the broader landscape of immigration policies.

As for Drost, she is pursuing degrees in public policy and law at the University of Tennessee, in Knoxville. She remains deeply engaged with American Muslim communities in Tennessee. When I asked her why she had chosen to study law, she said, "I want to go and learn the system, and be able to bring that back to the community and work to make Tennessee the state that it should be. I feel like I know this place. . . . And if I want to save the world, I want to start at home."

5

Disruptors and Bridge Builders

In twenty-first-century America, South Asian, Arab, Hindu, Muslim, and Sikh immigrants are among the groups transforming our country's racial landscape. In the public imagination, these communities feature in seemingly contradictory narratives. On the one hand, they are touted as spelling bee winners and Silicon Valley entrepreneurs, as individuals making their mark on every sector and industry from the White House to Hollywood and in between. On the other hand, South Asian, Arab, Muslim, and Sikh immigrants continue to be seen as national security risks, foreigners, and economic threats. In coming decades, the roles of these communities are certain to become even more complicated. Their lives and bodies will become the sites where the rights of people of color and immigrants are negotiated, diminished, denied, and compromised. Simultaneously, they will be invited to reinforce and maintain systems of White supremacy and the divisive racial hierarchy in our country.

Newspaper headlines in 2015 reveal the existence of these patterns already, especially related to Islamophobia and xenophobia. In January, anti-Muslim ads appeared on Muni buses in San Francisco.[1] That same month, after the *Charlie Hebdo* terrorist attack in Paris, Vanderbilt University law professor Carol Swain's op-ed in

The Tennessean stirred outrage among students on campus when she asked, "What horrendous attack would finally convince us that Islam is not like other religions in the United States, that it poses an absolute danger to us and our children unless it is monitored better than it has been under the Obama administration?"[2] The month ended with an incident in Texas where protesters harassed a group of Muslims preparing to visit their legislators at the state Capitol by shouting, "Go home! ISIS will gladly take you!"[3]

Other narratives are also emerging about South Asian and Arab communities. Take the case of Purvi Patel, a thirty-three-year-old Indian American immigrant who became the first person in the country's history to be convicted and sentenced for feticide and neglect of a dependent in March 2015. Patel had gone to an emergency room in St. Joseph, Indiana, in July 2013 to seek assistance for heavy vaginal bleeding. A few hours after she received medical treatment, local police arrived to interrogate her. Patel said that she had miscarried, believed that the fetus was not alive, and placed it in a bag in a Dumpster. Local police decided to investigate further and found text messages indicating that Patel may have ordered drugs to terminate the pregnancy. Although toxicology results revealed no record of drugs in Patel's blood samples, the state of Indiana decided to charge Patel with neglect of a dependent and feticide. She was convicted of both charges at a jury trial.

Patel received a sentence of forty-one years from a judge in South Bend, Indiana; she will serve twenty years, with an additional ten suspended.[4] Her treatment by the state of Indiana outraged many in the United States and around the world who were concerned that women could be criminalized for seeking health care after suffering pregnancy complications. Did the fact that Patel is a woman of color and immigrant make her more vulnerable to being investigated and charged with criminal violations? What role did cultural norms play in the assumptions the state made about her and her ability to make reproductive choices? Purvi Patel, a South Asian woman, has become the face of state-sanctioned race and gender discrimination against pregnant women.

About two hundred miles from South Bend, Indiana, where Patel stood trial, Rasmea Odeh, a sixty-seven-year-old Palestinian American community leader, awaited her sentence in federal court. Odeh had been charged by the federal government for failing to disclose a 1969 terrorism conviction in Israeli military court on her immigration application. She claimed that she had been forced to confess to crimes that she did not commit after undergoing weeks of torture and sexual assault by Israeli interrogators. Decades later, Odeh moved to Chicago to build a life for herself, working at the Arab American Action Network, a nonprofit organization. Her life was upended when she was charged with immigration fraud. In March 2015, a federal judge stripped Odeh of her U.S. citizenship and sentenced her to eighteen months in prison. She faces deportation to Jordan after serving the sentence. Her appeal is pending.

Within a month after the Odeh sentencing, newspaper headlines focused on Indian American Vijay Chokalingam, the brother of Mindy Kaling, an American actress of South Asian descent. In his book *Almost Black*, Chokalingam claims that he posed as a Black student in order to gain admission to medical school. He believes that affirmative action "destroys the dreams of millions of Indian-American, Asian American, and white applicants for employment and higher education."[5] Affirmative action is just one of the racial controversies in which South Asians will be inserted — and characterized essentially as White.

In the coming decades, South Asian, Arab, Muslim, and Sikh immigrants will face their share of racial dilemmas at the intersections of gender, faith, immigration status, sexual orientation, and nationality. That is why it is critical to become clear about the roles and identities that these communities must hold and articulate in the new American racial landscape. South Asian, Arab, Hindu, Muslim, and Sikh immigrants must disrupt the racial hierarchy in America, dismantle the systems of White supremacy, and dispel the narratives of cultural exceptionalism that hinder empathy and unity with other people of color. We must make it our responsibility to be both disruptors and bridge builders in movements for justice, from the post-9/11 moment and beyond.

"9/11 Racialized Us"

In the post-9/11 environment, South Asian, Arab, Muslim, and Sikh immigrants became the "other." "Whether we wanted to be or not, 9/11 racialized us," Linda Sarsour, executive director of the Arab American Association of New York, is fond of saying. This process of racialization after 9/11, during which faith and national origin became proxies for race, unfolded in different ways. For example, many Indians, Pakistanis, Bangladeshis, Nepalis, and Sri Lankans, especially those who are the children of the second wave of post-1965 immigrants, began more commonly to refer to themselves as "South Asian" to assert a unified racial identity in post-9/11 America. In addition, Arab, South Asian, Muslim, and Sikh communities were grouped together under a new racial categorization called "AMEMSA," which stands for Arab, Middle Eastern, Muslim, and South Asian.

Racial identity is constantly evolving, whether in one's own understanding of it or in a group's collective sense of it. Scholar and writer Vijay Prashad has questioned, for example, whether an authentic South Asian American identity can even exist given the tremendous differences among South Asian groups and in the absence of shared political goals. With the vast ethnic, faith, socioeconomic, and linguistic diversity among South Asians, uniting under a broad identity could erase fundamental distinctions and differences among and between groups. Indeed, the 3.4 million

South Asians in America trace their origins to Bangladesh, Bhutan, India, the Maldives, Nepal, Pakistan, Sri Lanka, and the South Asian diaspora (referring to those who are descended from South Asians who originally settled in other parts of the world such as Africa, Canada, the Caribbean, Europe, the Middle East, and other parts of Asia and the Pacific Islands).[6] Beyond national origin diversity, there are disparities among South Asians in terms of socioeconomic status, language proficiency, and immigration status, among others.

Prashad's questions about the authenticity of a South Asian American identity in light of these differences are apt ones: "Is it possible then to craft solidarities that might include an entrepreneur, a taxi driver, a domestic worker and a political activist? Is the only thing that unites them, their ancestry, enough to forge a community? What would be the values in such a community? Is it worthwhile to deploy categories that include people whose political goals are irreconcilable?"[7]

In post-9/11 America, some of Prashad's questions have been answered through the racial politics of many South Asian communities and the organizations that represent them. Some groups have identified a common set of political goals, as Prashad calls them, that center South Asians as people of color rooted in a history of racial injustice *and* linked to other movements for change. The personal or organizational decision to embrace a South Asian identity became not merely an exercise in identity politics; it was a political statement that recognized that the post-9/11 backlash and targeting had created a compelling reason to unite under a broader racial banner.

A political ethos and purpose can often motivate identity formation. In their seminal book *Racial Formation in the United States*, Michael Omi and Howard Winant explain that race is an "unstable and 'decentered' complex of social meanings constantly being transformed by political struggle."[8] In the post-9/11 climate, South

Asians reconstructed their own racial identities in light of the political moments they witnessed and endured in order to articulate solidarity with one another. This pan–South Asian category did not supplant cultural or faith-based affiliations; rather, it enabled community members to hold multiple layers of identities, creating a myriad of possibilities of connecting with each other around shared political values and goals.

The ways in which South Asians and Arabs have shaped their personal and group identities in post-9/11 America can provide insights into how racial classifications may shift as our country becomes a majority people-of-color population in the coming decades. A starting place is to understand how the U.S. Census Bureau collects and classifies information on race.[9] Government and nonprofit stakeholders rely on disaggregated racial data from the census to allocate resources and funds, build roads and bridges, demarcate congressional districts, and enforce civil rights laws. The race categories used by the Census Bureau today include Black, African American, or Negro;[10] American Indian or Alaska Native;[11] Asian; Native Hawaiian or Other Pacific Islander;[12] and White.[13] Given that people of Hispanic or Latino origin can be of any race—and can choose the one with which they identify on census forms—the Census Bureau classifies Hispanic and Latino as an ethnicity.[14] Individuals can also select Some Other Race if these categories do not apply or choose more than one race group if they are multiracial. The census does not collect information on religious affiliation.

Racial classifications have dramatically changed since the first census of 1790. For example, South Asians have been classified as Hindu, White, and Other at different points in time by the federal government.[15] Currently, South Asians are categorized as Asian if they choose one of the listed subgroups, such as Indian or Pakistani, or write in Bangladeshi, Bhutanese, Nepali, Sri Lankan, Indo Caribbean, or Indo Guyanese.[16]

The Census Bureau classifies Arabs and Middle Easterners as White/Caucasian for purposes of race tabulation.[17] This includes people from the Middle East and North Africa who trace their ancestry to countries such as Algeria, Iraq, Egypt, Jordan, Kuwait, Lebanon, Libya, Morocco, Palestine, Saudi Arabia, Syria, or Tunisia. According to Maya Berry, the executive director of the Arab American Institute, a national organization that encourages Arab American participation in civic life, "Arabs have complicated responses to racial identity, and it depends on their generation, the amount of time in America, their nationality and faith." Khaled Beydoun, assistant professor of law at Barry University, agrees. "Significant numbers of Arabs are Christian and are more likely to embrace the White racial category," Beydoun explained. "But Arab American Muslims find the assignment of per se Whiteness absurd, paradoxical, and not aligned with their treatment in the United States pre- and post-9/11."

The cultivation of minority consciousness among Arab Muslims in particular means that they identify with a people-of-color status rather than with the assigned census classification of White. This is the case for Drost Kokoye from Nashville. Kurds like Drost are currently classified as White under Census classifications. But Drost thinks of herself as a person of color because of her own political struggles as a Kurdish refugee and a Muslim in the United States. "As refugees, we're told to choose White when we come here," she said. "Whenever you get one of these forms, choose White. And so you start to believe that—that you are White."

But Drost came to understand that checking White on a form did not provide her with any of the racial privileges of Whiteness, due to her refugee status and her faith. "I don't experience Whiteness or White privilege," Drost explained. "I feel more connected to the experiences that people of color have. And that is why on these forms, I will always check Other before White." The experiences of being treated as a minority in the United States and connecting to the political struggles of other groups who face similar stigmas have led young people like Drost to embrace the broader category of "people of color," regardless of the government's classifications.

To create additional options beyond non-White classification, Arab American advocacy groups have proposed that the Census Bureau create a new race category called MENA, Middle Eastern and North African. Berry believes that this category will provide more accurate numbers for the Arab American population. According to data from the 2010 American Community Survey, about 1.9 million Arab Americans lived in the United States. AAI estimates that a higher number of Arab Americans—more than 3.6 million—reside in the country today, and that the inclusion of the MENA category will allow for more accurate demographic information to be collected about the community.[18] In addition, Berry believes that the MENA category will appeal to Arab and North African community members who have shared experiences of discrimination and who want to identify as people of color rather than White. Due to a positive community response to adding the MENA racial category, the Census Bureau may well test it out in coming years. Similar initiatives may occur with respect to faith-based communities, including Hindus, Sikhs, and Muslims, who seek disaggregated data about their groups.

As our country's demographics change, racial classifications will inevitably be in flux. Demographers and government agencies will need to reconfigure racial categories so that they align more closely with the ways in which people characterize their own racial identities. In addition, the racial concepts of "people of color" and "White" may expand and shift based on political views or struggles. The experiences of many South Asian, Arab, Muslim, and Sikh immigrants reveal that a reconceptualization of individual and group identity is already under way.

Collective Racial Identities in Post-9/11 America

The process of individual and group "racialization" that occurred after 9/11 included another component: political alliance building. Within weeks after 9/11, a new racial category called AMEMSA (Arab, Middle Eastern, Muslim, and South Asian) or MASA (Muslim, Arab, and South Asian) began to take shape. This category included the groups identified by the federal government as communities of interest in national security investigations. Organizations working with South Asian, Arab, Muslim, and Sikh immigrants accepted the AMEMSA/MASA category in order to emphasize that they experienced the post-9/11 climate in similar ways. "The AMEMSA [formation] is a natural alliance of groups in the post-9/11 environment to refer to common issues that we face," explained Berry. "It refers to a constituency and solidarity that is different from other communities because of the 9/11 experiences that connect Arabs, Muslims, Sikhs, and South Asians."

At the same time, community leaders also recognized the limitations of the AMEMSA/MASA identity. "The acronyms haven't caught on internally within our communities," said Zahra Billoo, the executive director of the Bay Area office of the Council on American-Islamic Relations. "Many people still identify by their country of origin or faith only. But community leaders and spokespersons use AMEMSA or MASA to describe the constituencies affected by issues like profiling and surveillance and to build solidarity." The AMEMSA/MASA identity may never be a point of daily reference for community members. Instead, it may well continue to exist as a racial construct that enables organizations and spokespersons to refer to communities with similar experiences and policy goals related to the post-9/11 environment.

One of the glaring limitations of the AMEMSA category is its exclusion of Black Muslims, who make up a third of the American Muslim population. This was especially true in the immediate aftermath of 9/11 when the experiences of *immigrant* Muslims became a proxy for the experiences of all Muslims. Additionally, organizations working with South Asian, Arab, Muslim, and Sikh communities framed post-9/11 issues in a national security and immigration framework rather than in a racial justice context. As a result, many Black Muslims feel that their own post-9/11 experiences took a backseat.

"All of a sudden after 9/11, Islam started to be foreign," explained Kameelah Mu'Min Rashad, an interfaith fellow and a Muslim chaplain at the University of Pennsylvania. "It became associated with war and foreign policy despite its long history in America. And if Islam becomes foreign, then Black Muslims don't even exist."

These tensions also have consequences in terms of alliance building. Many historical connections that could have been made to the civil rights struggle and to surveillance before 9/11 were missed, according to Dawud Walid, the executive director of the Michigan chapter of the Council on American-Islamic Relations. Walid explained, "South Asians and Arabs got racialized *after* 9/11. But Black Muslims have been racialized since day one. We never stopped being Black. The elders in the Black Muslim community remember COINTELPRO"—the FBI's counterintelligence programs in the 1950s and 1960s that spied on and disrupted activities of different organized groups—"they remember how our mosques were infiltrated." By not connecting to these histories of Black Muslims, AMEMSA communities may have missed the opportunities to draw upon lessons from racial justice struggles and to connect with Black communities more broadly.

In recent years, South Asian, Arab, and Muslim immigrants have understood the importance of altering these racial dynamics. For example, Namira Islam, a South Asian Muslim, and Margari Hill, a Black Muslim, co-founded the Muslim Anti-Racism Collaborative (MuslimARC) to challenge anti-Black racism within immigrant Muslim communities. "There is a superiority that some

South Asian and Arab immigrant Muslims have," explained Hill. "It comes out as colorism, where Black Muslim children get harassed or bullied because they are darker. It also comes out in the use of racial slurs that immigrant Muslims use." Two of these slurs are the Arabic word *abeed* and the Hindi word *kallu*, both derogatory slurs that demean Black people. Walid has initiated online conversations about the use of these racial slurs by South Asians and Arabs that led to a campaign called #DropTheAWord curated by MuslimARC. These efforts have sparked multiple dialogues, particularly among younger Muslims, South Asians, and Arabs, about the roots and ongoing impact of anti-Black racism.

Looking ahead, it will be important for AMEMSA organizations and supportive stakeholders to remove the national security frame from the experiences of communities and replace it with one that evokes racial justice movements. If Arabs, South Asians, Muslims, and Sikhs are perceived as national security threats, their lives will be disposable and their rights expendable. When advocates utilize a racial justice framework instead, they are able to more effectively connect the experiences of South Asian, Arab, Muslim, and Sikh community members to deeper and broader histories of racial struggles in America, and incorporate effective strategies, lessons, and messages.

Despite its limitations, the AMEMSA identity may be helpful in illuminating the need for organizations to nimbly build multiple alliances in response to political moments. For South Asians in particular, the AMEMSA coalitions became significant coalitions because existing racial identities such as "Asian American" could not fully encompass the complexities of post-9/11 America. South Asians have long acknowledged the discomfort they sometimes feel in being categorized under the broad and often unwieldy "Asian American" racial construct, which attempts to unite more than twenty different ethnic groups with different immigration and refugee histories, cultures, and languages. On what bases do

Pakistanis and Indians find common cause with Filipinos and Koreans, for example? Are the experiences of being seen as foreigners and outsiders sufficient to maintain a political identity between these vastly different ethnic groups?

These tensions were negotiated and explored in the post-9/11 climate. Many Asian American organizations took on important roles in providing legal services and advocacy on behalf of South Asians. For example, the Asian American Legal Defense and Education Fund in New York City and Asian Americans Advancing Justice–Asian Law Caucus in the Bay Area represented community members facing deportation proceedings. At the national level, groups such as Asian Americans Advancing Justice in Washington, D.C., documented stories of hate violence and pressed for legislation to restore civil liberties.

Still, there are points of healthy tension and opportunities for growth, given that pan–Asian American organizations do not naturally and instinctively embrace post-9/11-related issues. In order for the Asian American racial identity to hold together in coming decades, advocates must acknowledge that it is a tenuous racial construct that is not monolithic. Simultaneously, Asian American groups must strengthen the capacity of organizations that organize around ethnicity and find natural entry points for them to unite around issues and campaigns. For example, Nepali and Filipino domestic workers have forged alliances to press for fairer work conditions, given the increasing presence of these communities in the care industry. Southeast Asians and South Asians could form deeper alliances to address the deportation and immigration enforcement crises affecting both their communities, spurred on by the 1996 immigration laws and post-9/11 policies.

In addition, Asian American leaders and organizations could centralize the experiences of those communities that are often at the margins or that face significant threats from the state, including

Southeast Asians and South Asians. The cornerstone of pan–Asian American organizing has rested historically upon subverting the "model minority myth" or telling a monolithic Asian American history rooted in East Asian experiences. Broadening Asian American narratives, centralizing communities at the margins, and building interethnic solidarity through issue-based campaigns can strengthen collective Asian American racial and political identity.

Saying No to the Racial Bribe

In America's changing racial landscape, South Asian, Arab, Muslim, and Sikh immigrants and the organizations that represent them must make the choice every day, time and again, to actively disrupt the racial hierarchy in America and dispel the narratives of cultural exceptionalism. Doing so also involves confronting the systems of White supremacy articulated by Andrea Smith, an intellectual, feminist, and antiviolence activist who identifies as a Cherokee. According to Smith, when an institution, law, or system supports White supremacy, it results in the preservation of benefits, entitlements, and rights to White elites, who then wield greater influence over the political, ideological, cultural, and economic conditions in our nation.

Smith writes, "White supremacy is constituted by separate and distinct, but still interrelated, logics. Envision three pillars, one labeled Slavery/Capitalism, another labeled Genocide/Colonialism, and the last one labeled Orientalism/War, as well as arrows connecting each of the pillars together."[19] Each of these pillars devalues communities of color by positioning them as exploitable property (Black people's labor being used without compensation, for example), disposable (indigenous people seen as objects whose histories and struggles can be erased), or inferior subjects to be conquered through hostility, violence, and war (Latinos, Asians, and Arabs).

Given the post-9/11 environment, we could offer another pillar to this framework, one called Islamophobia/National Security that derogates Muslims and anyone perceived to be Muslim in order to preserve the illusion of collective safety. These pillars of White supremacy enable the United States to go to war; to deny people rights to their languages, histories, and homes; to militarize police forces in our cities; and to enact laws that profile, target, imprison, detain, and deport communities of color and immigrants.

At times, non-Black communities of color have colluded, consciously and unwittingly, to maintain White supremacy and its racial hierarchy in place. Our positions on the racial ladder in America dictate the opportunities, privileges, and entitlements that are available to us. Blacks are at the bottom, while Whites maintain the top position. Latinos, Arabs, and Asians fall in middle positions. The racial ladder preserves White privilege while propagating anti-Black racism. Racial groups in the middle maintain and reinforce this structure, sometimes with their consent. For example, immigrants of various racial backgrounds internalize racist attitudes toward Black Americans in the process of becoming "Americanized." In her 1993 essay "On the Backs of Blacks," author Toni Morrison explains that "the move into mainstream America always means buying into the notion of American blacks as the real aliens. Whatever the ethnicity or nationality of the immigrant, his nemesis is understood to be African American."[20] In other words, the process of Americanization and the journey toward cultural or legal citizenship inevitably includes accepting, internalizing, and perpetuating racist ideas and narratives of African Americans.

As our country's demographics change, our positions on the racial ladder will be cause for even greater anxiety. In order to maintain the position of groups in the racial hierarchy, we can expect to see efforts that expand the category of White to buttress the numbers of Whites and to convey the false impression that Whiteness can include racial diversity—that is, the claim that Whiteness could be based not merely on phenotypical racial identity but also on supposed nonracial factors that signify social and political power, including the attainment of higher economic and educational status. This creeping Whiteness inevitably means that some people of color will be invited to join the White category, with the promise of attaining the privileges of Whiteness. South Asians, Arabs, and other Asians have historically been tempted to take this racial bribe in order to advance to higher positions on the racial hierarchy. We must firmly decline this invitation. When we do so, we can begin to dismantle the racial ladder altogether.

In their book *The Miner's Canary*, Lani Guinier and Gerald Torres explain that the racial bribe has four goals: "(1) to defuse the previously marginalized group's oppositional agenda, (2) to offer incentives that discourage the group from affiliating with black people, (3) to secure high status for individual group members within existing hierarchies, and (4) to make the social position of 'Whiteness' appear more racially or ethnically diverse."[21] That is, non-Black communities of color are often invited to take the racial bribe in order to make the status of Whiteness more appealing and to signal Whites' openness to diversity.

But the White category does not confer any of the privileges of Whiteness. The false embrace of racial privilege provides only temporary comfort because of the structural and individual prejudices that disadvantage people of color regardless of their socioeconomic or educational status or attainment of U.S. citizenship. For example, while some South Asians have been able to avoid discrimination at an individual level thanks to economic and educational privilege, they cannot escape the negative public perceptions that exist about them generally or the prevalence of systemic racism in institutions of power.

Why are South Asians especially vulnerable to the racial bribe? The myth of cultural exceptionalism is partly to blame. It promotes the idea that South Asians possess innate cultural characteristics that propel them to succeed and thrive more than other minority groups. This narrative is tied closely to the model minority concept that purports similar views of the intellectual superiority of Asian Americans. The nuanced difference between these two narratives is that cultural exceptionalism is less focused on explicit racial comparisons to other groups, while the model minority narrative explicitly creates a wedge between Asian American and Black communities. Policy makers often exploit the model minority narrative to deny access to benefits to people of color as a whole by claiming that Asian Americans do not need them.

Often it is not culture but different forms of privilege—linguistic, educational, immigration, and economic—that provide some South Asians with the ability to make advances in professional and educational arenas. Rinku Sen, the president of Race Forward and publisher of *Colorlines*, uses a personal story to make this point. In seventh grade, Sen, an Indian American immigrant, scored quite high on an intelligence test. The school guidance counselor asked her why the Asian kids in school tended to outpace everyone else. Sen responded, "We have a culture that values education." But, as Sen noted in hindsight, "That was a naive response on my part as a seventh grader, which I came to understand later. What culture doesn't value education for their kids?" Sen came to recognize that her family, like many others, had received a helping hand along the way. "My family was among many essentially selected by Congress to come to this country when the immigration laws changed in 1965. And we arrived with a lot of privilege and lots of capital already built up. I got here speaking three languages, including English. I had a leg up in many ways." Sen recognized that her family had received the benefits of the 1965 immigration law, which paved the way for many South Asian families to find success in the United States.

When South Asians are touted as cultural success stories across the board, the community's experiences become homogeneous. For example, while the achievements of South Asians who are Silicon

Valley CEOs, spelling bee champions, and science whizzes should be celebrated and lauded at every turn, they should not be presented as the only or prevailing narrative about the experiences of South Asian communities. We must challenge representations that imply all South Asians have the same privileges as those who have attained high levels of success. Otherwise we effectively render invisible the experiences and needs of the Nepali domestic worker who makes the Indian CEO's success possible or the Bangladeshi taxi driver who takes the Pakistani Wall Street banker to work.

Consider the example of Sangeeta Richard, a domestic worker who mustered up the courage to press charges against her employer, Indian deputy consul general Devyani Khobragade, in December 2013. Preet Bharara, the Indian American U.S. attorney for the Southern District of New York, alleged that Khobragade had submitted fraudulent documents in order to bring Richard into the United States to work in her home and care for her children.[22] The government also alleged that Khobragade had exploited Richard by paying her just $3.31 an hour, significantly below the required minimum wage or what Richard had originally been promised.[23]

Within days, the case drew national and international attention.[24] Khobragade claimed that during the arrest authorities stripsearched her, which led to a diplomatic spat between India and the United States.[25] Reactions to the case revealed that many Indian Americans were more concerned with Khobragade's treatment than with Richard's plight.[26] In a rightfully indignant statement, Bharara wondered why "there is so much outrage about the alleged treatment of the Indian national accused of perpetrating these acts, but precious little outrage about the alleged treatment of the Indian victim and her spouse?"[27]

The answer might partly lie in the interest that some Indian Americans have in preserving the perception of economic and racial privilege, even at the cost of marginalizing people from within their own community. The devaluation of certain types of work, such as housekeeping, cooking, and babysitting, also leads to these negative perceptions. According to Ashwini Jaisingh, a twenty-eight-year-old Indian American organizer who works with domestic workers at CASA de Maryland, the Khobragade-Richard story provides insights into how economic privilege operates within South Asian American communities. "We have some real class issues to address in the South Asian community," Jaisingh explained. "Some perceptions are brought from home countries, but others are built and perpetuated here to preserve racial privilege. There is this sense that domestic workers do low-wage work, so we should treat them accordingly, with fewer rights and benefits." These divisions prevent South Asians from understanding and advocating for the rights of the least privileged in our communities.

The costs of accepting the racial bribe are significant. Doing so hinders the ability of South Asian communities to find solidarity with one another. Instead, South Asians should choose to build intracommunity solidarity across class lines. This means that South Asians must empathize with the experiences of people like Sangeeta Richard rather than marginalize or dismiss them outright. It means that South Asians must reject opportunities to create divisions between undocumented South Asians working in the shadow economy and skilled workers with H-1B visas in Silicon Valley—and instead find common ground based on the immigration system's deficiencies and on a collective vision about the conditions that all immigrants deserve for their work. It means that South Asians must rally behind campaigns led by South Asian workers, such as the taxi drivers of the New York Taxi Workers Alliance and guest workers who are often trafficked into this country and face workplace exploitation. Rejecting the racial bribe means finding solidarity with one another and other people of color rather than separating ourselves in order to preserve self-interests.

South Asian cultural, professional, student, and business associations have important roles to play in refusing the racial bribe and dismantling the narrative of exceptionalism. Often such groups choose to avoid issues such as Islamophobia or immigration reform by claiming that they are too divisive, controversial, or political. Yet these issues affect the daily lives of many South Asians. Ignoring them means that we deny the lived experiences of community members and become complicit in accepting the laws and systems that disadvantage them. Instead, all South Asian groups must take on political issues with greater regularity.

For example, a South Asian college organization could invite to its cultural events artists who use art or comedy to engage political issues, including D'Lo, a transgender Tamil queer Sri Lankan American actor, writer, and comedian; Dark Matter, a trans South Asian performance art duo comprised of Alok Vaid-Menon and Janani Balasubramanian whose performances integrate themes of colonialism, 9/11, and multiracial communities; or Anu Yadav, an actress, writer, and theater-based educator who tells stories of people on the social and economic margins of America. Community artists who address political issues could jump-start conversations on campuses is about the racial realities facing South Asians.

Additionally, a South Asian association of attorneys could use a racial justice analysis to document the systemic barriers that community members face in accessing legal services and host regular legal clinics at places of worship. A South Asian chamber of commerce could issue a statement around the need for immigration reform that recognizes both business and worker interests. A South Asian cultural or faith-based organization could ask civic, nonprofit, and political groups to table at their events. With such acts, these organizations can lead the way in rejecting the myth of cultural exceptionalism and interrupting the racial hierarchy in the United States.

The Future of Community Building

In 2004, I traveled with staff and board members at South Asian Americans Leading Together (SAALT) to different cities around the country for listening sessions. We wanted to hear directly from community members and organizational leaders about the pressing needs facing South Asian communities in the first few years after 9/11. In community dialogues that we held in cities such as Chicago, Houston, Jersey City, the Washington, D.C., metropolitan area, New York, and San Francisco, we heard similar themes and refrains from South Asian organizational leaders including Seema Agnani from Chhaya CDC, Maneesha Kelkar from Manavi, Aparna Sharma from South Asian Progressive Action Collective (SAPAC), Monami Maulik from Desis Rising Up and Moving (now called DRUM–South Asian Organizing Center), Amardeep Singh from the Sikh Coalition, and Aparna Bhattacharyya from Raksha. They emphasized the need for local community-based organizations to be connected to one another in order to amplify their voices nationally, to have the capacity to address the far-ranging needs emerging among South Asians through multilayered strategies, and to change inequitable conditions affecting the lives of South Asians.

One lesson we learned through the community dialogues is that the landscape of South Asian organizations looked vastly different after 9/11. The bulk of pre-9/11 nonprofit groups included South Asian women's organizations that were created in the 1980s and 1990s by feminists who realized that South Asian women facing violence had few options, especially if they were dependent on an abuser's immigration or financial status. Groups such as Manavi (New Jersey), Raksha (Atlanta), Apna Ghar (Chicago), Sakhi for South Asian Women (New York City), and Maitri (Bay Area) had become lifelines for many South Asians over the years.

As the South Asian population in the United States began to increase and change in the late 1990s and early 2000s, regional social

service organizations emerged to respond to the needs of community members, primarily those who were new immigrants, working
class, and not fully proficient in English. These included groups
such as the South Asian Network (Southern California-based), the
Indo-American Center (Chicago-based), Desis Rising Up and Moving (New York City), Chhaya CDC (New York City), the Sikh American Legal Defense and Education Fund (national), and SAALT
(national). In 2007, many of these organizations came together to
form the National Coalition of South Asian Organizations (NCSO),
coordinated by SAALT, to amplify their voices at the national level
on policy issues using a progressive lens and intersectional analyses.

In the years after 9/11, Arab American and Muslim organizational infrastructure was a bit further along. More established
groups such as the American-Arab Anti Discrimination Commit
tee (formed in 1980) and the Arab American Institute (formed
in 1985) helped South Asian, Sikh, and Muslim groups navigate
Washington, D.C.'s government agencies in the aftermath of 9/11.
In 2002, staff at the Arab Community Center for Economic and
Social Services in Dearborn, Michigan, began to develop the vision for the National Network of Arab American Communities
(NNAAC). NNAAC brings together Arab American community-based organizations around the country and takes policy stances
on issues such as civil and immigrant rights. Immigrant Muslim
communities relied on national organizations such as the Islamic
Circle of North America (founded in 1968), the Muslim Public
Affairs Council (founded in 1986), KARAMAH, Muslim Women
Lawyers for Human Rights (founded in 1993), and the Council
on American-Islamic Relations or CAIR (founded in 1994). Over
time, groups like Muslim Advocates and the American Muslim
Civic Leadership Institute formed.

When 9/11 occurred, many of these South Asian, Arab, Muslim, and Sikh organizations were just beginning to build infrastructure and gain a foothold in the nonprofit sector and their own

communities. In the weeks and months afterward, they scrambled to address the evolving crisis. Seema Agnani, who served as executive director of Chhaya CDC in New York City, recounted: "Immediately after 9/11, our phones were ringing off the hook. The calls were about hate crimes happening in neighborhoods, people getting fired from their jobs. I remember hearing from a group of Pakistani bus drivers who were all fired at once. We were not equipped to handle all the issues, so we would refer many community members to groups like AALDEF [the Asian American Legal Defense and Education Fund]. We focused on helping taxi drivers who worked in Lower Manhattan obtain assistance from FEMA [Federal Emergency and Management Agency] so they could pay their rents and make their mortgage payments. After NSEERS, we started noticing that a lot of the tenants in buildings that we were organizing in would just disappear. Women would be left on their own without income sources, without even knowing where their spouses were."

For many years after 9/11, many South Asian, Arab, Muslim, and Sikh nonprofit organizations existed in this cycle of crisis response, pivoting to the range of needs presented by clients and community members while also advocating against harmful government policies and divisive public narratives. But South Asian, Arab, Muslim, and Sikh immigrants are no longer just "post-9/11 communities." While we continue to face hate violence, surveillance, and anti-Muslim rhetoric, additional challenges lie before us as our numbers increase in America. In particular, socioeconomic differences, educational barriers, lack of accessible health care, and limited English proficiency hamper the opportunities of many community members. In addition, internal community divides along class, faith, and gender lines continue to pose challenges.

Given the increase in needs presented by South Asians, it is critical to support the capacity of local nonprofit organizations, which are often on the front lines in our communities. Currently, South Asian nonprofits engage in a range of social change strategies to empower South Asian, Arab, Muslim, and Sikh communities, including policy and media advocacy, civic and political empowerment, leadership development, alliance building with other communities, and social service provision. If we are to build the community's power in a deeper and more sustainable way, then grassroots organizing and coalition building must become core strategies for community-based groups.

Grassroots organizing grounds itself in the lived experiences and the leadership of individuals who face class, gender, immigration, and racial inequities. They include working-class, poor, and un-documented people who experience multiple levels of individual discrimination and systemic injustice. Grassroots organizing also builds a base of people equipped and ready to create and mobilize around campaigns. It need not be a strategy limited to organizations with members. For example, traditional social service agencies can integrate organizing strategies in English as a Second Language classes, naturalization workshops, and after-school programs to bring people together and facilitate their own leadership to change neighborhoods and workplaces.

This is at the heart of the work of DRUM–South Asian Organizing Center in Queens, which organizes undocumented and working-class communities in New York City who have been at the forefront of campaigns for economic and immigrant justice. One of DRUM's core programs is YouthPower!, led by working-class people ages thirteen to twenty-one. YouthPower! members have been active participants in the Dignity in Schools program to raise awareness about the school-to-prison and low-wage-jobs pipelines. "The only way that working-class communities—the most directly affected, we often say—can be involved is through organizing," Fahd Ahmed, the executive director of DRUM–South Asian Organizing Center, explained. "A young South Asian going to a sub-standard school that's a pipeline to the criminal justice system isn't going to be ready to talk education policy immediately. Through an organizing model, we are able to invite more people that are directly impacted by struggle. We then connect our members with other communities of color facing similar struggles."

Adhikaar, a membership-based organization for Nepali-speaking communities in New York City, also places a strong emphasis on grassroots organizing and working in broader coalitions. Many of Adhikaar's members are domestic workers and nail salon workers. "Our members work as nannies, cooks, housekeepers. They care for seniors. But some of our members live in slavelike conditions," explained Narbada Chhetri, a former domestic worker and the director of organizing and advocacy at Adhikaar. "These women work long hours and get little money, sleep in basements without windows, and cannot take off when they are sick. But they are ready to organize to change their lives." Many of Adhikaar's members actively participate in economic justice campaigns to press for laws that change workplace conditions for domestic workers. Adhikaar also works closely with larger and multiracial networks such as the National Domestic Workers Alliance. "When we all come together from different backgrounds, we feel empowered," Chhetri said.

Organizing groups like DRUM and Adhikaar understand clearly that their members may experience discrimination in a myriad of ways beyond race and class. South Asians, like other minority groups, often carry multiple identities—a woman who is also undocumented or a Hindu woman who is also lesbian—which means that they face discrimination at all of the points where those identities intersect. This awareness of "race plus" discrimination guides the work of the Muslim Alliance for Sexual and Gender Diversity (MASGD, pronounced "masjid," the Arabic word for mosque) which emerged in 2011 to support, empower, and connect LGBTQ Muslims in the United States. "It's hard to come out as queer in a Muslim space, and it's hard to come out in the mainstream LGBTQ space because of the perceptions of Islam," explained Urooj Arshad, a steering committee member of MASGD. The conversations held at annual MASGD retreats often revolve around the multiple layers of oppression that queer Muslims face. "Since 9/11, it's become clear that being Muslim is a racialized identity," Arshad said. "At our retreats, we always talk about the impact of Islamophobia on us, what it means to face it when you are queer *and* Muslim." MASGD also sees itself as part of broader people-of-color LGBTQ movements for social justice. "We participate in multiracial coalitions like the National Queer Asian Pacific Islander Alliance. We insert analysis about being Muslim and queer at conferences organized by more mainstream LGBTQ organizations." In these ways, MASGD plays the role of being an interlocutor and bridge builder in movements for racial justice and LGBTQ equality.

Even social service providers are in the midst of transforming their work in response to the changing needs of their clients. Neha Gill, executive director of Apna Ghar in Chicago, explained that their organization's services have expanded well beyond domestic abuse. "We are connecting with domestic workers, undocumented families, same-sex partnerships in which there is violence, and individuals who have been trafficked to work in the small South Asian–owned franchises on Devon Avenue," Gill said. "We are also advocating around reproductive justice and health issues facing immigrant women."

Similarly, Moumita Zaman, a twenty-nine-year-old Bangladeshi American and the director of outreach and advocacy at Sapna NYC, hears daily about the experiences of South Asian immigrant families living in the Westchester Square and Parkchester neighborhoods of the Bronx. Sapna NYC has supported the work of Bangladeshi women to engage in participatory research campaigns and peer-education workshops around a range of issues that they have identified, including mental health and socioeconomic barriers. "Our work is very place-based, and it involves the residents of these neighborhoods," Zaman said. "We facilitate asset building in the community so that people have the tools to change their lives and their neighborhoods for the better." In coming years, Sapna NYC plans to facilitate worker cooperatives for South Asian women interested in using their existing resources, skills, and knowledge to build their collective economic power.

Outside New York City, many South Asian organizations face uphill battles as they struggle to be responsive to the needs of their communities. For example, Aparna Bhattacharyya, executive director at Raksha in Atlanta, explained that South Asians in Georgia contact her organization, which focuses on addressing gender violence, for help with a host of issues. "We are the only South Asian social service organization in the state," she explained. "So, many times, we become the first call for people in different crisis situations." Bhattacharyya recalled one of these crisis situations that occurred in 2005, when federal and local law enforcement charged South Asian convenience store owners and clerks in northwest Georgia with illegally selling items that would be used to produce methamphetamine. Operation Meth Merchant, as it was known, resulted in indictments of 20 percent of the South Asian store owners in the area.[28]

Raksha became a resource for store owners and clerks who believed that they had been targeted unfairly by law enforcement. "We got criticism about our role, with people asking us why a domestic violence group was getting involved with an issue of racial profiling," Bhattacharyya recounted. "But we just couldn't stand by when everyone arrested were South Asians. We had to develop a vocabulary around the criminal justice system and develop relationships we didn't have at the time in order to connect people who were affected to the right resources."

Raksha also lent assistance to a group of Indian migrant workers who had been trafficked into Texas and Mississippi after Hurricanes Rita and Katrina in 2006 to repair oil facilities owned by Signal International, a shipbuilding company. Claiming that there was a shortage of skilled workers, Signal used the H2-B guest worker program to bring in workers to the Gulf Coast. Around five hundred men were lured to the United States on H2-B guest worker visas with false promises that they would receive green cards. The men were instead subjected to inhumane living conditions in cramped and guarded camps and had to pay $1,050 to Signal International each month. Many of the workers began to organize with the help of the New Orleans Workers' Center for Racial Justice and obtained legal representation from the American Civil Liberties Union and the Southern Poverty Law Center. Five of the men received $14 million in damages from a federal jury in Louisiana in February 2015. More than two hundred additional claims are still pending against Signal International.[29]

Given that some organizations are able to be more nimble than others in responding to the various needs of community members, the role of activists and volunteers becomes even more important. Community activists are even exploring informal strategies outside traditional nonprofit structures. One approach includes organizing through faith-based institutions such as mosques, gurdwaras, and temples, which reach a wider swath of community members than most nonprofit groups. Partnerships between faith leaders and activists can have a tremendous impact.

Zahra Billoo, the thirty-one-year-old executive director of the Bay Area office of the Council on Arab-Islamic Relations, explained that successful campaigns and initiatives in Muslim communities often blend political issues in faith spaces. She noted that when imams and religious spokespersons at mosques engage their constituents on political and civic issues, the response within community members is far-reaching. "If the *khutbah* [sermon] could be on joining the Ferguson movement or getting registered to vote, more people will respond to it and apply it in their lives," Billoo said.

Faith-based models of grassroots engagement are also evolving in the Hindu community. Aminta Kilawan, a twenty-six-year-old founding board member of Sadhana: Coalition of Progressive Hindus, explained that her group regularly engages with Hindus at temples, particularly in the Richmond Hill and South Ozone Park neighborhoods in Queens, New York. "There are as many temples as roti shops in South Ozone Park," Kilawan, who is Indo-Guyanese, said, only half jokingly. "We want to mobilize community members where they are, as progressive Hindus for social change." Sadhana also supports other communities of faith who are often targeted, including Sikhs and Muslims. "We want to stand alongside them," Kilawan explained. "We believe that our overall cause is stronger when there is a progressive Hindu group that speaks up on issues facing other faith communities."

Not surprisingly, civic and political participation will be a major priority in the coming decades for South Asians. "Naturalization workshops and civic and political engagement training are becoming integral parts of our work," said Manju Kulkarni, the executive director of the South Asian Network in Southern California. That's not surprising given that South Asians are becoming an increasingly visible segment of the rising American electorate. The numbers of South Asian U.S. citizens of voting age increased rapidly between 2000 and 2010. For example, the percentage of U.S. citizens of Bangladeshi descent who are of voting age rose by 471 percent. For Indians, Pakistanis, and Sri Lankans, the percentage changes were 99 percent, 205 percent, and 143 percent, respectively.[30] In addition, the numbers of citizens-in-waiting—including green card holders who may become U.S. citizens in the future—are on the rise.

In the decade ahead, South Asian activists and organizations must invest time and energy toward registering voters and informing South Asians about their electoral rights and responsibilities. Political organizations and candidates are certain to reach out to this segment of the rising American electorate. In the past two presidential elections, the Republican and Democratic Parties targeted South Asians through advertisements in ethnic media and events for young professionals. As South Asian organizations and activists prepare for future election cycles, political education workshops and trainings must also become an important priority, especially for new voters, to convey information about the American political process, the issues at stake in elections, and accountability mechanisms to effectively assess candidates and elected officials.

In years to come, South Asians are also likely to increase their involvement with transnational struggles for gender rights and interfaith solidarity, antiwar efforts, the treatment of migrants and refugees, the Palestinian liberation movement, and environmental causes, just to name a few issues. In other words, demonstrations of diaspora solidarity may become just as important as issues within the United States. For example, groups including Brown and Green: South Asian Americans for Climate Justice and Eco Sikh organized a visible presence at the People's Climate March in September 2014. These organizations have also been raising awareness about the impact of climate change in both South Asia and the United States.

When South Asians, Arabs, Muslims, and Sikhs center themselves firmly in a collective racial identity, challenge the myth of cultural exceptionalism and disrupt the racial order, we can transform our movements for racial justice and equity. When South Asians resist the racial bribe and align with Black communities, we can disrupt the racial hierarchy. And when South Asians, Arabs, and other Asians refuse to uphold racial dynamics that pit communities of color against one another and frame their interests in opposition to one another, we can chip away at the foundations of White supremacy. As discussed in the following chapters, the rights of undocumented immigrants and the campaigns against police brutality are opportunities for South Asian, Arab, and Muslim immigrants to engage with issues that are beginning to define the twenty-first-century racial justice movement.

6

Undocumented Youth Rise Up

Early on an August morning in the summer of 2008, Yves Gomes's family awakened to knocks on the door of their house in Silver Spring, Maryland. The early morning visitors were law enforcement agents from Immigration and Customs Enforcement (ICE), the arm of the Department of Homeland Security that enforces immigration laws. The agents entered the family home, checked all the rooms, and questioned Yves's father, Robin, about his immigration status. They then handcuffed Robin in front of his family and said they were taking him to a detention facility because he had no legal authorization to be present in the United States. As he was taken away, Robin told Yves: "Be strong for your mother and brother." Within weeks, the U.S. government deported Robin to Bangladesh.

Yves's entire world turned upside down that summer. Born in India, Yves had arrived in the United States on a tourist visa with his father, a Bangladeshi Christian, and his mother, an Indian Christian, when he was a little over a year old. Robin and Cecilia Gomes settled near other family members in Silver Spring and began to build their lives. Yves's father worked as a waiter at the Crowne Plaza and Hilton hotels in Washington, D.C., and his mother taught computer science at Northern Virginia Community

College while working toward her doctorate. The family became active in Saint Camillus Church, a multicultural Catholic parish, in Silver Spring. Yves and his younger brother, Aaron, hung out often with their cousins and friends. Yves learned English by watching *The Fresh Prince of Bel-Air* and *Full House* with them.

As a child, Yves was unaware that his family's immigration status was precarious. His father had applied for asylum based on a fear of religious persecution, but for twelve years the case languished in immigration courts. In 2006, the government denied Robin's asylum claim. Robin, Cecilia, and Yves immediately became undocumented and deportable. Aaron, born in Maryland, is a U.S. citizen.

Yves's life changed when he came to realize that he and his parents were undocumented. The family was always worried about being detained by law enforcement. But voluntarily returning to India or Bangladesh with their children was not a viable choice for Robin and Cecilia Gomes. Yves had spent all but fourteen months of his life in Silver Spring, and Aaron had been born in the United States. The brothers had no connection to anyplace other than Maryland. Yves's parents knew that they had to find a way to continue their lives in America—even if it meant living without immigration status and dealing with the constant fear of being discovered. The knowledge that he and his parents were undocumented shaped Yves's critiques of U.S. immigration policies. "Two years of living like that, like many undocumented people do every day, opened my eyes for the first time," Yves told me. "I began to realize how problematic our immigration laws are."

The Gomes family's worst fears came true during the summer of 2008. In August of that year, local police stopped Yves's father for driving with a faulty taillight. That traffic stop set the Gomes family on a collision course with the immigration system. It led to the ICE raid of Yves's home and the detention of his father. After holding him in detention for six months, the U.S. government deported Yves's father to Bangladesh. Yves's mother, also undocumented, was placed in an "alternative to detention" program called the Intensive Supervision Appearance Program.[1] Under this program, Cecilia Gomes had to wear an electronic ankle monitor every day for a year.[2] "I think that was the toughest part for me, to watch my mother struggle like that," Yves remembered. His mother had to routinely check in with an immigration office in Baltimore "just to show that she wasn't doing anything crazy," he said. Then, she drove to northern Virginia for her job so that she could continue to support Yves and his younger brother.

In July 2009, Yves's mother was deported. From India, she applied for a job to teach at a women's college in the United Arab Emirates and sponsored her husband to join her in Abu Dhabi. Yves and Aaron have stayed in touch with their parents over the years through weekly Skype conversations.

"Undocumented, Unapologetic, Unafraid"

Typically, the public, media, and policy makers think of South Asian immigration issues through the lens of family reunification or the H-1B "skilled worker" visa program. Yet the reality is much more complex, and it is one that includes growing numbers of undocumented South Asians. In 2012, approximately 11.4 million undocumented people resided in the United States, with nearly 2 million under the age of eighteen. Most come from Mexico, El Salvador, Guatemala, Honduras, the Philippines, India, Korea, China, Ecuador, and Vietnam.[3] In 2015, approximately 450,000 undocumented individuals from India resided in the United States, making up the fourth-largest undocumented population in the nation.[4]

Many undocumented immigrants work, live, and study in the shadows, fearful of being discovered and often ashamed of revealing their lack of immigration status. Although the construction, agriculture, food service, and private home care industries rely on the labor of undocumented immigrants, they face tremendous

barriers. Immigration policies at state and federal levels criminalize and endanger undocumented immigrants by limiting the provision of driver's licenses[5] or health care,[6] by denying traditional
employment benefits such as medical insurance or unemployment
compensation,[7] and by enabling the profiling of immigrants by law
enforcement.[8]

In the South Asian community, the stigma of being undocumented has a myriad of consequences. Many South Asian undocumented immigrants feel that they have done something wrong,
shameful, or criminal by being out of status. Yet South Asians
fall out of immigration status for a range of reasons. The undocumented South Asian community includes H1-B workers who lost
their status due to layoffs, elderly immigrants who overstay their
visitor visas, workers in the shadow economy whose employers are
unwilling to sponsor them, students whose visas expire after they
receive their degrees, individuals who are recruited and trafficked
into the country, and people like Yves and his parents whose claims
for asylum status are denied after years of waiting.

For South Asian undocumented youth, the psychological and
emotional impact of being out of status can be particularly severe.
Undocumented youth often realize in high school that they are different from their peers when they cannot apply for college scholar-
ships, in-state tuition, or drivers' licenses. Prerna Lal, co-founder of
Dream Activist, a network connecting undocumented youth, and a
staff attorney with Asian Americans Advancing Justice, explained
that before she joined the undocumented youth movement, she
had felt isolated. "I was around fifteen years old when I came to
the U.S. I used to hide. I was told by my family not to tell anyone,"
she said. "I found my community online through a portal for undocumented youth. I was shocked that there were undocumented
kids from all over the world just like me."

Stories of people like Yves and Prerna reveal that South Asians
can have a range of experiences with the U.S. immigration system.

They also give courage to other South Asians who wish to reveal their immigration statuses and challenges more publicly. That has been the case with Bupendra ("Bupen") Ram, a twenty-nine-year-old Fijian Indian living in Los Angeles.

In 1988, when Bupen was two years old, his parents made a decision to escape the political unrest targeting Indians in Fiji. Bupen's parents, Tota and Kamala Ram, wished to move to the United States to provide a better life for their five children. In good faith, they trusted a recruiter who told them that he could transport them to Los Angeles and acquire legal immigration papers for a lump sum of $10,000. Bupen's parents sold their possessions in Fiji, provided the payment, and boarded an airplane for Los Angeles on tourist visas. Once they got to Los Angeles, they received fake immigration papers. By the time Bupen's parents realized that the papers were false, the family had already overstayed their tourist visas.

For years, Bupen's family, just like Yves's, maintained lives in the shadows and under the radar. Bupen's parents took various jobs to make ends meet. His father worked as a security guard and performed Hindu religious services for the Fijian Indian community in the area. Kamala worked as a sous-chef at a restaurant and in customer service at Los Angeles International Airport. Even at a young age, Bupen was aware that he was undocumented. Some of his earliest memories involve waiting in line at the Los Angeles immigration office and going to meetings that his parents had with lawyers. As he grew up, Bupen followed an unspoken code of behavior. "I knew there were certain things I could and couldn't do," he told me. "I always had a sense of fear about meeting new people, about what I should disclose."

In college at California State University, Fullerton, Bupen experienced years of isolation that came from having to hide not only his immigration status but also his sexual orientation. "I thought I was all alone, because I was both undocumented and queer," he explained. Slowly, Bupen began to find a community of queer un-documented youth like him. He heard about Prerna, who is also Fijian Indian, undocumented, and queer, and felt a deep connection to her personal story. He began to volunteer with Dream Team Los Angeles to raise public awareness about the challenges facing undocumented youth.

Within the undocumented youth movement, Bupen realized he no longer had to hide his sexual orientation or his immigration status. "For the longest time, I've tried to segregate my identities," he said. "Only queer in one space and only undocumented in another space. As I've gotten more involved with different organizations, I've been able to integrate these identities."

While the undocumented youth movement is primarily led and organized by Latino youth, South Asians like Yves, Prerna, and Bupen have become visible participants. By 2010, several organizations and networks had come together to create infrastructure around undocumented youth, calling them "Dreamers," a term that refers to their hopes and aspirations, many of which could not be attained even though they had lived much of their lives in the United States like other young Americans. Networks of undocumented youth began to take shape nationally, online, and on college campuses through the assistance of organizations such as Dream Activist and the National Immigration Law Center. The country's largest youth-led immigrant organization, United We Dream, has a base of more than one hundred thousand youth and allies and fifty-five affiliate groups across twenty-six states. These groups organized to help undocumented youth fight their deportations, and mobilized around the proposal of the DREAM Act in Congress in 2010. The DREAM Act sought to provide undocumented high school graduates who had entered the United States when they were fifteen years of age or younger with the opportunity to eventually obtain permanent residency if they completed two years of college or served in the military.

Even though the DREAM Act failed in the U.S. Senate—by just five votes—it empowered undocumented youth. The DREAM Act had captured the attention of the public and the media in large part due to the visible involvement of undocumented youth who claimed that they were "undocumented, unapologetic, and un-afraid." In recent years, undocumented youth have continued to organize to draw attention to the high rates of immigration en-forcement in the United States and the need for executive action by President Obama in light of Congress's inadequate efforts to pass immigration reform legislation.

Non-Latino undocumented youth have been playing small but important roles in these efforts. For example, Asian American undocumented youth started to organize formally in recent years through organizations such as Asian Students Promoting Immi-grant Rights through Education (ASPIRE)—based in the Bay Area (in coordination with Asian Americans Advancing Justice–Asian Law Caucus) and in Los Angeles (in coordination with Asian Americans Advancing Justice–Los Angeles)—and Revolutionizing Asian American Immigrant Stories on the East Coast (RAISE), in coordination with the New York City–based Asian American Legal Defense and Education Fund. These groups started as spaces where undocumented Asian American youth could find support and refuge, build their leadership skills, and connect with broader campaigns organized by networks like United We Dream.

As undocumented youth build a movement in the United States to reshape narratives about immigrants and reform immigration laws, the inclusion of non-Latino young people must be a priority. Greisa Martinez, a field organizer for United We Dream, regularly includes stories of non-Latino youth to mobilize undocumented im-migrant youth of various backgrounds at college campuses around the nation. "People still see immigration as a Latino issue," she explained. "Latinos might be able to secure some policy wins on immigration on their own given our numbers. But we want to build a movement that is bigger than short-term policy change, one that's about mobilizing all young people who have an undocumented experience and want a better life for themselves and their families."

Martinez believes that, in order to build a more inclusive grassroots movement of undocumented youth, Latino-led organizations must recruit non-Latino immigrant youth and create welcoming spaces for them. "Groups like United We Dream tend to be primarily Latino in terms of our membership and leadership because of the ways we have organized and the sheer numbers of Latino undocumented youth. But we have a deep commitment to being more inclusive," she said. "People like Yves and Rishi Singh"—an undocumented youth member of DRUM: South Asian Organizing Center—"remind us that our spaces need to be more culturally and linguistically welcoming to non-Latinos and non-Spanish speakers. We also want to support the growth and capacity of groups that organize Asian and South Asian undocumented youth."

The presence of Asian undocumented youth in immigrant rights organizations and coalitions also helps to challenge the misleading perceptions that exist about the monolithic immigrant experiences of Asian Americans overall. "Even in the undocumented youth movement, there is this notion that Asians have the same amount of privilege as Whites," Yves observed. "But it's not always the case—a lot of undocumented Asians are working fifteen-hour shifts, struggling every day, making less than minimum wage. Asians aren't all living the same lives. We need to have these conversations within the undocumented community about Asians—to say, look, we are not the model minority."

Changing such assumptions about South Asian undocumented immigrants became a by-product of Hina Naveed's work at El Centro del Inmigrante, where she helped to start the Staten Island DREAM Coalition. Hina, an undocumented Pakistani and Muslim student at the College of Staten Island, believes that her presence at a predominantly Latino organization altered people's preconceptions about the types of issues that South Asian immigrants face. "I was different-looking, being Pakistani and wearing a hijab, but people slowly understood that I had the same concerns as they did about being undocumented," she explained. "We had the same problems and the same hopes."

My Introduction to the Movement Was Not by Choice

Often undocumented youth become involved in the immigrant rights movement while they navigate their own deportation struggles. This was the case for Yves, who began to grapple with his own deportation as he began his senior year at Paint Branch High School in Silver Spring, Maryland. The prospect of being deported to India did not stop him from applying to colleges. During the process, Yves decided to come out publicly about his undocumented status to his high school counselor. "I felt really ashamed and scared of how she would react," he remembered. Her reaction surprised him. She empathized with Yves's situation, reassured him that he would be heading to college, and even encouraged him to apply to the Maryland Distinguished Scholar program. He graduated from Paint Branch High School with honors in June 2010.

Looming ahead was August 13, 2010, the date of Yves's scheduled deportation. As it neared, Yves decided that he had to raise public awareness and support. His family and friends sprang into action. His cousin, Harold, launched an online campaign to draw attention to Yves's impending deportation. The priest at Saint Camillus's church connected Yves with the Center for Community Change, which compiled a video story of Yves's family that received wide public attention. Yves's friends created a Facebook page to spread information about his case, started online petitions, and asked organizations to send letters of support on his behalf.

Just three days before his deportation date, Yves's attorney, Cynthia Groomes Katz, surprised him at his home with reporters from a local television station in tow. Katz told Yves and his family that the government had issued an order for deferred action that provided him relief from deportation for two years. "It was the support of so many people that helped me," Yves recalled. "That made me want to help others in the same position as well."

Yves would make good on that promise as an undergraduate student at Montgomery College's Rockville, Maryland, campus. There he met Jonathan Jayes-Green, a fellow undocumented student. Jonathan had come from Panama to Silver Spring when he was thirteen years old and had read about Yves in the paper. "I was excited to meet him, but Yves was pretty humble," Jonathan remembered. They became good friends, connected by their undocumented status and their activism. Together they started an organization for undocumented students on campus and became involved with efforts to support passage of the Maryland Dream Act. The state legislature passed this bill in 2011, but it was challenged and then placed on a referendum in the 2012 general election.[9]

Yves and Jonathan worked with CASA de Maryland, a statewide advocacy and organizing group, to raise awareness about the referendum by speaking to voters around the state, often highlighting their own stories. In addition to voting on the Maryland Dream Act, voters in the 2012 general election had to weigh in on a same-sex marriage referendum that would enable same-sex couples to obtain a civil marriage license in Maryland. Jonathan linked the two issues together in speaking engagements around the state. "As someone who is queer and undocumented, I could talk to different audiences about coming out of two closets," he explained. Doing so provided an opening for LGBTQ communities and immigrant communities to understand that there were similarities in their experiences of marginalization and in their political goals. Maryland voters approved both referenda in the 2012 general election. Under the Maryland Dream Act, undocumented high school graduates can qualify for lower tuition rates at Maryland's public colleges.[10]

For Yves, immigrant activism has become a way of life, a commitment that is at the core of his values. "My introduction to the movement was not by choice," he told me. "But it's a big part of who I am now." Yves's courage has inspired many others, including Jonathan. "Yves was a pillar among undocumented youth in Maryland," Jonathan said. "Because Yves was one of the first to publicly come out as undocumented, a lot of us felt more comfortable doing so. And I felt accountable when Yves would get up and share his story: I felt that I had a responsibility to do it as well, to share my own story."

Deportation Nation

Under President Obama's administration, nearly 2 million people have been deported.[11] Despite the government's insistence that its focus is on deporting violent offenders, gang members, and terrorists, the truth of the matter is that many of the people being detained and deported include those who commit minor or nonviolent crimes. According to the Immigration Policy Center, of the 368,644 immigrants who were deported in 2013, only one-fifth were classified as violent criminals.[12] "Many people who are deported have families, live in communities, or are working," explained Paromita Shah, associate director of the National Immigration Project. "Sadly, they are caught in the net of harsh immigration enforcement policies. We are at a point where people like Yves's dad can be placed in deportation just for having a faulty taillight because the local police can check whether immigrants are authorized to be here or not."

It is not lost on advocates like Shah and undocumented youth activists that the push toward immigration enforcement in the United States draws upon decades of criminalization of Black communities in particular. "The mass deportation culture draws upon the trends we see in the criminal justice system," Shah explained.

"The United States has the largest prison population in the world. The terrible habits that have infected our criminal justice system, such as the lack of transparency or accountability or prosecutorial discretion, have also permeated immigration enforcement."

Immigration enforcement has become a national priority over the past thirty years as a result of laws and policies that seek to deter undocumented immigrants from entering the United States. It includes programs like Section 287(g), created by Congress in 1996, that gives local police departments the authority to enforce immigration laws.[13] Under the program, local police officers are able to verify whether a person they stopped or interrogated had valid immigration status by comparing that person's identification information with federal databases. By 2010, the Immigration Policy Center found that more than 1,075 local police officers across twenty-four states had been trained and certified to identify and apprehend immigrants under the 287(g) program.[14]

Advocates have criticized the 287(g) program because of the possibility of rampant profiling by law enforcement and the lack of civil rights protections available to immigrants. According to Paromita Shah, Section 287(g) has contributed to the national culture of enforcement and criminalization. "Section 287(g) might be in effect in only some jurisdictions, but it fuels a mass deportation culture around the country," Shah explained. "Enforcement has always been happening at the borders, but 287(g) allowed it to move into the interior of America. These programs make police officers feel like they are immigration agents, but they don't act in line with civil rights standards." For example, police officers may use criteria such as skin color, accent, and lack of proficiency in English as markers of undocumented status rather than relying on individualized behavior. Policies like 287(g) place a large number of people of particular racial and ethnic backgrounds—regardless of their immigration status—in fear of going about daily activities, such as driving to work or school or traveling, because they might be detained or questioned by law enforcement.

Similarly, some state legislatures have targeted undocumented immigrants through anti-immigrant policies. In 2010, the state of Arizona passed S.B. 1070, which allowed law enforcement to ask for proof of legal immigration status if they suspected that someone was undocumented. Advocates and community leaders objected to the law, claiming that it would lead to profiling of Latino and Asian immigrants based on their accents or skin color. Five states—Alabama, Georgia, Indiana, South Carolina, and Utah—followed Arizona's example and passed copycat bills. All included similar provisions that required or authorized police to demand documentation showing proof of citizenship or immigration status if they suspected that an individual whom they encountered was undocumented. While the U.S. Supreme Court struck down several parts of the Arizona's law, it held that the controversial "show me your papers" provision was constitutional. Key provisions in the five copycat laws have been blocked upon legal challenge.[15]

The practice of criminalizing immigrants through these divisive policies and narratives has a long history in our country. The government relies on the simplistic categorization of immigrants as "good/desirable/welcome" or "bad/disposable/unwelcome" in order to justify actions that advantage one group of people over another for the purposes of receiving immigration benefits or migration preferences. On one hand, we rely on immigrant labor, whether that means Silicon Valley engineers, apple pickers, or domestic workers; we appreciate the diversity of cuisines, customs, and cultures that immigrants bring to our neighborhoods and schools; and we celebrate immigrant success stories. Yet on the other hand, we maintain a high level of anxiety about how America might change when people from other countries, especially those speaking non-English languages and practicing non-Christian faiths, populate our neighborhoods, schools, and workplaces. Additionally, the arguments for limiting migration and denying services and benefits to immigrants rely on the misleading narrative of scarcity, which assumes that resources are already limited and should be preserved for "Americans" only.

Asian immigrants in particular have been puppets on the immigration stage, vacillating between the statuses of undesirable/inadmissible and acceptable/welcomed. At the turn of the twentieth century, for example, immigrants from India were viewed as the "brown horde," often represented in American newspapers as turbaned invaders with the odious intent of taking away American jobs and infiltrating the country with their uncouth customs and traditions.

Media narratives and policy makers reinforced these perceptions. A March 1910 article in *Collier's: The National Weekly* insisted that Indian immigrants had neither the skills that the United States needed nor the proclivity to properly assimilate. It also created artificial separations between Indian and Chinese immigrants even though both groups were treated as outsiders. "They are, on the whole, inferior workmen," declared the *Collier's* article. "They manifest no interest in the country or its customs; and they differ from the unobtrusive Chinaman by being sullen and uncompromising in adhering to their habits."[16]

Not surprisingly, these nativist views extended to federal policy as well. National origin quotas restricted the number of visas that could be provided to those seeking to migrate from a part of the world called the "barred Asiatic zone."[17] Indians who were able to come to the United States to work or attend school faced severe restrictions in terms of their ability to own and sell land or become citizens. In 1908, Naturalization Division chief Richard K. Campbell announced opposition to naturalization by East Indians and "Hindoos" following previous denials of citizenship to Japanese and Chinese immigrants.[18] In a series of court cases in the early 1900s, a new legal jurisprudence began to emerge that posited Whiteness as a criterion for citizenship.

The 1923 case of *United States v. Thind* settled the question of whether Indians or Hindus could become citizens.[19] It involved a request for naturalization from Bhagat Singh Thind, an immigrant who had come to Oregon from India in 1913. Thind worked in lumber mills, paid his way through the University of California at Berkeley, and enlisted in the U.S. Army in 1918.[20] He insisted that he should be naturalized because he was Caucasian, thereby meeting the legal requirements of Whiteness that courts had decided were prerequisites for naturalization. It is important to note that Thind, like many other Asians seeking naturalization, did not challenge the racial construct of Whiteness altogether in his quest for U.S. citizenship by claiming that it was discriminatory or racist overall. Thind's legal arguments in support of his naturalization ultimately rested not upon dismantling the racist jurisprudence of Whiteness but rather upon fitting within it.

The Supreme Court denied Thind's claims. The court found that, in order to be a citizen, one had to demonstrate Whiteness as it is commonly understood. Associate Justice George Sutherland, writing for the majority, noted:

It is a matter of familiar observation and knowledge that the physical group characteristics of the Hindus render them readily distinguishable from the various groups of persons in this country commonly recognized as white. The children of English, French, German, Italian, Scandinavian, and other European parentage, quickly merge into the mass of our population and lose the distinctive hallmarks of their European origin. On the other hand, it cannot be doubted that the children born in this country of Hindu parents would retain indefinitely the clear evidence of their ancestry.[21]

According to the Supreme Court, Whiteness could be extended only to those who shared particular phenotypic characteristics or had the potential for full assimilation into American life. Indian immigrants failed this test. For Thind, a Sikh from India, the decision was a significant personal blow. Even though he seemed to possess the experiences that Americans desired—a job, a college education, military service, and an honorable discharge from the U.S. Army—his skin color, country of origin, and cultural and religious background could not overcome the Court's racist criteria for assessing Whiteness, citizenship, and entry into American society. Preventing Thind and others like him from gaining citizenship provided another means for the government to exploit the labor of immigrants without providing any benefits in return.

It would take Thind another thirteen years before he could obtain U.S. citizenship.[22] But it would take decades longer for Congress to remove all the racial restrictions on immigration and naturalization. The push to change immigration policies would not have occurred without the civil rights movement led by Black communities in the 1960s. Federal policy makers realized that it would be politically untenable to continue to condone racist immigration policies while advancing civil rights for people of color in America. In addition, U.S. employers wanted to recruit individuals with skills that were in shorter supply in various industries including science, engineering, and medicine. Consequently, the Immigration and Nationality Act of 1965 opened America's doors to skilled, educated immigrants and their families.[23]

With the passage of this legislation, Asian immigrants benefited from the popular belief that they were "good" immigrants. This perception worked hand in hand with the dangerous "model minority" narrative, which posited that Asian Americans were culturally inclined toward educational and economic success and superior to other minority groups.[24] These frameworks sent the inaccurate and misleading message that other communities of color did not culturally value education in the way that Asians did. They created divisions between Asian Americans and other people of color—in particular, Blacks. They also masked the tremendous disparities that exist within Asian American communities along socioeconomic and educational attainment lines by peddling a monolithic, one-size-fits-all narrative about Asian American values and lifestyles.

"Mr. President, You Have the Power!"

Since 1965, immigration laws such as the Illegal Immigration Reform and Immigrant Responsibility Act of 1996 (IIRIRA), harsh border and interior enforcement policies, and increasing family and employment visa backlogs have created a broken immigration system.[25] For decades, immigrant rights advocates have courageously called for changes to this broken system. Their actions have escalated in recent years. The mass marches in 2006, the sit-ins at congressional offices by undocumented youth in graduation caps and gowns, and the protests at detention facilities have all created a sense of urgency to reform the immigration system.

Undocumented youth have been at the forefront of this movement, urging changes not only for themselves but for families torn apart by harsh immigration enforcement policies. "As the most privileged of the undocumented population, it's important for us 'Dreamers' to bring others along, especially those who are seen as 'criminals' in the eyes of the system and put into deportation proceedings for minor offenses that they have already served time for in many cases," explained Prerna Lal.

The public pressure worked. In June 2012, President Obama announced the Deferred Action for Childhood Arrivals (DACA) program, which provided certain qualified youth with the ability to temporarily stay and work in the United States.[26] If eligible for

DACA status, undocumented youth could stay in the United States for two years and receive authorization to work. The status could be renewed for another two years after it expired.[27] Immigrant rights advocates have credited the implementation of DACA to the undocumented youth movement. "Deferred action in 2012 came about because of the undocumented youth who risked their lives by sitting in front of detention centers and at border stops to draw attention to the inequities of our immigration system," said Shah. Undocumented youth, including Bupen and Hina, have benefited from the DACA program.

The implementation of DACA and the introduction of immigration reform legislation in the Senate fueled the momentum of the immigrant rights movement. Asian Americans participated in many of the actions and campaigns calling for immigration reform. This is not a surprise, given that three-fourths of Asian Americans were born outside the United States.[28] As immigrants or children of immigrants, Asian Americans interface with every aspect of the immigration system—as workers, family members, entrepreneurs and innovators, students, asylum seekers and refugees, and detainees.

In May 2013, leaders of Asian American organizations had the opportunity to meet directly with President Obama at the White House to discuss a range of issues, including immigration. We outlined for the president the ways in which the immigration system fails Asian immigrants daily. We highlighted the tremendous backlog of family visas that prevent reunification between family members, leading to waits of up to twelve years for those being sponsored from India and twenty-four years for those being sponsored from the Philippines. We identified ways to reform the employment visa system, including the need to ensure that immigrants are not trafficked into the United States and exploited by unscrupulous employers. We outlined our support for the path to legalization for undocumented immigrants and rejected harsh enforcement practices that targeted immigrants and separated them from their loved ones.[29] In turn, President Obama reiterated his commitment to fixing the immigration system and to working with lawmakers to do so.

By the end of 2013, however, it was clear that Congress would not be passing immigration reform legislation. The pressure again was on President Obama to use his executive powers and grant immigration relief for undocumented people. In the Bay Area, ASPIRE (Asian Students Promoting Immigrant Rights through Education) members began participating in civil disobedience actions and campaigns to press for broader executive action by President Obama. "We are trying to shift the mind-set from DREAMers—from just helping me or us," explained Wei Lee, an ASPIRE member who is ethnically Chinese and was born and raised in Brazil. "We want to build a movement that goes beyond us."

ASPIRE members played a role in highlighting the more ambitious policy asks of the movement when President Obama visited San Francisco to speak at the Betty Ong Rec Center in November 2013. Some members held demonstrations outside the center to raise awareness about the effects of deportations. Inside the center that day, an undocumented Asian American youth and ASPIRE member named Ju Hong interrupted President Obama's speech, shouting, "Mr. Obama, my family has been separated for nineteen months now. You have a power to stop deportation for all undocumented immigrants in this country."[30]

These actions surrounding the president's appearance in San Francisco moved the needle forward on the possibility of executive action on immigration. While the president did not use his power to stop all deportations, his administration made significant changes to different parts of the immigration system through executive actions announced a year after Ju's impassioned appeal.

In November 2014, President Obama expanded the DACA

program and created a new Deferred Action for Parental Account-ability (DAPA) program aimed at parents of U.S. citizens or lawful permanent residents. He also announced new enforcement pri-orities to guide detention and deportation practices.[31] The White House has estimated that up to 5 million immigrants could be positively affected by these wide-reaching policy changes.[32] While advocates were grateful to President Obama for initiating immigra-tion relief, many have provided feedback on changing the messages that the White House used in describing the new actions. "Presi-dent Obama said that the programs are not going to help felons, but families, not gang members, but moms working hard," Yves said. "But it's not a black or white line. My own mother was seen as a felon. She had to wear an ankle bracelet for a year. But she was also working hard to take care of her kids. You can be both—a felon, because that's how the system sees you, *and* a mom."

In February 2015, a federal judge in Texas blocked implementa-tion of the expanded DACA and DAPA programs after twenty-six states challenged the president's executive action in court. The government appealed. In May 2015, a split federal appeals court declined to lift the injunction, continuing to leave nearly 5 million people who stand to benefit from DACA and DAPA in limbo.[33]

Undocumented young people like Bupen, Hina, and Yves are di-versifying the immigrant rights movement with their presence and stories and expanding its scope and reach. Hina works as a neigh-borhood organizer in Staten Island and engages in public outreach around New York City's municipal identification program. One of her priorities is to ensure that more undocumented people sign up to obtain the photo identification card.

In April 2014, Bupen participated in a ribbon-cutting ceremony to open the Titan Dreamers Resource Center at California State Uni-versity, Fullerton, his alma mater. The center offers undocumented students services and programs including academic and emotional support. For Bupen, whose college experience had been lonely and challenging, the presence of the Titan Dreamers Resource Center represents a victory that is connected to his own personal struggle.

In December 2014, I joined several of Yves's classmates, professors, friends, and family members at his graduation from the University of Maryland. Yves acknowledged our loud cheers and yells with a big smile as he walked across the stage to accept his hard-earned degree in biochemistry. His personal story of triumph over our country's flawed and unjust immigration system is a testament to his courage and to the mass movement of undocumented youth seeking justice. That is why, at Yves's commencement, we were celebrating more than his tremendous achievements. We were also sending a public statement that Yves and young undocumented people like him deserve fair and equal treatment. Yves's friend Jonathan Jayes-Green captured our sentiments as he held a sign that read "We Are ALL Yves."

7

Ferguson Is Everywhere

On a chilly Saturday morning in October 2014, a diverse crowd gathered in downtown St. Louis, ready to march through the streets in the name of Michael Brown, an eighteen-year-old Black teenager who had been killed two months earlier by Darren Wilson, a White police officer, in Ferguson, Missouri. I joined the solidarity march in St. Louis, along with Gregory Cendana and Johanna Hester of the Asian Pacific American Labor Alliance, Tejal Mankad of Asian Americans Advancing Justice–Asian Law Caucus, and Linda Sarsour of the Arab American Association of New York. We were all there to participate in #OctoberFerguson events organized by young people to raise awareness about the national epidemic of police violence targeting Black communities.

Michael Brown's murder in Ferguson sparked a protest movement that drew worldwide attention. As Ferguson residents engaged in peaceful demonstrations, local and state law enforcement intimidated and attacked them in the name of public safety. Night after night for weeks in August 2014, police officers donned riot gear, drove tanks down city streets, used tear gas and rubber pellets against protesters, and imposed evening curfews. Millions of people around the United States and the world watched as live video streams from Ferguson displayed images of a war zone in the heartland of America.

What happened in Ferguson brought into sharp focus the alarming outcomes that Black men, women, and children often face in encounters with law enforcement. A study by ProPublica, a nonprofit investigative journalism organization, found that between 2010 and 2012, young Black men were twenty-one times more likely as Whites to be killed by police.[1] Nationwide, the numbers of Black people likely to be stopped, frisked, and arrested are also higher than any other racial group. A November 2014 analysis by *USA Today* of national arrest rate records in 2011 and 2012 found that seventy police departments around the country tended to arrest Black people at a rate ten times higher than non-Blacks.[2] While Black men face higher rates of arrests, stop-and-frisks, assaults, and deaths at the hands of law enforcement, Black women, children, and transgender people are not immune. The names of Michael Brown, Eric Garner, Rekia Boyd, John Crawford, Ezell Ford, Freddie Gray, Akai Gurley, Mya Hall, Trayvon Martin, Tamir Rice, Walter Scott, and Aiyana Stanley-Jones make up just part of a distressingly long list of Black men, women, and children who have lost their lives in encounters with law enforcement.

By the time we arrived in St. Louis for #OctoberFerguson, the youth-led movement that started in Ferguson had spread around the country. Our guide in St. Louis was Mustafa Abdullah, a twenty-seven-year-old program associate at the American Civil Liberties Union (ACLU) of Missouri. When we met in person I could immediately sense Mustafa's inexhaustible energy and determination. He introduced us to local Arab and South Asian immigrant business owners and Black organizers in Ferguson. He marched with us through the streets of St. Louis. During our group dinner one night, Mustafa fielded calls and messages from legal observers he had trained to document the treatment of peaceful protesters on the streets of Ferguson, while at the same time providing us with historical context about policing in St. Louis.

Mustafa is well aware that his presence as an Arab American and Muslim in police accountability efforts sends an important message about multiracial solidarity. Born in Cairo, Mustafa and his family moved to western Massachusetts when he was just a year old. At the age of twelve, Mustafa's family relocated to Winston-Salem, North Carolina, where his parents enrolled him in a private Baptist school. "If you weren't White, wealthy, Christian, you stuck out as a sore thumb," he recalled of his middle school experience. The events of 9/11, which occurred when Mustafa was in eighth grade, only exacerbated this feeling.

"The day after 9/11, everyone in my English class seemed to have figured out the narrative," he told me. "It was clear who our enemies were, who was in the right and who was in the wrong. A lot of that was confusing to me. At the end of the class, the teacher looked at me and said, 'Mustafa, do you have anything to say as a Muslim student?' I felt that I was being asked to represent the entire Muslim community. I said nothing." In the months that followed, Mustafa made the decision to delve deeper into a study of Islam. "I wasn't comfortable with my own identity and didn't want to have conversations with my peers. I felt more comfortable being invisible."

The one place where Mustafa, who is six feet ten, felt that he truly belonged was on the basketball court. "On the court, I didn't have to talk about anything else. It facilitated relationships. It kept me from being ostracized," he said. But the basketball court was not immune from racial bias. During one game, Mustafa remembers that he wasn't able to get to the ball because he was being held by his arms and blocked by the opposing team's players. At the end of the first half, he approached the referee to complain about this treatment. The referee turned to him and said loudly, "Shut up, you big monkey." Mustafa was shocked that the referee had used a racial slur against him. Immediately, his coach spoke up on his behalf and berated the referee. "Those experiences of other people standing up for me had an impact on me," Mustafa remembered. "And I wanted to do that for others. I didn't want any more eighth-grade Mustafas to experience anything like that."

After college, Mustafa worked for a local interfaith organization called CHANGE (Communities Helping All Neighbors Gain Empowerment). He engaged in outreach to Muslim leaders, organized in Latino and Black neighborhoods, and learned about the common issues that affected people of color and faith communities in Winston-Salem. In June 2013, Mustafa relocated to St. Louis and started his work at the ACLU. Little did he know then that in less than a year he would become involved in one of the most significant racial justice movements today.

On the Monday after Michael Brown's death, Mustafa came to work to find his voicemail full of messages. One of the calls he took that morning was from Linda Sarsour. "She asked where the local Muslim community was on what had happened to Mike Brown," Mustafa said. "That really centered me. Of course, Muslims had to speak up." Within days, Mustafa, Sarsour, Dawud Walid (executive director of the Michigan chapter of the Council on American-Islamic Relations), and Muhammed Malik (a community activist in Miami, Florida) started a group called Muslims for Ferguson. Over the coming weeks and months, they held national calls attended by hundreds of people, amplified the demands from Ferguson organizers and protesters, and participated in solidarity actions around the country.

Another swift response came from the St. Louis Palestine Solidarity Committee (STL-PSC), which had been founded in 2009 to support equal rights and freedom for people living in Palestine. Suhad Khatib, a St. Louis resident and daughter of a Palestinian refugee, said that over the years, STL-PSC and local Black community leaders had been building stronger relationships. For example, the Organization for Black Struggle and other Black leadership groups and leaders had joined a campaign led by STL-PSC to prevent the city of St. Louis from entering into a contract with a multinational company whose Israeli subsidiary operates in an illegal Jewish-only settlement. Black organizers had also attended events organized by STL-PSC to support the residents of Gaza. "By the time everything started to happen after Mike Brown's death, we already had personal relationships with Black organizations and leaders in St. Louis," Khatib said. "There was no doubt that we would support them." That support even came from Palestine. "We saw this remarkable exchange between Palestinian young people and Ferguson protesters over social media," Khatib recalled. "They were tweeting safety precautions on how to deal with being teargassed by the police in Ferguson."

The painful understanding of how state violence affects people has led to solidarity between Palestinian Americans around the nation and Ferguson residents. "We aren't equating Ferguson with Palestine," explained Mustafa. "But we are trying to draw the link that state violence is wrong—no matter where it happens." That sentiment was visible when we marched through the streets of St. Louis with the Palestinian American contingent during #OctoberFerguson. Young Black and Palestinian activists held signs that read "From Palestine to Ferguson: Resistance Is Not a Crime." At the rally concluding the march, Khatib spoke. Her declaration that "Black liberation in America will lead to liberation everywhere" drew loud cheers from the audience.

What Does It Mean to Stand with Ferguson?

In the wake of Ferguson, an opportunity for authentic and sustained multiracial solidarity has emerged. As I write, the Ferguson movement continues to evolve. Yet even in its beginning stages, important messaging points, actions, questions, and interventions have arisen. For South Asian, Arab, and Muslim immigrants, solidarity with Ferguson means supporting the message behind Black Lives Matter without co-opting or expanding it. It means articulating the pervasiveness of anti-Blackness in our society through the lens of both individual discrimination and systemic racism. It means becoming active participants (rather than bystanders or mere allies) in the movement to end police brutality by recognizing the impact of discriminatory law enforcement actions on people of color. And it means working within our own communities to address the role of anti-Black racism and White supremacy.

Alicia Garza, who co-founded the message that "Black Lives Matter" along with Patrisse Cullors and Opal Tometi, has written about the roots of the phrase. She describes it as an "ideological and political intervention in a world where Black lives are systematically and intentionally targeted for demise. It is an affirmation of Black folks' contributions to this society, our humanity, and our resilience in the face of deadly oppression."[3] The Black Lives Matter movement demands that we confront the ways in which Black communities disproportionately face violence at the hands of the state not only in the context of police encounters but also in terms of decades of educational segregation; poverty; income inequality; lack of access to jobs, housing, and public transportation; and a prison system that incarcerates Black people at alarming rates. The movement has also forced national conversations about the inescapable role of anti-Blackness in policies, practices, and decisions that have led to long-term disinvestment in Black neighborhoods from Ferguson to Oakland to Baltimore. Authentic and sustainable solidarity efforts must be premised on this broader understanding of why Black lives matter, why they have not mattered historically, and why they still do not matter today, as they should. Centralizing Black communities in the current moment is how genuine solidarity begins. South Asian, Arab, and Muslim activists have been careful not to co-opt or expand this premise by applying it to their communities—by stating "All Lives Matter" or "South Asian Lives Matter," for example. This stems from the knowledge that when Black lives actually matter, when Black people are not seen as disposable commodities, then all lives will truly matter. In other words, when Black people, who are at the bottom of America's divisive racial ladder, are free, it will be impossible for systems and policies to engage in discrimination and racism against other communities of color.

South Asian, Arab, and Muslim activists have demonstrated this understanding in their messages and actions. Youth members of DRUM–South Asian Organizing Center made a powerful statement in the wake of Michael Brown's death when they marched through the streets of Jackson Heights, Queens, holding their hands up and shouting, "Hands Up, Don't Shoot." In Oakland, South Asians joined other Asian Americans with signs that read "Model Minority Mutiny!" to encourage the subversion of the framework that creates divisions between Black and Asian American communities. Student groups, such as Muslim Students Associations and Students for Justice in Palestine, participated in die-ins on college campuses around the nation. With these actions and messages, South Asian, Arab, and Muslim activists have amplified the experiences of Black people without conflating them with the struggles of non-Black communities.

"We Are All Criminalized"

How can both Black and non-Black activists center experiences of Black people with law enforcement while also acknowledging the ways in which state violence affects non-Black people of color? Dante Barry, a twenty-six-year-old African American organizer who is the executive director of the Million Hoodies Movement for Justice, believes that Black and Brown organizers must find collaborative yet distinct ways of talking about police violence. "Yes, there are common threads—the growth of the prison-industrial complex and the detention facilities, the surveillance of Muslims and the War on Drugs," Barry said. "There are commonalities in how these mechanisms mistreat Black and Brown people. But the challenge before us is this: how do we talk about anti-Black racism and anti-Brown racism as similar—but different? How can we leave room for these communities to build on their own—and together?"

Answering these questions will involve candid conversations between Brown and Black activists, as well as trial and error in terms of practices and messages. For Brown activists, solidarity with Black Lives Matter must not come at the cost of negating or erasing the experiences that their own communities have with state violence. After all, Asian and Arab Americans, Native Americans, and Latinos are no strangers to police violence and profiling based on skin color, accent, language, immigration status, or faith. Between 1999 and 2013, indigenous people were killed by police officers at rates nearly identical to that of Blacks.[4] For years, Latinos, along with African Americans, have been the disproportionate targets of the New York Police Department's stop-and-frisk tactics.[5] In their ongoing war on undocumented immigration, federal and state law enforcement agencies have engaged in rampant profiling of Latino and Asian American communities. Federal programs such as Secure Communities[6] and "Show Me Your Papers" laws[7] enacted in Arizona, Alabama, Georgia, Indiana, South Carolina, and Utah have led to stops and detentions of people based on their accent or skin color and deepened the fears of immigrants in engaging with law enforcement. In addition, South Asians, Arabs and Muslims have been subjected to unchecked surveillance by local and federal law enforcement in the years following 9/11. These patterns and examples of discriminatory policing and violence demonstrate that all people of color have a stake in the efforts to bring about reform and accountability on the part of law enforcement.

For example, in February 2015, the assault of a fifty-seven-year-old Indian American grandfather named Sureshbhai Patel by a white police officer squarely thrust South Asians into the charged national conversations about police accountability. Patel, who was visiting his son in Madison, Alabama, was taking a walk in his son's neighborhood when cops approached him. The police officers had been dispatched on the basis of a 9/11 call from someone who claimed that a "skinny black guy" was walking around the neighborhood, making him nervous.[8] Police accosted Patel on a residential street and engaged in the following dialogue:

Officer: "What's going on, sir?"
Officer: "You what?"
Patel: "India."
Officer: "Where you heading?"
Officer: "Where?"
Officer: "I can't understand you, sir."
Officer: "Where's your address?"
Officer: "Do you have any ID?"
Patel: "India?"
Officer: "Do you live here?"
Officer: "Sir, sir, come here."
Officer: "Do not jerk away from me again, or I will put you on the ground. Do you understand?"

After this exchange, during which it became clear that Patel was not proficient in English, officers placed Patel's hands behind his back. One of them yanked his arm and slammed him onto the ground. Patel became partially paralyzed as a result of this assault.

South Asians around the nation were outraged upon hearing about the incident. Organizations such as Asha Kiran, a local Alabama group, and South Asian Americans Leading Together (SAALT) in Washington, D.C., called upon the federal government and the Madison police department to investigate the incident and bring legal charges against the police officer, Eric Parker. After the video footage of the incident was released, the Madison police department fired Parker. The Indian government expressed its outrage, which led to the governor of Alabama making a public apology for the officer's use of excessive force. Community members signed petitions, wrote letters of support to Patel, and placed the assault in the larger context of police brutality in the United States.

In March 2015, the U.S. Department of Justice announced that a federal grand jury had indicted Eric Parker for using unreasonable force against Sureshbhai Patel.[9] Indictments of individual police officers cannot by themselves undo the systemic racism that permeates many police departments in our nation. Yet they do send important messages about the limits and boundaries of action that our society will tolerate from public officials and provide some amount of justice for the families of those who have been affected.

In the wake of what happened to Patel, different perspectives emerged within the South Asian American community about what the case meant in terms of South Asian solidarity with Black communities. Should the incident be characterized solely as an example of the insidious and pervasive nature of anti-Black racism, given the tip that prompted the police action was from a community member who said that he was worried about "a skinny black guy" walking around the neighborhood? Or should Patel's immigration status and limited English proficiency be identified as unique factors that played a role in the response by the police officers? Should the incident be a launching pad to address the internal racist attitudes that some South Asians hold toward Black people? The answer is that it is important to do all of the above.

In the wake of Ferguson, South Asians supported the movement for Black lives because it is moral and right to do so. At the same time, it is important to recognize that reasons in addition to the legal, systemic, and cultural frameworks of anti-Blackness—such as immigration status, language ability, and national origin—often lead to discrimination against their own communities. South Asians lose no political or moral ground in holding both of these positions.

The desire to build solidarity and alliances with Black communities—which must be fostered and prioritized at every turn—cannot be fulfilled at the expense of disregarding and discounting the ways in which racism and discriminatory treatment occur to non-Black community members. In the case of Sureshbhai Patel, framing his actual lived experiences of state violence only in the context of anti-Black racism discounts and marginalizes them. His encounter with law enforcement was sparked and catalyzed by anti-Black racism, but his nationality and his limited English ability were contributing factors as well. In standing against White supremacy and in solidarity with Black communities, South Asians and other communities of color must not erase their own experiences confronting racism in the United States. This is the time to be both supporters *and* active, respectful participants in the conversations and actions to end police brutality. As Dante Barry says, "Black people need co-conspirators, not allies. Let's scheme together to all get free!"

South Asian, Arab, and Muslim organizations and advocates have begun to take important steps to connect Black and Brown communities as "co-conspirators." For example, Palestinian American activist Linda Sarsour is a core member of the Justice League of New York City, a task force of criminal justice experts, artists, and formerly incarcerated individuals that has mobilized communities in the wake of the decision not to charge Officer Daniel Pantaleo in the chokehold death of Eric Garner in 2014. Sarsour represents Muslim and Arab communities in the Justice League. "I'm able to talk about surveillance and post-9/11 War on Terror issues. The exchange of information helps to build relationships and helps us see how systemic racism is playing itself out on all our communities," Sarsour explained. In fact, the connections between Black and Brown communities got even closer as news reports in December 2014 revealed that an FBI Joint Terrorism Task Force in Minnesota was monitoring a protest related to Black Lives Matter at the Mall of America. After the protest occurred, eleven participants were arrested for misdemeanors, including unlawful assembly.[10] The tools of the War on Terror are increasingly being used to

intimidate activists in movements such as Black Lives Matter—
another point of collaboration among activists.

Arab and Muslim community leaders have extended information
exchanges with Black activists outside the United States as well. In
2015, thirty-year-old Ahmad Abuznaid, the chief operating officer
of the Dream Defenders, an organization created in the aftermath of
the Trayvon Martin murder in 2012, led a delegation of activists to
Palestine. Abuznaid, a Palestinian American and Muslim, believes
in the importance of understanding shared histories of oppression.
In January 2015, he organized a group of activists from Ferguson,
New York City, and the Dream Defenders to visit Palestine and
meet with community leaders there. "I believe that we will see a
future where marginalized communities can stand together against
dehumanization, imperialism, and injustice," Abuznaid explained.
"But that means we have to also really understand each other's own
historical and contemporary experiences with injustice."

Ciara Taylor, the twenty-five-year-old director of political consciousness at the Dream Defenders, was part of the delegation
that visited Palestine. For Taylor, solidarity among Black and Arab,
Muslim, and South Asian communities is possible because community members share similar stigmas and perceptions. "We are
all criminalized somehow—whether it is as thugs, troublemakers,
or terrorists," she said. "We need to build a practice of expressing our solidarity. It's not just about holding signs at each other's
protests. It's about building relationships with each other through
understanding our histories and cultures, and taking part in
anti-oppression trainings and popular education workshops."

The Mike Browns of the World Are Not Our Enemies

Solidarity practices between South Asian, Arab, Muslim, and Black
communities can be effective only to the extent that notions of
anti-Blackness and the system of White supremacy that reinforces

them can be disrupted. This includes having difficult conversations with friends, families, and community members about racist perceptions of Blacks within non-Black communities. "A lot of our people feel that the Mike Browns of the world are our enemies," Abuznaid explained. "We need to build bridges to change those perceptions."

To help facilitate these conversations, South Asian, Arab, and Muslim community members and organizations are creating curricula and gathering together in forums and workshops around the nation. For example, the Queer South Asian Network produced a curriculum called *It Starts at Home: Confronting Anti-Blackness in South Asian Communities*, which is being used in small group conversations to better identify how people become socialized into integrating anti-Black narratives. The authors write that addressing anti-Black racism within South Asian communities "should not be the work of Black people; this is our work, and it always has been."[11]

Organizations have also been holding community forums to address anti-Black racism. The National Network for Arab American Communities (NNAAC), a consortium of local Arab American organizations, began their work to bridge misunderstandings between Arab and Black communities in 2014. NNAAC held town hall meetings in Detroit and Brooklyn that brought Black and Arab communities together. Nadia Tonova, NNAAC's director, described the town halls as "race dialogues where Arab communities listened to Black experiences and voices and responded to them." NNAAC is committed to continuing these discussions. "At a community level, we still have a long way to go to build trust between people," Tonova said.

Matt Stiffler, the research and content manager at the Arab American National Museum in Dearborn, Michigan, attended the Black/Arab town hall in Detroit. He explained that it was an important start to a conversation that was long overdue. "In Detroit, a significant number of liquor stores and gas stations are owned by immigrants from Iraq or Lebanon. There have always been tensions there. African Americans have complained about how they aren't hired in these stores, or that Arabic is spoken when they come inside the store, or that they are overcharged," Stiffler said. "On the flip side, there is also a lot of crime targeting immigrant small-business owners. We have to stop this cycle of misperceptions and misunderstandings that often leads to violence."

Interestingly, Ferguson and St. Louis may provide starting points for these important conversations between immigrant small-business owners and Black residents. In Ferguson, as in many places around the nation that have concentrated Black populations, a high percentage of the small businesses are actually owned and operated by Asian, Arab, and South Asian immigrants. For example, an Indian businessman, Mike Patel, owns the Ferguson Market and Liquor and leases several stores to other immigrants, some of whom are Arab American. While in St. Louis for #OctoberFerguson, Mustafa Abdullah introduced us to several of these small-business owners. We met Zuhdi Masri, a Palestinian American who has owned Yeatman Market on the North Side of St. Louis for thirty-two years. Working closely with local African American leaders, including the Metro St. Louis Coalition for Inclusion and Equity's Ramona Williams, Masri has been able to broker agreements between area gangs. Seemingly simple acts such as building a gazebo outside his store or creating an area for people to sit and have conversations inside the store have led to transformative changes in the neighborhood and in the relationships between residents.

A slightly different situation awaited us on Ferguson's West Florissant Avenue, where many small businesses—beauty supply shops, take-out restaurants, small markets, and liquor marts—still had reminders of the August unrest on their storefronts. Sheets of plywood with spray-painted messages such as "Open for Business" covered parts of the stores. We stopped for a while at the Ferguson

Market and Liquor. I noticed immediately the rapport between the Indian immigrant workers and Black customers. The clerks knew the types of items that their regular customers wanted, and the customers called the clerks by name. One of the Indian clerks told me that even though the store suffered damage during the unrest, some Black customers had stood guard outside the store to protect it. When I asked about racial tensions between the immigrant store-owners and Black residents, he shrugged it off. There's some shoplifting and name-calling here and there, he said, "but the real problem is with cops who stop African Americans" without cause.

The Ferguson Market and Liquor clerk and other immigrant workers were not participants in Ferguson-related protests, but they seemed to share an understanding of the racial realities in the city, especially when it comes to law enforcement activities. There also seemed to be tacit support of the call for justice, which might be the opening to have deeper and broader conversations. In fact, in the aftermath of Ferguson, Neelu Panth and DeBorah Ahmed, who work with Better Family Life, Inc., in St. Louis, and Mustafa from the ACLU planned to hold roundtables between immigrant small-business owners and African American leaders in the area.[12]

Black Lives Matter may become the most significant racial justice movement of the twenty-first century. It has mobilized thousands of people around the world and led to important policy conversations about the role of law enforcement and the inequities in our criminal justice system. It has also created openings for people of color to build alliances with one another in ways that my generation has not witnessed. South Asian, Arab, and Muslim communities must be visible and supportive partners and engaged actors in the Black Lives Matter movement. How we build together now will influence movements for racial justice and solidarity for decades to come.

8

We Too Sing America

By 2043, America will become a "majority-minority" nation for the first time in its history.[1] This pivotal moment is the result of a steady demographic transformation that has already started in many parts of the nation and that will reach its peak in 2060. In 2012, about 116.2 million people belonging to minority groups lived in the United States, constituting 37 percent of the total population. By 2060, people of color will represent approximately 57 percent of the total population, numbering 241.3 million out of a total population of 420.3 million.[2] Simultaneously, the White population will stay the same until 2040, when it will begin to decrease. (See appendix B, Table 1, on projected population changes between 2020 and 2060). Latinos and Asians are driving the demographic growth among minority groups. According to the Pew Research Center, the Latino population is on the rise due to a record number of U.S. births, while immigration is the primary reason behind Asian American growth.[3]

These demographic changes are already visible around us. In September 2014, the U.S. Department of Education reported that the number of students of color surpassed that of white students in public schools for the first time.[4] Additionally, many of our counties and metropolitan areas have become multiracial jurisdictions already. As of 2013, the ten largest metropolitan areas where the percentage of people of color was greater than 50 percent of the overall population included New York, Los Angeles, Houston, Miami, Dallas, the D.C.-Maryland-Virginia area, Riverside, Atlanta, San Francisco, and San Diego. (See appendix B, Table 2, on the top ten metropolitan areas with majority-minority populations.)

Changes in migration flows are also responsible for these changes. Since 1960, the foreign-born population has steadily become a larger percentage of the total U.S. population year after year. In 2013, there were 41.3 million foreign-born residents living in the nation, making up approximately 13 percent of the total population.[5] The foreign-born population has also transformed in terms of race and ethnicity over the past fifty years. In 1960, 75 percent of the immigrant population was from European countries due to policies that favored them. In 2010, the top five countries of birth for foreign-born residents in the United States were Mexico, China, India, the Philippines, and Vietnam. In fact, more than 80 percent of the foreign-born now come from Latin America or Asia.[6] The refugee populations from non-European countries are also on the rise. In 2013, of the nearly seventy thousand refugees admitted into the United States, 75 percent came from Iraq, Burma, Bhutan, and Somalia.[7]

As immigrants and people of color transform our workplaces, schools, and neighborhoods over the coming decades, the future is full of promise and possibility. These demographic changes will generate a variety of responses from our nation's cultural, political, legal, and media spaces. At the same time, we must be vigilant and prepared to face the racial flash points that will inevitably accompany the transformation taking place in our country.

For example, the new landscape will give rise to racial anxiety about the perceived loss of an imagined "American" culture on the part of White communities and even of people of color with "honorary white" status. Demographic changes are likely to threaten the small group of elites who enjoy benefits, entitlements, and privileges in political, social, educational, residential, and workplace contexts. Indeed, research shows that the diminishment of majority-group status, even when it is three decades away, moves some White people toward positions of political conservatism, especially around race-related policies. In a series of experiments by Northwestern University's Department of Psychology and Institute for Policy Research, Maureen Craig and Jennifer Richeson studied how Whites responded to information about the changing racial demographics from a political standpoint. Their research revealed that White respondents unaffiliated with a political party were motivated to support conservative policies and candidates, as well as conservative positions on race-related and race-neutral policies, *after* learning about the demographic changes occurring around the nation.[8]

Concerns about losing power or having to share higher positions on the ladder of racial hierarchy will also shape negative state policies and public attitudes toward communities of color. We could see even greater erosion of legal rights at the voting booth and in workplaces and schools. We could see the introduction of English-only policies that deprive non-English-speaking immigrants of critical benefits and services. We could also witness political rhetoric that emphasizes diversity and multiculturalism in the "majority-minority" nation but glosses over the importance of addressing systemic racial inequities. We could begin to see visible and organized pushback against immigrants, in the vein of the movement that has emerged in parts of Europe called Pegida (Patriotic Europeans Against Islamisation of the West), which couches its xenophobic rhetoric in a focus on Muslim immigrants in particular. And as we have seen through the experiences of South Asian, Arab, Muslim, and Sikh communities, racial anxiety could lead to a rise in hate groups and anti-immigrant sentiment that leads to the "othering" of particular communities.

In light of these racial realities in America, we must recommit to our pursuit of equity and justice with vigor, empathy, and vigilance. We must expand and deepen the Black or White racial binary that has guided our understanding of racial justice in decades past. Additionally, the multiple ways in which people of color, faith communities, and immigrants experience discrimination mean that we must utilize "race plus" frameworks and enhance existing antidiscrimination laws. The systemic barriers that plague people of color and immigrant communities when it comes to educational and job attainment, income levels, health benefits, and English-language proficiency indicate that we cannot abandon our ongoing struggles to address systemic racial inequities. Lastly, we must develop, organize, and support regional multi-issue, multiracial coalitions that center, organize, and mobilize communities of color, working class and poor people, women, LGBTQ communities, and immigrants to aggressively push back against far-right efforts that seek to strip away hard-won rights and benefits.

These strategies depend first on dismantling the myths that accompany the notion of a "majority-minority" nation. The phrase "majority-minority nation" is itself misleading. A more precise description of the demographic changes under way in our country is that America is evolving into a multiracial nation, with no single racial group occupying a majority. Census data bears this out. In 2060, the non-Hispanic White population is still projected to be the largest single race segment of the U.S. population, at 43.6 percent; followed by the Hispanic population, at 28.6 percent; the Black population, at 13 percent; the Asian population, at 9.1 percent; the American Indian and Alaska Native population; at 0.6 percent; and the Native Hawaiian and Pacific Islander population, at 0.2 percent. Americans who identify themselves as being more than one race will make up 4.9 percent of the total U.S. population by 2060. (See appendix B, Table 3.)

Using the phrase "multiracial" rather than "majority-minority" to describe the demographic transformation in the United States also places importance on the type of country we aspire to become. It welcomes White communities, individuals who identify as being more than one race, and people who may be ambivalent about their own racial identities. Transforming into a multiracial nation connotes a collective journey—one that is inclusive and hopeful—we take in order to create an America for future generations.

From Majority-Minority to Multiracial

As discussed, earlier, the term *majority-minority* is inaccurate for a host of reasons, yet its allure is also hard to ignore. For example, conservative forces will certainly rely on the myth of the "majority-minority nation" to shift public attention away from the tremendous systemic inequities that continue to exist along racial lines. They will point to the demographic changes as proof positive that we are transforming into a color-blind or postracial society and that efforts to understand and eliminate racial disparities through policy changes, race-conscious initiatives, or disaggregated racial data collection can be disbanded. They will call attention to the existence of minority representation in political, corporate, entertainment, and media sectors as markers of the growing influence of communities of color.

But conservatives are not the only ones likely to reinforce the myth of the majority-minority nation for political purposes. Progressives, including people of color, are not immune to buying into the assumption that racial politics will change and that racial injustice will disappear as demographics shift. In focus groups I held in preparation for this book with people under the age of thirty, I heard many people of color state such opinions. One participant said, "Once people of color have the numbers, we will have power in every arena. Racism won't be an issue. We won't need to talk about race anymore." Other participants mentioned that as people of color ascend to leadership in various sectors, from politics to corporate America to the media, they will take on the responsibility of changing systems that have historically been rife with racial disparities. Still others placed their faith in the ability of the rising American electorate—which includes women, people of color, and millennials—to flex their political muscles and use the ballot box to bring about solutions to racial inequities.

We must critically examine these assumptions. We can start by calling into question the term *majority-minority* and what it implies. The phrase mistakenly suggests that minority populations will gain power and influence due to their numbers. But sheer numbers will not drive racial equality, economic equity, or political power. Numerical dominance will not mean that attitudes and systems that lead to racial oppression will disappear or that people of color will be able to exercise power over their political and economic conditions.

The experiences of communities of color in South Africa provide important lessons on this point. Garth Stevens, assistant dean for research at the University of Witwatersrand in Johannesburg, told me that after apartheid was dismantled in South Africa, the notion of a "rainbow nation" began to emerge. "The 'rainbow nation' became a positive metaphor that captured the public imagination," Stevens said, much like the majority-minority narrative does. "But people quickly understood that this wasn't true, because the material conditions for many, especially Black and working-class people, had not fundamentally altered. Twenty years later, the idea of a singular nation that is egalitarian does not exist in South Africa." It does not exist partly because systemic and institutional racism continues to persist in South Africa, creating different outcomes for Blacks and other people of color than for Whites.

Unless we meaningfully confront similar institutional and systemic racial disparities in America, it is highly unlikely that minority populations will occupy a markedly different status in coming decades than they do today. Racial inequities show up in various contexts, from education to housing to income levels. According to a Pew Research Center analysis of the Federal Reserve's Survey of Consumer Finances, in 2013 the wealth of White households was thirteen times the median wealth of Black households and ten times the wealth of Latino households.[9] Similarly, in the context of education attainment, while 8.3 percent of the White population had less than a high school diploma in 2013, the numbers were significantly higher for some minority populations, such as 18.3 percent for American Indian and Alaska Natives and 12.7 percent for Native Hawaiian and Pacific Islanders. (See appendix B, Table 4.)

While Asian Americans are often held up as an example of high educational attainment, there are many Asian ethnic groups who are struggling. For example, the 2013 American Community Survey shows that Burmese, Hmong, Laotian, and Cambodian groups have high percentages of community members with less than a high school diploma. (See appendix B, Table 5.) Limited English proficiency, immigration status, and higher poverty rates could contribute to lower rates of educational attainment among some Asian ethnic groups. In addition, the treatment of students of color in many school districts is a factor in educational success. Zero-tolerance disciplinary policies instituted in schools around the country disproportionately punish students of color at higher rates, leading to suspensions for minor infractions.[10]

Unless government, civic, philanthropic, and community stakeholders tackle the roots of these disparities through responsive public policies and proper reallocation of resources, people of color will continue to experience inequitable outcomes regardless of their population power. We must recommit ourselves to identifying and implementing solutions to address systemic racial inequities instead of glossing over them in the belief that they will automatically disappear as our nation's demographics shift.

One way to do this is by incentivizing corporations, institutions of higher education, government agencies, and political leaders to apply a racial equity framework in their programs and initiatives. This means that in addition to focusing on representation of people of color—assessed by diversity and inclusion benchmarks in hiring, promotion, and recruitment—companies and government agencies pay attention to how their services, programs, and initiatives can change outcomes for communities of color. The Government Alliance on Race and Equity (GARE) is a program that works with a cohort of municipalities around the country to do just that.[11] Government agencies and municipalities that participate in GARE develop a shared language to understand and convey the meaning of racial equity or identify tools to assess how their programs are altering the lives of communities of color. "As our racial demographics change, it is vital for government agencies to incorporate racial equity frames," explained Julie Nelson, the director of GARE. "That means that they think about the impact on communities of color when they put a budget together or run an agency program." Racial equity frameworks equip government agencies with benchmarks to assess the impact of their services on people of color.

Programs like GARE can also be replicated in private sector industries and institutions of higher learning committed to racial equity. Rinku Sen from Race Forward believes that the private sector in particular must rethink its corporate practices around diversity benchmarks. "Companies are beginning to understand that in many cases, they are no further along on actually being more diverse than they were before. They've got a revolving door of people of color because it's about more than recruitment and hiring," she said. "If ten CEOs made a commitment not only to diversity but to racial equity and actually looking into how it works within their companies, there could be a transformative effect across the sector."

Similarly, many institutions of higher learning have become attuned to the importance of recruiting and retaining students of color and creating more inclusive campus environments. In addition, requiring all college students to take classes on diversity and ethnic studies and mandating that the leaders of college associations, including fraternities and sororities, attend regular trainings on understanding how privilege, implicit bias, and systemic racism operate on campus could be helpful practices.

Racial equity has a role in the ways in which elected officials govern as well. Sayu Bhojwani, the founder and president of the New American Leaders Project (NALP), explained that political leaders who are comfortable with seeing their own lived experiences through the lens of gender, sexuality, or race are more likely to have approaches to governance and policy change that reflect racial- and gender-justice values. NALP works with first- and second-generation immigrants to prepare them for civic leadership. "We train immigrant leaders who already have deep and clear connections to their communities and a track record of civic engagement," Bhojwani said. "Their identities and experiences—whether around gender, race, sexuality, or immigration background—can affect the way that they perceive issues when they get into positions in government or occupy political office."

Bhojwani pointed to South Asian, Arab, Muslim, and Sikh political representatives including Ravinder Singh Bhalla (member of the Hoboken City Council), Aruna Miller (delegate to the Maryland legislature), Rashida Tlaib (former representative in the Michigan legislature), and Pramila Jayapal (state senator in the Washington legislature) as examples of political leaders whose own life experiences as people of color, women, or immigrants have shaped their policies, stances, and inclusion of issues affecting marginalized communities.

2043 Won't Be a "Kumbaya Moment"

"The moment when people of color become the majority in the United States sounds great, but it's not going to be a kumbaya moment," said Tia Oso, the national coordinator for the Black Immigration Network. "It won't mean that people of color will all of a sudden have power." Oso is right. The looming questions for activists and organizations shaping our nation's twenty-first-century movements for economic, racial, and gender justice revolves around what communities of color will stand for and whether we will stand together. "Will communities of color be able to hold together around shared values?" asks Glenn Harris, the president and CEO of the Center for Social Inclusion, a national organization that addresses structural racial inequity. Marisa Franco, the director of the #Not1MoreDeportation campaign, has similar questions for Latino communities. "Will we just fight for diversity or try to elect someone with a Spanish surname? Or will we come together to push a pro–civil rights, pro-women, pro-immigrant political agenda?"

As we become a more multiracial nation, we will continue to contend with these questions as well as with racial politics designed to turn communities of color against one another. Will Black communities resist the xenophobic rhetoric about immigrants taking away jobs in order to unite with Brown communities in the fight for immigration reform? Will Asian Americans push back against those within their own communities who criticize affirmative action policies? Will Latinos and Native Americans denounce Islamophobia? As we grapple with these questions and others in the years to come, organizers and activists can begin to articulate inclusive racial justice frameworks and identify points of collaboration that will bring about transformative—not merely transactional—solidarity among communities of color.

One such message involves recognizing that racial politics in America today extends well beyond prevailing frameworks. We have become accustomed to thinking about race issues through a Black or White binary or about immigration through the lens of Latinos, for example. The experiences of emerging minority faith and immigrant communities, including South Asian, Arab, Muslim, and Sikh community members in post-9/11 America, require us to revise and adjust these frameworks. When we do so, we can create more effective multiracial coalitions that recognize the unique ways in which various communities of color experience racism in America.

In addition, racial justice advocates must both centralize race and articulate the additional ways that communities of color experience discrimination. As we know from South Asian, Arab, Muslim, and Sikh immigrants in post-9/11 America, discrimination also occurs on the bases of faith and nationality, which are often used as proxies for racial bias. Factors such as class, gender, sexuality, disability, and faith must be part of our work to advance racial equity. According to Rinku Sen, while we must not "de-race" America, we cannot focus on race as the only basis for inequity. "If we want to modernize a racial justice ethic, practice, and movement, then we don't gain much from insisting that it's all about race or even that race is the number one element and other factors are secondary," she said. By using a "race plus" approach, we can make space for the multiple levels of oppression that people face and centralize racial injustice at the same time.

Lastly, racial justice advocates must call upon the expansion of our arsenal of civil rights and antidiscrimination laws. The hardwon civil rights struggles of the 1960s necessarily emphasized the need for laws to protect the rights of individuals who faced discrimination at workplaces, at schools, and at the voting booth. Over the years, many of these laws have been expanded to prohibit discrimination on the basis of national origin, gender, sexual orientation, disability, citizenship status, or color, among other characteristics.

These legal protections convey the message that our society values equality and eschews acts of discrimination.

Yet, in many instances, the current architecture of antidiscrimination laws does not reflect the ways in which people of color experience injustice today. Our laws must address the emerging proxies for race such as faith, immigration status, and language ability that are used as bases for discriminating against many people of color and immigrants today. In addition, the high legal thresholds necessary to bring federal civil rights claims are often difficult to meet. This has been abundantly clear in the difficulties that the Department of Justice has had in bringing civil rights complaints in police brutality or hate crimes cases. Policy makers must amend current civil rights laws by changing these high thresholds so that enforcement agencies can more frequently bring investigations and claims. Without systemic solutions that address the far-reaching and longitudinal effects of structural racism, individual rights rhetoric can only go so far.

Race Talk

In speaking with activists around the nation who are engaged in movements for justice, I found one concept that emerged time and again: the need for us to develop empathy by being in deep conversation with one another. Many racial justice activists say that engaging in conversations and dialogues with one another about our experiences with racial identity, oppression, and injustice can help us understand that we have linked fates and futures.

Organizations and movements have long used versions of race talks to build understanding and respect among people of various backgrounds. For example, at the William Winter Institute for Racial Reconciliation at the University of Mississippi, executive director Susan Glisson and her team use the concept of the "Welcome

Table" to generate conversations among communities. Many of these Welcome Table conversations connect Black and White residents in Mississippi, a state with a deep history of racial segregation and hostility. "People share their experiences, and sometimes they are having painful ones. They might not use the word *race* explicitly all the time, but that's what they are talking about—racial bias and racial injustice," Glisson explained. Through sustained conversations, participants at Welcome Tables develop collective strategies and practices to achieve racial equity in their neighborhood or city.

The inclusion of White communities in Welcome Table projects has been particularly effective in developing their comfort with discussing race and cultivating alliances, according to Glisson. She noted that in the South, while low-income White communities have much at stake in identifying solutions to address inequity, they do not engage in conversations through a racial lens to understand the similarities in experiences with their Black neighbors. "There are issues where we can build power together," she explained. "For example, the educational system in Mississippi and other parts of the South is abysmal. It affects poor White kids, working-class White kids—as well as Black children. It's an opportunity to bring people together." By connecting White and Black communities together for storytelling and dialogue, the Winter Institute advances collaborative solutions to address race and class inequities.

Tia Oso from the Black Immigration Network also identified the importance of integrating dialogues about historic oppression in antiracist trainings and workshops. "There is a lack of trust and understanding of one another's stories and histories, especially between some Black immigrants and African American communities," Oso said. "Immigrants don't learn African American history. And, more often than not, history in America is not taught through a multiracial lens, so most Americans don't learn about immigrant experiences."

In Houston, Cherry Steinwender, a spirited seventy-three-year-old activist and the executive director of the Center for the Healing of Racism in Houston, uses intergroup dialogues to develop personal relationships between community members. "When we build authentic relationships, we can dismantle the 'divide and conquer' strategy that keeps us apart from each other," Steinwender explained. She also believes that simple acts such as sharing meals or inviting people from different racial backgrounds to her home regularly—"going through the seasons of life together," as she puts it—can foster individual understanding and group alliances.

By integrating race talks into conversations with family members and friends, at our workplaces, on our campuses, and inside our organizations, we can lay the groundwork to find common ground in addressing the pressing issues facing our nation. Appendix A contains information to help you organize and conduct your own race talks.

Conclusion

As I finished writing this book, I received news that three young Muslims in Chapel Hill, North Carolina, had been murdered in a triple homicide. Yusor Abu-Salha, her husband, Deah Barakat, and her sister Razan Abu-Salha were murdered on February 10, 2015, by their neighbor Craig Hicks in Chapel Hill, North Carolina. Hicks is facing the death penalty for the murders, which the victims' family members claim were racially motivated.[12]

In the days immediately after this horrible tragedy, people began to report other acts of violence around the nation. On February 13, 2015, a man started a fire at the Quba Islamic Institute in Houston, Texas; he has since been charged with first-degree arson.[13] The Islamic School of Rhode Island was vandalized on February 14, 2015, with the words "Now this is a hate crime" and "pigs" written on the school walls.[14] The Hindu Temple and Cultural Center in Bothell, Washington, was vandalized around February 15, 2015, with a Nazi swastika and the words "Get Out" spray painted on the building. On the same day, also in Bothell, Washington, Skyview Junior High School was vandalized with the words "Muslims get out" and a swastika.[15] On February 28, 2015, Mukhtar Ahmed, a Pakistani man, was shot in the head and killed while driving on the interstate I-71 in Kentucky.[16] And in Dallas, Texas, Ahmed al-Jumaili, who had immigrated to the United States from Iraq just one month earlier, was shot to death on March 5, 2015, as he was taking pictures of the snow outside his apartment with his wife and brother-in-law.[17]

This barrage of incidents occurring in the first few months of 2015 sent shock waves through South Asian, Arab, Muslim, and Sikh communities. But at the same time, community organizations sprang into rapid-response mode, engaging in actions that have sadly become all too familiar over the past decade and a half—comforting families of loved ones, liaising with government agencies, disseminating safety kits for community members, and amplifying positive messages in mainstream media outlets.

In spite of the forces of racial anxiety, Islamophobia, and xenophobia, South Asian, Arab, Muslim, and Sikh communities have developed tremendous resilience to withstand, resist, and overcome. Our resolve to move America toward a different course, an alternative direction, remains intact.

The activists and organizers featured in this book offer us all the strength and inspiration to hold fast to this resolve and commitment to shaping a multiracial and equitable America, even in the face of hateful attacks, vilification, and turmoil. Their examples can move us all to act with conviction and courage. Together we can walk boldly toward a vision of a more inclusive and equitable future, one in which there are no more "others"—one in which there is a place for all of our beloved communities.

Appendix A:
Race Talks

What is your vision for a multiracial and equitable America? You can convene a race talk with friends in your own home, as a topic for a general meeting of your campus group, as a conversation for an affinity group of professionals at your company, at a book club, as a brown-bag lunch conversation at your organization, or as a workshop at a conference. Here are some ideas to get you started:

- Commit to convening three race talks in the next twelve months.
- Identify the venue and format for your race talk. Instead of convening a panel with speakers, host an informal dialogue that allows people to share their experiences and ideas. Race talks are ideal if they occur in groups of four to fifteen people and last for an hour at minimum.
- Come up with a set of questions that you will explore during your race talk. See below for sample ones.
- Ask your group to read a chapter or chapters in *We Too Sing America* and to come prepared with questions that arose while reading.
- Race talks should end with one action step that your group will take based on what you discussed and a commitment to meet again within three months.

- You will find more resources and information at www. deepaiyer.com to help you coordinate your race talks and to share ideas and feedback with people around the nation.

Here are some questions to get you started with your race talk.

- Why are race talks important to each of us? Why are we here?
- What was your point of entry into racial consciousness? What incident or event triggered your understanding that racial identity plays a role in your lives?
- Which person featured in *We Too Sing America* spoke to you the most and why?
- In *We Too Sing America*, Drost Kokoye from Nashville talks about how she identifies as a person of color even though she would be classified as White by the government. What role do racial classifications play in your life? How do you think the government should categorize racial identities as America's racial landscape changes?
- *We Too Sing America* traces the impact of xenophobia and Islamophobia in the decade and a half since 9/11. How has post-9/11 America affected you? How have your views of South Asian, Arab, Muslim, and Sikh communities changed over the past fifteen years?
- Does your community receive the "racial bribe" or the invitation to climb the racial ladder? How can you and your group help community members decline the racial bribe?
- Reflect on your workplace, company, campus, or organization. How does it engage with building multiracial and equitable spaces? What one action step do you think it could take?

- During the 2016 election cycle, we heard more about structural and systemic racism, thanks in large part to the Movement for Black Lives. In light of the 2016 election outcome, which removed the veneer of civility and diversity in America to reveal deep racial wounds, what types of conversations must we have? Who are the people we must reach?

- Envision *your* multiracial America. What does it look like? The "it" could be your own campus or neighborhood, a particular industry, or the country as a whole. *(Tip: Ask participants to put together the cover of a magazine in 2043, when the country becomes a multiracial nation. Encourage participants to draw or include cutout pictures in order to create headlines and stories, and then share their visions with each other.)*

- What are common themes that emerge among the visions that people identified? What is one step that can be taken now to move toward your vision, either individually or collectively? Set a time for your next gathering and share a short summary of your race talk at www.deepaiyer.com.

Together, we can use storytelling, dialogue, and ideas to transform our communities.

Appendix B:
Disruptors and Bridge Builders:
5 Steps to Take Now

Culled from the responses of people I met on the *We Too Sing America* book tour, and from the examples of positive actions happening around the country, below are five ways to take action now to demonstrate that it is vital—and possible—to point our country in an alternative direction, one based on a shared vision of respect, justice, equity, and solidarity.

1. **Statements matter.** "I will ask my organization, my elected official, or my place of worship to make statements of support and solidarity to protect the rights of Muslim, South Asian, and Arab communities."

2. **Prevention matters.** "As a parent, I am going to ask my school counselor and principal how they are planning to address bullying and bias against Muslim, Arab, Sikh, and South Asian students."

    We can attempt to stem the tide of hate violence and bias incidents in schools, communities, and workplaces with **three R's** in mind: ensuring that communities being targeted are aware of their **rights**; ensuring that government agencies and public stakeholders publicly articulate and vigorously enforce their **responsibilities** under anti-discrimination laws; and ensuring that **resources** are made available to assist communities in need. For example:

- Ask your local civil and human rights commission to release in-language fact sheets about the legal protections that exist on the basis of national origin and faith.
- Ask your city council to hold a hearing on the impact of today's climate on Muslim, Arab, and South Asian communities that reflects the voices and experiences of local community members and leaders.
- If you are a parent, ask your school principal and counselors about their plans to ensure that policies and resources are in place to address bullying.

3. **Conversations matter.** "I will have a conversation about race and Islamophobia with my colleagues at work." "I will challenge my relatives who make anti-Muslim statements." The messiest and most difficult conversations are often the ones we have with the people in our closest circles of colleagues, family members, and friends to raise awareness and shift viewpoints.

4. **Supporting organizations and grassroots efforts matters.** Crisis response has been a daily phenomenon for groups working with Muslim, Arab, South Asian, and Sikh communities, including local community-based organizations and places of worship in your area. As the book indicates, building a mass movement of communities is critical in shaping and influencing our democracy.

5. **Showing up matters.** Coming together with Muslim, Arab, and South Asian communities for a press conference, a civic action, a march on campus, or a solidarity event at a mosque sends a powerful message at this moment. Prepare for or

follow up on solidarity events with an awareness and strategy session with the membership of your own organizations and representatives of Muslim, Arab, and South Asian groups. At all times, it is important to connect with and take the lead from groups working directly with affected communities to reflect their voices and expertise on messaging.

Appendix C:
Data on Race in America

Table 1. Projected Population Changes Between 2020 and 2060

Race	2020	2030	2040	2050	2060
Hispanic	63,551,224	77,463,178	91,626,191	105,550,298	119,044,452
Not Hispanic					
Asian	19,254,656	23,598,577	28,756,431	33,391,092	37,878,862
Black	41,593,636	45,318,448	48,161,993	51,005,521	54,028,173
American Indian/ Alaska Native	2,431,860	2,555,499	2,623,103	2,641,125	2,637,144
Native Hawaiian and Pacific Islander	594,717	685,131	765,342	836,326	900,198
White	199,399,832	199,403,343	195,197,015	188,418,849	181,929,597
More than one race	7,677,533	10,178,018	13,089,127	16,485,138	20,376,184
	334,503,458	359,402,194	380,219,202	398,328,349	416,794,610

Source: U.S. Census Bureau, Population Division, 2014 National Population Projections. Data courtesy of Howard Shih, director of policy and research at the Asian American Federation.

Table 2. Top Ten Metropolitan Statistical Areas with Majority-Minority Populations Ranked by Total Minority Population

Geography	Total population	White Alone, Not Hispanic or Latino	Percentage of White Alone, Not Hispanic	Minority Population
New York, NY–Newark, NJ–Jersey City, NJ–PA, Metro Area	19,949,502	9,583,209	48%	10,366,293
Los Angeles–Long Beach–Anaheim, CA, Metro Area	13,131,431	4,025,519	31%	9,105,912
Houston–The Woodlands–Sugar Land, TX, Metro Area	6,313,158	2,415,820	38%	3,897,338
Miami–Fort Lauderdale–West Palm Beach, FL, Metro Area	5,828,191	1,933,229	33%	3,894,962
Dallas–Fort Worth–Arlington, TX, Metro Area	6,812,373	3,334,245	49%	3,478,128
Washington, DC–Arlington, VA–Alexandria, VA–MID–WV, Metro Area	5,950,214	2,822,941	47%	3,127,273
Riverside–San Bernardino–Ontario, CA, Metro Area	4,380,878	1,521,153	35%	2,859,725
Atlanta–Sandy Springs–Roswell, GA, Metro Area	5,524,693	2,729,679	49%	2,795,014
San Francisco–Oakland–Hayward, CA, Metro Area	4,516,276	1,864,501	41%	2,651,775
San Diego–Carlsbad, CA, Metro Area	3,211,252	1,510,757	47%	1,700,495

Source: U.S. Census Bureau, 2013 American Community Survey, Table DP05 ACS (Demographic and Housing Estimates).

Table 3. Projected Population Share Changes Between 2020 and 2060

Race	2020	2030	2040	2050	2060
Hispanic	19.0%	21.6%	24.1%	26.5%	28.6%
Not Hispanic					
Asian	5.8%	6.7%	7.6%	8.4%	9.1%
Black	12.4%	12.6%	12.7%	12.8%	13.0%
American Indian and Alaska Native	0.7%	0.7%	0.7%	0.7%	0.6%
Native Hawaiian and Pacific Islander	0.2%	0.2%	0.2%	0.2%	0.2%
White	59.6%	55.5%	51.3%	47.3%	43.6%
More than one race	2.3%	2.8%	3.4%	4.1%	4.9%

Source: U.S. Census Bureau, Population Division, 2014 National Population Projections, December 2014.

Table 4. Educational Attainment by Race Group, 2013 American Community Survey

Population Group	Population 25 years and over	Less than high school diploma	High school graduate (includes equiv.)	Some college or associate's degree	Bachelor's degree	Graduate or professional degree
Arab	1,071,579	11.0%	18.1%	24.0%	28.8%	18.1%
Asian (Including Hispanic)	11,043,022	13.8%	15.3%	19.6%	29.7%	21.6%
Hispanic	29,673,441	35.3%	27.1%	23.5%	9.5%	4.4%
Not Hispanic						
American Indian and Alaska Native	1,260,457	18.3%	32.2%	35.2%	9.5%	4.8%
Asian	10,949,392	13.8%	15.3%	19.4%	29.8%	21.7%
Black	24,046,438	16.1%	31.2%	33.3%	12.3%	7.1%
Native Hawaiian and other Pacific Islander	296,721	12.7%	36.7%	34.7%	11.8%	4.2%
White	141,478,073	8.3%	28.4%	30.2%	20.5%	12.5%
Some other race	342,203	16.7%	25.5%	25.3%	19.1%	13.3%
Two or more races	2,863,890	10.1%	23.0%	35.6%	19.6%	11.6%

Source: U.S. Census Bureau, 2013 American Community Survey, Table S0201, Selected Population Profile in the United States.

Table 5. Educational Attainment by Asian Ethnic Groups, 2013 American Community Survey

Population Group	Population 25 years and over	Less than high school diploma	High school graduate (includes equiv.)	Some college or associate's degree	Bachelor's degree	Graduate or professional degree
Bangladeshi	99,714	17.7%	17.5%	16.1%	26.3%	22.4%
Burmese	71,236	45.1%	15.2%	11.6%	20.2%	7.9%
Cambodian	175,821	34.2%	26.2%	23.7%	12.5%	3.4%
Chinese	2,646,568	18.2%	13.5%	14.6%	26.6%	26.8%
Chinese (except Taiwanese)	2,533,383	18.7%	14.2%	14.6%	26.3%	26.1%
Taiwanese	113,185	5.7%	7.1%	14.1%	31.7%	41.5%
Filipino	1,947,177	7.3%	14.8%	30.0%	38.7%	9.1%
Hmong	119,724	30.3%	24.8%	28.8%	13.1%	3.0%
Indian	2,172,451	7.9%	8.7%	10.4%	32.3%	40.6%
Indonesian	50,317	5.2%	20.7%	28.8%	30.2%	15.0%
Japanese	667,840	4.9%	19.6%	26.8%	31.8%	17.0%
Korean	1,040,140	7.6%	17.6%	20.9%	33.6%	20.3%
Laotian	138,785	30.6%	27.6%	27.8%	11.0%	3.0%
Nepalese	55,636	29.0%	14.1%	15.0%	22.8%	19.2%
Pakistani	258,947	11.9%	15.1%	17.4%	31.0%	24.6
Thai	143,285	15.1%	17.3%	23.2%	28.6%	15.9%
Vietnamese	1,135,631	26.9%	22.5%	22.7%	20.1%	7.8%

Source: U.S. Census Bureau, 2013 American Community Survey, Table S0201, Selected Population Profile in the United States.

Appendix D:
Race Talk Resources

This is a list *in formation*! Below are preliminary resources that provide background information and talking points to assist with race talks. They come from organizations that are featured in *We Too Sing America* and/or sponsor the book. Please email deepa@deepaiyer.com to add to this list with additional suggestions.

General Resources Related to Race

The Advancement Project

Mission. The Advancement Project is a next-generation, multi-racial civil rights organization. Rooted in the great human rights struggles for equality and justice, it exists to fulfill America's promise of a caring, inclusive and just democracy. It uses innovative tools and strategies to strengthen social movements and achieve high impact policy change.

Website: http://www.advancementproject.org

Race talk resources:

- *The Social Justice Phrase Guide*: http://b.3cdn.net /advancement/94da835bcf2d3e7631_bfm6yh5kg.pdf
- Brochure on the school-to-prison pipeline: http://b.3cdn .net/advancement/03721750a0812a95bd_6im6ih8ns.pdf

Race Forward

Mission: Race Forward advances racial justice through research, media, and practice. Founded in 1981, Race Forward brings systemic analysis and an innovative approach to complex race issues to help people take effective action toward racial equity. Race Forward publishes the daily news site *Colorlines* and presents Facing Race, the country's largest multiracial conference on racial justice.

Website: www.raceforward.org

Race talk resources:

- Participate in Racial Justice Leadership Institutes: https://www.raceforward.org/trainings
- *What Is Systemic Racism?* Short video series featuring Jay Smooth: https://www.raceforward.org/videos /systemic-racism

Center for New Community

Mission: The Center for New Community remains committed to countering the reality of racism and bigotry in America. It was founded on the principle that a concerted, long-term effort to address issues of social, economic, and racial justice is both necessary and achievable.

Website: http://newcomm.org

Race talk resources:

- Reports on activities of racist, nativist, and xenophobic leaders and organizations in the United Sates: http://newcomm.org/resources
- Blog: http://imagine2050.newcomm.org

Center for Social Inclusion

Mission: The Center for Social Inclusion works to identify and support policy strategies to transform structural inequity and exclusion into structural fairness and inclusion. It works with community groups and national organizations to develop policy ideas, foster effective leadership, and develop communications tools for an opportunity-rich world in which we all will thrive no matter our race or ethnicity.

Website: www.thecsi.org

Race talk resource:

- *Let's Talk Race: How Racially Explicit Messaging Can Advance Equity*: http://www.centerforsocialinclusion.org /lets-talk-about-race-how-racially-explicit-messaging-can -advance-equity

Teaching Tolerance: A Project of the Southern Poverty Law Center

Mission: Teaching Tolerance is dedicated to reducing prejudice, improving intergroup relations, and supporting equitable school experiences for our nation's children.

Website: www.tolerance.org

Race talk resources especially for educators and parents:

- Perspectives for a diverse America: anti-bias social justice content with the rigor of the Common Core State Standards: http://perspectives.tolerance.org
- Classroom resources and lesson plans on a variety of topics including religion, the civil rights movement, and more: http://www.tolerance.org/classroom-resources

Showing Up for Racial Justice

Mission: SURJ is a national network of groups and individuals organizing White people for racial justice. Through community organizing, mobilizing, and education, SURJ moves White people to act as part of a multiracial majority for justice with passion and accountability. The network works to connect people across the country while supporting and collaborating with local and national racial justice organizing efforts. SURJ provides a space to build relationships, skills, and political analysis to act for change, envisioning a society where we struggle together with love, for justice, human dignity, and a sustainable world.

Website: http://www.showingupforracialjustice.org

Race talk resource:

- Resources for organizing, campaigns, leadership: http://www.showingupforracialjustice.org/resources

Million Hoodies Movement for Justice

Mission: Million Hoodies Movement for Justice is a Black- and Brown-led racial justice network that builds next generation leaders to end mass criminalization and gun violence. It is a mass organization of human rights leaders confronting anti-Black racism and systemic violence through grassroots organizing, advocacy, and education.

Website: http://millionhoodies.net

Race talk resource:

- Blog: http://millionhoodies.net/blog

Resources from Muslim, Arab, and South Asian Organizations

DRUM–South Asian Organizing Center

Mission: DRUM–South Asian Organizing Center (formerly Desis Rising Up and Moving) is a multigenerational, membership led organization of low-wage South Asian immigrant workers and youth in New York City.

Website: www.drumnyc.org

Race talk resource:

- *Education Not Deportation* report: https://cdp.urbanjustice .org/sites/default/files/Education_Not_Deportation_ Report_06jun06.pdf

Muslim Advocates

Mission: Muslim Advocates envisions a world in which equality, liberty, and justice are guaranteed for all, regardless of faith, and in which the Muslim American legal community is vital to promoting and protecting these values. In pursuit of this vision, Muslim Advocates' mission is to promote equality, liberty, and justice for all by providing leadership through legal advocacy, policy engagement, and civic education, and by serving as a legal resource to promote the full and meaningful participation of Muslims in American public life.

Website: https://www.muslimadvocates.org

Race talk resources:

- Pair MA's report *Losing Liberty: The State of Freedom 10 Years After the Patriot Act* with Chapter 2 of *We Too Sing America* to discuss the national security and immigration policies that have affected communities since 9/11: https://www.muslimadvocates.org/ten_years_after _patriot_act_time_to_restore_america_s_freedoms
- Pair the report with a viewing of *Whose Children Are These?*, a documentary directed by filmmaker Theresa Thanjan about the impact of the special registration program on families and children

Council on American-Islamic Relations (CAIR)

Mission: CAIR's mission is to enhance understanding of Islam, encourage dialogue, protect civil liberties, empower American Muslims, and build coalitions that promote justice and mutual understanding.

Website: www.cair.com

Race talk resource:

- Anti-prejudice tools: http://www.islamophobia.org /anti-prejudice-tools.html

- *Know Your Rights* brochure for Muslim youth in school: https://ca.cair.com/sfba/wp-content/uploads/2014/09 /Kids-Know-Your-Rights-Pocket-Guide.pdf Islamophobia pocket guide: http://www.cair.com/images/pdf /Islamophobia-Pocket-Guide.pdf
- Basic facts about Islam: http://www.cair.com /publications/about-islam.html

National Network for Arab American Communities (NNAAC)

Mission: The NNAAC's mission is the development of Arab American community-based nonprofit organizations that understand, meet the needs, and represent the concerns of Arab Americans at a local level, while also collectively addressing those issues at a national level.

Website: http://www.nnaac.org

Race talk resource:

- Advocacy and civic engagement resources.: http://www .nnaac.org/advocacy_and_civic_engagement_resource

Sikh American Legal Defense and Education Fund (SALDEF)

Mission: SALDEF seeks to empower Sikh Americans by building dialogue, deepening understanding, promoting civic and political participation, and upholding social justice and religious freedom for all Americans.

Website: www.saldef.org

Race talk resource:

- *Turban Myths*, the first public perception assessment of Sikh Americans: http://online.wsj.com/public/resources /documents/TurbanMyths.pdf

South Asian Americans Leading Together (SAALT)
Mission: SAALT is a national, nonpartisan, nonprofit organization that elevates the voices and perspectives of South Asian individuals and organizations to build a more just and inclusive society in the United States.
Website: www.saalt.org
Race talk resources:

- Factsheets about South Asians: http://saalt.org/resources /reports-and-publications/#factsheets
- Campus sessions, 60–90 minute workshop, presentation, or panel led by SAALT staff or community member, focusing on issues affecting South Asian students and developing tools and resources for campus advocacy: http://saalt.org/programs/campus-session
- Briefs, statements, and reports on racial justice, including two reports that track xenophobic political rhetoric since 9/11: http://saalt.org/policy-change/racial-justice

Notes

1. "Not Our American Dream":
The Oak Creek Massacre and Hate Violence

1. Linda Edwards, *A Brief Guide to Beliefs: Ideas, Theologies, Mysteries, and Movements* (Louisville, KY: Westminister John Knox Press, 2001); Simran Jeet Singh, "10 Things I Wish Everyone Knew About Sikhism," *On Faith*, November 28, 2014, http://www.faithstreet.com/onfaith/2014/11/18/10-things-i-wish-everyone-knew-about-sikhism/35075; Pew Research Center, *How Many U.S. Sikhs?*, August 6, 2012, http://www.pewresearch.org/2012/08/06/ask-the-expert-how-many-us-sikhs/. It is important to note that scholars and nonprofit organizations estimate the population of U.S. Sikhs as 500,000 or higher.

2. *Hate Crimes and the Threat of Domestic Extremism: Hearing Before the Subcommittee on Constitution, Civil Rights and Human Rights, Committee on the Judiciary, United States Senate*, 112th Cong. (2012) (statement of Harpreet Singh Saini).

3. "Gunman, Six Others Dead at Wisconsin Sikh Temple," CNN.com, August 5, 2012, http://www.cnn.com/2012/08/05/us/wisconsin-temple-shooting/.

4. Bill Glauber, "Oak Creek Police Officers Remember Sikh Temple Shooting," *Milwaukee Journal Sentinel*, October 29, 2012, http://www.jsonline.com/news/wisconsin/oak-creek-police-officers-remember-day-of-sikh-temple-shooting-g47bt5k-176194591.html.

5. "Wisconsin Temple Shooter Killed Himself, FBI Says," CNN.com, August 8, 2012, http://news.blogs.cnn.com/2012/08/08/wisconsin-temple-shooter-killed-himself-fbi-says/.

6. Katie Delong, "Sikh Temple Shooting Victim Profiles," Fox 6 Milwaukee, August 7, 2012, http://fox6now.com/2012/08/07/sikh-temple-shooting-victim-profiles/.

7. Dinesh Ramde, "Sikh Son First Saw Father at Dad's Wis. Funeral," Yahoo! News, August 2, 2013, http://news.yahoo.com/sikh-son-first-saw-father-dads -wis-funeral-202821759.html.

8. South Asian Americans Leading Together, *Under Suspicion, Under Attack*, September 2014, appendix A, http://saalt.org/wp-content/uploads/2013 /06/SAALT_report_full_links1.pdf.

9. Ibid.

10. Human Rights Watch, *We Are Not the Enemy*, November 2002, http:// www.hrw.org/sites/default/files/reports/usa1102.pdf.

11. David Cahn, "The 1907 Bellingham Riots in Historical Context," Seattle Civil Rights & Labor History Project, accessed December 1, 2014, http:// depts.washington.edu/civilr/bham_history.htm#_ednref7.

12. "Our View: 100 Years After Riot Coverage: Our Apology," *Bellingham Herald*, September 2, 2007, http://www.bellinghamherald.com/2007/09/02 /169787/100-years-after-riot-coverage.html#storylink=cpy.

13. Ibid.

14. Bill Lann Lee and Christopher Punongbayan, "The Civil Rights Act Helped Asian Americans, Too," *The Progressive*, July 2, 2014, http://www .progressive.org/news/2014/07/187762/asian-americans-and-1964-civil -rights-act.

15. Civil Rights Act of 1964, Pub. L. No. 88-352, 78 Stat. 241 (1964) (codified as amended in scattered sections of 2 U.S.C., 28 U.S.C., and 42 U.S.C.); Voting Rights Act of 1965, Pub. L. No. 89-110, 79 Stat. 437 (1965) (codified as amended in scattered sections of 42 U.S.C.).

16. Immigration and Nationality Act of 1965, Pub. L. No. 89-236, 79 Stat. 911 (1965) (codified as amended in scattered sections of 8 U.S.C.).

17. Michel Marriott, "In Jersey City, Indians Protest Violence," *New York Times*, October 12, 1987, http://www.nytimes.com/1987/10/12/nyregion/in -jersey-city-indians-protest-violence.html.

18. Shekhar Gupta, "An Indian Nightmare," *India Today*, December 15, 1987, http://indiatoday.intoday.in/story/us-racist-dotbusters-go-berserk-in-jersey -city/1/337832.html.

19. Marriott, "In Jersey City, Indians Protest Violence."

20. Ibid.

21. National Asian Pacific American Legal Consortium, *Audit of Violence Against Asian Pacific Americans: Challenging the Invisibility of Hate*, 1999, http://www.advancingequality.org/sites/aajc/files/1999_Audit_2.pdf.

22. Queens District Attorney's Office, "South Ozone Park Man Sentenced to 8 Years in 1998 Bias Attack," news release, July 28, 2000, http://queensda .org/Press%20Releases/2000%20Press%20Releases/07-July/07-28-2000.htm.

23. Somini Sengupta, "Following Up; Putting a Life Together 2 Years After Attack," *New York Times*, September 17, 2000, http://www.nytimes.com/2000/09/17/nyregion/following-up-putting-a-life-together-2-years-after-attack.html.

24. Hate Crimes Act of 2000, NY CLS Penal § 485.05 (2000).

25. Queens District Attorney's Office, "Three Young Men Indicted in Alleged Bias Attack," news release, November 9, 1998, http://queensda.org/Press%20Releases/1998%20Press%20Releases/11-November/11-09-1998.htm.

26. Queens District Attorney's Office, "South Ozone Park Man Sentenced to 8 Years in 1998 Bias Attack."

27. Harold Hayes, "Baumhammers Wants Death Sentence Thrown Out," CBS Pittsburgh, September 13, 2011, http://pittsburgh.cbslocal.com/2011/09/13/baumhammers-wants-death-sentence-thrown-out/.

28. Anti-Defamation League, "The Consequences of Right Wing Extremism on the Internet," http://archive.adl.org/internet/extremism_rw/inspiring.html.

29. Francis X. Clines, "Shootings Leave Pittsburgh Suburbs Stunned," *New York Times*, April 30, 2000, http://www.nytimes.com/2000/04/30/us/shootings-leave-pittsburgh-suburbs-stunned.html.

30. Arthur J. Pais, " 'He Said Hey, and Just Shot Me . . . ,' " Rediff.com, May 2, 2001, http://www.rediff.com/news/2001/may/02us3.htm.

31. Brian Bowling, "Federal Judge Puts Baumhammers' Execution on Hold," *TribLive*, October 7, 2014, http://triblive.com/news/adminpage/6926109-74/baumhammers-federal-death#axzz3FzX0BQ6s.

32. Ibid.

33. South Asian Americans Leading Together, *American Backlash: Terrorists Bring War Home in More Ways Than One*, 2001, http://saalt.electricembers.net/wp-content/uploads/2012/09/American-Backlash-report.pdf.

34. Tamar Lewin, "Sikh Owner of Gas Station Is Fatally Shot in Rampage," *New York Times*, September 17, 2001, http://www.nytimes.com/2001/09/17/us/sikh-owner-of-gas-station-is-fatally-shot-in-rampage.html.

35. Sikh American Legal Defense and Education Fund, "The First 9/11 Backlash Fatality: The Murder of Balbir Singh Sodhi," August 30, 2011, http://saldef.org/issues/balbir-singh-sodhi/#.VDr4fOdN1c4.

36. Robert E. Pierre, "Victims of Hate, Now Feeling Forgotten," *Washington Post*, September 14, 2002, http://www.washingtonpost.com/wp-dyn/content/article/2002/09/14/AR2006031501323.html.

37. Jerome Taylor, "I Never Hated Mark. My Religion Teaches That Forgiveness Is Always Better than Vengeance,' " *The Independent*, July 9, 2011, http://www.independent.co.uk/news/world/americas/i-never-hated-mark-my

-religion-teaches-that-forgiveness-is-always-better-than-vengeance-2309526 .html.

38. White House, "'Islam Is Peace' Says President," news release, September 17, 2001, http://georgewbush-whitehouse.archives.gov/news/releases /2001/09/20010917-11.html.

39. Sikh American Legal Defense and Education Fund and Stanford University, *Turban Myths: The Opportunities and Challenges for Reframing Sikh American Identity in Post-9/11 America*, December 14, 2013, http://issuu.com /saldefmedia/docs/turbanmyths_121113.

40. Dawinder S. Sidhu and Neha Singh Gohil, *Civil Rights in Wartime: The Post-9/11 Sikh Experience* (Burlington, VT: Ashgate Publishing, 2009), 99–100.

41. U.S. Department of Justice, "Initiative to Combat Post-9/11 Discriminatory Backlash," accessed December 1, 2014, http://www.justice.gov/crt/legalinfo /nordwg_mission.php.

42. U.S. Equal Opportunity Employment Commission, "What You Should Know About the EEOC and Religious and National Origin Discrimination Involving the Muslim, Sikh, Arab, Middle Eastern and South Asian Communities," accessed October 12, 2014, http://www.eeoc.gov/eeoc/newsroom /wysk/religion_national_origin_9-11.cfm.

43. U.S. Equal Opportunity Employment Commission, "Former and Current Owners of the Sahara Hotel to Pay $100,000 to Settle EEOC National Origin Harassment & Retaliation Suit," news release, December 7, 2010, http://www1.eeoc.gov//eeoc/newsroom/release/12-7-2010b.cfm?renderfor print=1.

44. U.S. Supreme Court, "14-86, E.E.O.C. v. Abercrombie & Fitch Stores, Inc.," accessed June 2, 2015, http://www.supremecourt.gov/opinions /14pdf/14-86_p86b.pdf; Adam Liptak, "Muslim Woman Denied Job Over Head Scarf Wins in Supreme Court," *New York Times*, June 1, 2015, http:// www.nytimes.com/2015/06/02/us/supreme-court-rules-in-samantha-elauf -abercrombie-fitch-case.html.

45. U.S. Attorney's Office for the Northern District of Georgia, "The DeKalb County School District Reaches Settlement Agreement with Federal Authorities for Harassment Based on Religion and National Origin," news release, November 18, 2014, http://www.justice.gov/usao/gan/press/2014/11-18 -14.html.

46. Federal Bureau of Investigation, *Hate Crime Statistics, 2001*, http:// www.fbi.gov/about-us/cjis/ucr/hate-crime/2001/hatecrime01.pdf.

47. Federal Bureau of Investigation, *Hate Crime Statistics, 2004*, https:// www2.fbi.gov/ucr/hc2004/tables/HateCrime2004.pdf.

48. Federal Bureau of Investigation, *Hate Crime Statistics, 2008*, http:// www2.fbi.gov/ucr/hc2008/documents/incidentsandoffenses.pdf; Federal Bureau of Investigation, *Hate Crime Statistics, 2009*, http://www2.fbi.gov/ucr/hc 2009/documents/incidentsandoffenses.pdf; Federal Bureau of Investigation, *Hate Crime Statistics, 2013*, http://www.fbi.gov/about-us/cjis/ucr/hate-crime /2013/topic-pages/incidents-and-offenses/incidentsandoffenses_final.

49. Marc Santora, "Woman Is Charged with Murder as a Hate Crime in a Fatal Subway Push," *New York Times*, December 29, 2012, http://www .nytimes.com/2012/12/30/nyregion/woman-is-held-in-death-of-man-pushed -onto-subway-tracks-in-queens.html.

50. Joe Jackson, "Woman Sentenced to 24 Years After NYC Man Pushed into No. 7 Train," *Wall Street Journal*, May 20, 2015, http://blogs .wsj.com/metropolis/2015/05/20/woman-sentenced-to-24-years-after-nyc -man-pushed-into-no-7-train/.

51. U.S. Department of Justice, *Confronting Discrimination in the Post— 9/11 Era: Challenges and Opportunities Ten Years Later*, October 19, 2011, http://www.justice.gov/crt/publications/post911/post911summit_report _2012-04.pdf.

52. U.S. Department of Justice, "Attorney General Eric Holder Speaks at the Oak Creek Memorial Service," news release, August 10, 2012, http:// www.justice.gov/iso/opa/ag/speeches/2012/ag-speech-1208101.html.

53. Bureau of Justice Statistics, "Hate Crime Victimization, 2004–2012— Statistical Tables," Office of Justice Programs, U.S. Department of Justice, February 2014, http://www.bjs.gov/content/pub/pdf/hcv0412st.pdf.

54. Federal Bureau of Investigation, "Latest Hate Crime Statistics Report Released," news release, December 8, 2014, http://www.fbi.gov/news /stories/2014/december/latest-hate-crime-statistics-report-released/latest -hate-crime-statistics-report-released.

55. National Advocacy for Local LGBTQH Communities, "National Report on Hate Violence Against Lesbian, Gay, Bisexual, Transgender, Queer and HIV-Affected Communities Released Today," news release, May 29, 2014, http://www.avp.org/storage/documents/2013_mr_ncavp_hvreport.pdf.

56. Sikh American Legal and Defense Education Fund, "SALDEF December Advocate: Assailants in Sacramento Hate Crime Apprehended," December 16, 2010, http://saldef.org/uncategorized/saldef-december-advocate assailants-in-sacramento-hate-crime-apprehended//#.VIJ4YlXF_dc.

57. *Hate Crimes and the Threat of Domestic Extremism: Hearing Before the Subcommittee on Constitution, Civil Rights and Human Rights, Committee on the Judiciary, United States Senate*, 112th Cong. (2012) (statement of Harpreet Singh Saini), http://media.jsonline.com/documents/Saini.pdf.

58. Eric Holder, "Healing Communities and Remembering the Victims of Oak Creek," U.S. Department of Justice, August 2, 2013, http://www.justice.gov/opa/blog/healing-communities-and-remembering-victims-oak-creek.

59. Federal Bureau of Investigation, *Hate Crime Data Collection Guidelines and Training Manual*, February 27, 2015, http://www.fbi.gov/about-us/cjis/ucr/hate-crime-data-collection-guidelines-and-training-manual.pdf.

60. The Matthew Shepard and James Byrd, Jr., Hate Crimes Prevention Act of 2009, 18 U.S.C. § 249.

61. Yamiche Alcindor, "Holder: Standard in Civil Rights Cases 'Too High,'" *USA Today*, February 27, 2015, http://www.usatoday.com/story/news/2015/02/27/holder-standard-in-federal-civil-rights-cases-is-too-high/24108103/.

62. U.S. Census Bureau, "U.S. Census Bureau Projections Show a Slower Growing, Older, More Diverse Nation a Half Century from Now," news release, December 12, 2012, https://www.census.gov/newsroom/releases/archives/population/cb12-243.html.

63. Mark Potok, "The Year in Hate and Extremism," *Intelligence Report*, Spring 2014, http://www.splcenter.org/get-informed/intelligence-report/browse-all-issues/2014/spring/The-Year-in-Hate-and-Extremism.

64. Mark Potok, "The 'Patriot' Movement Explodes," *Intelligence Report*, Spring 2012, http://www.splcenter.org/get-informed/intelligence-report/browse-all-issues/2012/spring/the-year-in-hate-and-extremism; Southern Poverty Law Center, "FBI: Dramatic Spike in Hate Crimes Targeting Muslims," *Intelligence Report*, Spring 2012, http://www.splcenter.org/get-informed/intelligence-report/browse-all-issues/2012/spring/fbi-dramatic-spike-in-hate-crimes-targetin.

65. Mark Potok, "American Extremists Find Delight in September 11th Attacks," *Intelligence Report*, Spring 2002, http://www.splcenter.org/get-informed/intelligence-report/browse-all-issues/2002/spring/the-year-in-hate.

66. David Holthouse, "926 Hate Groups Active in 2008," *Intelligence Report*, Spring 2008, http://www.splcenter.org/get-informed/intelligence-report/browse-all-issues/2009/spring/the-year-in-hate.

67. Mark Potok, "The Year in Hate & Extremism, 2010," *Intelligence Report*, Spring 2011, http://www.splcenter.org/get-informed/intelligence-report/browse-all-issues/2011/spring/the-year-in-hate-extremism-2010; Mark Potok, "The Year in Hate and Extremism," *Intelligence Report*, Spring 2013, http://www.splcenter.org/home/2013/spring/the-year-in-hate-and-extremism.

68. Mark Potok, "The Year in Hate and Extremism," Southern Poverty Law Center, accessed April 12, 2015, http://www.splcenter.org/Year-in-Hate-and-Extremism.

69. Southern Poverty Law Center, "Active Patriot Groups in the United States in 2013," *Intelligence Report*, Spring 2014, http://www.splcenter.org /get-informed/intelligence-report/browse-all-issues/2014/spring/Active -Patriot-Groups-in-the-United-States.

70. Southern Poverty Law Center, "Anti-Immigrant," accessed December 5, 2014, http://www.splcenter.org/get-informed/intelligence-files/ideology /anti-immigrant.

71. Southern Poverty Law Center, "National Socialist Movement," accessed December 5, 2014, http://www.splcenter.org/get-informed/intelligence-files /groups/national-socialist-movement.

72. Marilyn Elias, "Sikh Temple Killer Wade Michael Page Radicalized in Army," *Intelligence Report*, Winter 2012, http://www.splcenter. org/get-informed/intelligence-report/browse-all-issues/2012/winter/ massacre-in-wisconsin.

73. Ibid.

74. Ibid.

75. Ibid.

76. Mark Potok, "The Year in Hate and Extremism," Southern Poverty Law Center, accessed April 12, 2015, http://www.splcenter.org/Year -in-Hate-and-Extremism.

77. Eli Lake and Audrey Hudson, "Federal Agency Warns of Radicals on Right," *Washington Times*, April 14, 2009, http://www.washingtontimes.com/ news/2009/apr/14/federal-agency-warns-of-radicals-on-right; Eli Lake and Audrey Hudson "Napolitano Stands by Controversial Report," *Washington Times*, April 16, 2009, http://www.washingtontimes.com/news/2009/apr/16 /napolitano-stands-rightwing-extremism/?page=all.

78. Annie-Rose Strasser, "Republicans Blasted Obama Administration for Warning About Right-Wing Domestic Terrorism," *ThinkProgress*, August 7, 2012, http://thinkprogress.org/politics/2012/08/07/645421/right-wing-extremism/.

79. White House, *Empowering Local Partners to Prevent Violent Extremism in the United States*, August 2011, http://www.whitehouse.gov/sites/default /files/empowering_local_partners.pdf.

80. Muslim Advocates, "Coalition Letter to Obama Administration on Countering Violent Extremism," December 18, 2014, http://www.muslim advocates.org/coalition-letter-to-obama-administration-on-countering-violent -extremism.

81. Traditionalist American Knights of the Ku Klux Klan, "KKK Ferguson Flier," http://www.scribd.com/doc/246369623/KKK-Ferguson-Flier.

82. Keegan Hankes, "Ku Klux Klan to 'Protect' White Businesses in Ferguson," Southern Poverty Law Center, August 19, 2014, http://

www.splcenter.org/blog/2014/08/19/ku-klux-klan-to-protect-white
-businesses-in-ferguson/.

83. Keegan Hankes, "KKK Joins Immigration Debate with Calls for 'Corpses' on the Border," Southern Poverty Law Center, July 31, 2014, http://www.splcenter.org/blog/2014/07/31/kkk-joins-immigration-debate-with -calls-for-corpses-on-the-border/.

84. Church Arson Prevention Act of 1996, Pub. L. No. 104-155, 110 Stat. 1392 (1996).

85. National Church Arson Task Force, "National Church Arson Task Force Issues Fourth Report: Number of Arsons at America's Houses of Worship Continues to Decline," news release, September 15, 2000, https://www .atf.gov/files/press/releases/2000/09/091500-atf-church-arson-task-force -report.pdf.

86. *Hate Crimes and the Threat of Domestic Terrorism: Hearing Before the Senate Committee on the Constitution, Civil Rights, & Human Rights*, 112th Cong. 2–6 (2012) (statement of Deepa Iyer, Executive Director of South Asian Americans Leading Together).

87. Cecilia Muñoz, "Commemorating the Fifth Anniversary of the Shep-ard-Byrd Hate Crimes Act," White House Blog, November 6, 2014, http://www.whitehouse.gov/blog/2014/11/06/commemorating-fifth-anniversary -shepard-byrd-hate-crimes-act.

88. Matt Campbell, "FBI Investigating Possible Hate Crime in Fatal Hit-and-Run of Muslim Boy in KC," *Kansas City Star*, December 4, 2014, http://www.kansascity.com/news/local/crime/article4285553.html.

2. Journeys in a Racial State

1. Uniting and Strengthening America by Providing Appropriate Tools Re-quired to Intercept and Obstruct Terrorism (USA PATRIOT ACT) Act of 2001, Pub. L. No. 107-56, 115 Stat.272 (2001) (hereafter Patriot Act).

2. Antiterrorism and Effective Death Penalty Act of 1996, Pub. L. No. 104-132, 110 Stat. 1214.

3. Natsu Taylor Saito, "Whose Liberty? Whose Security? The USA PATRIOT ACT in the Context of COINTELPRO and the Unlawful Repres-sion of Political Dissent," *Oregon Law Review* 81 (2002): 1109–10.

4. American Civil Liberties Union, "The USA PATRIOT ACT and Gov-ernment Actions That Threaten Our Civil Liberties," accessed Decem-ber 20, 2014, https://www.aclu.org/files/FilesPDFs/patriot%20act%20flyer .pdf.

5. Office of Justice Programs, "Uniting and Strengthening America by Pro-viding Appropriate Tools Required to Intercept and Obstruct Terrorism (USA

PATRIOT) Act of 2001," U.S. Department of Justice, accessed December 16, 2014, https://it.ojp.gov/default.aspx?area=privacy&page=1281; Eyder Peralta, "Parts of Patriot Act Expire, Even as Senate Moves on Bill Limiting Surveillance," *The Two-Way* blog, National Public Radio, May 31, 2015, http://www.npr.org/sections/thetwo-way/2015/05/31/411044789/live-blog-facing-midnight-deadline-the-senate-debates-parts-of-the-patriot-act.

6. "H.R.5005—Homeland Security Act of 2002," accessed December 20, 2014, https://www.congress.gov/bill/107th-congress/house-bill/5005; "Judging the Impact: A Post 9-11 America," National Public Radio, July 16, 2004, http://www.npr.org/911hearings/security_measures.html.

7. U.S. Department of Homeland Security, "Homeland Security Act of 2002," accessed December 20, 2014, http://www.dhs.gov/homeland-security-act-2002.

8. U.S. Department of Homeland Security, "Who Joined DHS," accessed December 20, 2014, http://www.dhs.gov/who-joined-dhs.

9. Custody Procedures, 66 Fed. Reg. 48334 (September 20, 2001).

10. U.S. Department of Justice, Office of the Inspector General, *The September 11 Detainees: A Review of the Treatment of Aliens Held on Immigration Charges in Connection with the Investigation of the September 11 Attacks,* April 2003, http://www.justice.gov/oig/special/0306/full.pdf.

11. American Civil Liberties Union, "Appeals Court Hears Arguments Today in Second ACLU Challenge to Secret Immigration Hearings," news release, September 17, 2002, https://www.aclu.org/national-security/appeals-court-hears-arguments-today-second-aclu-challenge-secret-immigration-heari.

12. American Civil Liberties Union, "End Government Use of Secret Evidence Against Immigrants," accessed December 20, 2014, https://www.aclu.org/end-government-use-secret-evidence-against-immigrants.

13. Human Rights Watch, *Presumption of Guilt: Human Rights Abuses of Post-September 11 Detainees,* August 2002, http://www.hrw.org/reports/2002/us911/USA0802.pdf.

14. U.S. General Accounting Office, *Report to Congressional Committees: Justice Department's Project to Interview Aliens After September 11, 2001,* April 2003, http://www.gao.gov/assets/240/237849.pdf.

15. Office of Inspector General, "An Assessment of United States Immigration and Customs Enforcement's Fugitive Operations Teams," U.S. Department of Homeland Security, March 2007, http://www.oig.dhs.gov/assets/Mgmt/OIG_07-34_Mar07.pdf.

16. *Department of Homeland Security Transition: Bureau of Immigration and Customs Enforcement: Hearing Before the Subcommittee on Immigration,*

Border Security, and Claims of the Committee on the Judiciary, 108th Cong. (2002) (statement of Honorable Asa Hutchinson, Undersecretary for Border and Transportation Security), http://www.gpo.gov/fdsys/pkg/CHRG -108hhrg86409/html/CHRG-108hhrg86409.htm.

17. Registration and Monitoring of Certain Nonimmigrants, 67 Fed. Reg. 52584 (August 12, 2002).

18. U.S. Department of Justice, "Attorney General Prepared Remarks on the National Security Entry-Exit Registration System," news release, June 6, 2002, http://www.justice.gov/archive/ag/speeches/2002/060502agprepared remarks.htm.

19. Removing Designated Countries from the National Security Entry-Exit Registration System (NSEERS), Notice, 76 Fed. Reg. 23830 (April 28, 2011), http://www.gpo.gov/fdsys/pkg/FR-2011-04-28/html/2011-10305.htm.

20. Registration and Monitoring of Certain Nonimmigrants, 67 Fed. Reg. 52584 (August 12, 2002).

21. Megan Garvey, Martha Groves, and Henry Weinstein, "Hundreds Are Detained After Visits to INS," *Los Angeles Times*, December 19, 2002, http:// articles.latimes.com/2002/dec/19/local/me-register19.

22. Asian American Legal Defense and Education Fund, *Special Registration: Discrimination and Xenophobia as Government Policy*, January 2004, http://www.aaldef.org/docs/AALDEF-Special-Registration-2004.pdf.

23. American Civil Liberties Union, "Immigrants Targeted for Deportation After Participating in INS Special Registration Program Speak Out," news release, July 1, 2003, https://www.aclu.org/national-security/immigrants -targeted-deportation-after-participating-ins-special-registration-progr.

24. Muzzaffar Chishti and Claire Bergeron, "DHS Announces End to Controversial Post- 9/11 Immigrant Registration and Tracking Program," Migration Policy Institute, news release, May 17, 2011, http://www.migration policy.org/article/dhs-announces-end-controversial-post-911-immigrant -registration-and-tracking-program.

25. South Asian Americans Leading Together, "SAALT Testimony for Hearing on Comprehensive Immigration Reform," May 22, 2007, http:// saalt.electricembers.net/wp-content/uploads/2012/09/SAALTs-Testimony -before-House-Subcommittee-on-Immigration-Refugees-and-Citizenship -May-2007.pdf.

26. Removing Designated Countries from the National Security Entry-Exit Registration System (NSEERS).

27. Ibid.; Office of Inspector General, *Information Sharing on Foreign Nationals: Border Security*, U.S. Department of Homeland Security, February 2012, http://www.oig.dhs.gov/assets/Mgmt/2012/OIGr_12-39_Feb12.pdf.

28. Leadership Conference, *Restoring a National Consensus: The Need to End Racial Profiling in America*, March 2011, http://www.civilrights.org/publications/reports/racial-profiling2011/racial_profiling2011.pdf.

29. United States v. Montero-Camargo, 208 F.3d 1122 (9th Cir. 2000).

30. Leadership Conference, *Restoring a National Consensus*.

31. Muslim Advocates, "Muslim Advocates Testifies Before US Senate Judiciary Subcommittee on Laptop Seizures & Other Privacy Violations," news release, June 25, 2008, http://www.muslimadvocates.org/muslim-advocates-testifies-before-us-senate-judiciary-subcommittee-on-laptop-seizures-other-privacy-violations/.

32. American Civil Liberties Union, "Factsheet: The ACLU's Challenge to the U.S. Government's 'No Fly List,'" accessed December 20, 2014, https://www.aclu.org/national-security/factsheet-aclus-challenge-us-governments-no-fly-list.

33. Latif v. Holder, 2014 U.S. Dist. LEXIS 85450, 2014 WL 2871346 (D. Or. June 24, 2014); American Civil Liberties Union, "Latif, et al. v. Holder, et al.—ACLU Challenge to Government No Fly List," accessed December 1, 2014, https://www.aclu.org/national-security/latif-et-al-v-holder-et-al-aclu-challenge-government-no-fly-list.

34. Eileen Sullivan, "US to Tell Certain Travelers If on No-Fly List," Yahoo! News, April 14, 2015, http://news.yahoo.com/us-tell-certain-travelers-no-fly-list-152706755—politics.html.

35. Civil Rights Division, "Guidance Regarding the Use of Race by Federal Law Enforcement," U.S. Department of Justice, June 2003, http://www.justice.gov/crt/about/spl/documents/guidance_on_race.pdf.

36. Ibid.

37. U.S. Department of Justice, "Guidance for Federal Law Enforcement Agencies Regarding the Use of Race, Ethnicity, Gender, National Origin, Religion, Sexual Orientation, or Gender Identity," December 2014, http://www.justice.gov/sites/default/files/ag/pages/attachments/2014/12/08/use-of-race-policy.pdf.

38. American Civil Liberties Union, "ACLU Response to Revised DOJ Guidance on the Use of Race by Federal Law Enforcement Agencies," news release, December 8, 2014, https://www.aclu.org/criminal-law-reform-racial-justice/aclu-response-revised-doj-guidance-use-race-federal-law-enforceme.

39. U.S. Department of Justice, "Guidance for Federal Law Enforcement Agencies Regarding the Use of Race, Ethnicity, Gender, National Origin, Religion, Sexual Orientation, or Gender Identity."

40. South Asian Americans Leading Together, "Practice of Profiling: Traveling While Brown," March 2010, http://saalt.electricembers.net/wp-content

/uploads/2012/09/SAALT-Issue-Briefs-Travel-March-2010.pdf; Muslim Advocates, *Losing Liberty: The State of Freedom 10 Years After the Patriot Act*, October 2011, http://d3n8a8pro7vhmx.cloudfront.net/muslimadvocates/pages/47/attachments/original/Losing_Liberty_The_State_of_Freedom_10_Years_After_the_PATRIOT_Act.pdf?1330650785.

41. American Civil Liberties Union, "Border Communities Under Siege: Border Patrol Agents Ride Roughshod Over Civil Rights," accessed December 20, 2014, https://www.aclu.org/border-communities-under-siege-border-patrol-agents-ride-roughshod-over-civil-rights.

42. South Asian Americans Leading Together et al., *In Our Own Words: Narratives of South Asian New Yorkers Affected by Racial and Religious Profiling*, March 2012, http://saalt.electricembers.net/wp-content/uploads/2012/09/In-Our-Own-Words-Narratives-of-South-Asian-New-Yorkers-Affected-by-Racial-and-Religious-Profiling2.pdf.

43. South Asian Americans Leading Together, *From Macacas to Turban Toppers: The Rise in Xenophobic and Racist Rhetoric in American Political Discourse*, October 2010, 13, 17, http://saalt.org/wp-content/uploads/2012/09/From-Macacas-to-Turban-Toppers-Report.small_.pdf.

44. "National Briefing | South: Louisiana: Apology from Congressman," *New York Times*, September 21, 2001, http://www.nytimes.com/2001/09/21/us/national-briefing-south-louisiana-apology-from-congressman.html.

45. South Asian Americans Leading Together, *From Macacas to Turban Toppers*.

46. *Compilation of Hearings on Islamist Radicalization—Volume I: Hearings Before the Committee on Homeland Security, House of Representatives*, 112th Cong., 1st sess. (March 10, 2011), http://homeland.house.gov/hearing/hearing-%E2%80%9C-extent-radicalization-american-muslim-community-and-communitys-response%E2%80%9D.

47. Jillian Rayfield, "Joe Walsh: Profile 'Young Muslim Men,'" *Salon*, April 23, 2013, http://www.salon.com/2013/04/23/joe_walsh_profile_young_muslim_men/.

48. Mona Shadia and Paloma Esquivel, "Villa Park Councilwoman Deborah Pauly Ignites Controversy with Speech at Islamic Charity Event," *Los Angeles Times*, March 24, 2011, http://articles.latimes.com/2011/mar/24/local/la-me-0324-villa-park-20110324.

49. Neil T. Gotanda, "Citizenship Nullification: The Impossibility of Asian American Politics," in *Asian Americans and Politics: Perspectives, Experiences, Prospects*, ed. Gordon H. Chang (Washington, DC: Woodrow Wilson Center Press, 2001).

50. National Park Service, "The War Relocation Centers of World War II: When Fear Was Stronger than Justice," accessed January 25, 2015, http://www.nps.gov/nr/twhp/wwwlps/lessons/89manzanar/89manzanar.htm.

51. Korematsu v. United States, 323 U.S. 214, 218 (1944).

52. Civil Liberties Act of 1988, Pub. L. No. 100-383, 102 Stat. 904 (1988).

53. Neal Katyal, "Confession of Error: The Solicitor General's Mistakes During the Japanese-American Internment Cases," Justice Blogs, U.S. Department of Justice, May 20, 2011, http://www.justice.gov/opa/blog/confession-error-solicitor-generals-mistakes-during-japanese-american-internment-cases.

54. United Nations Committee on Elimination of Racial Discrimination, "Consideration of Reports Submitted by States Parties Under Article 9 of the Convention: Concluding Observations of the Committee on the Elimination of Racial Discrimination," 72nd sess., May 2008, http://www.state.gov/documents/organization/107361.pdf.

55. Leadership Conference on Civil and Human Rights, "Japanese American Redress Bill," *Civil Rights Monitor* 5, no. 1 (June 1986), http://www.civilrights.org/monitor/june1986/art8p1.html.

56. Eric K. Yamamoto, "Racial Reparations: Japanese American Redress and African American Claims," *Boston College Third World Law Journal* 19, no. 1 (1998): 477–523, http://lawdigitalcommons.bc.edu/cgi/viewcontent.cgi?article=1190&context=twlj.

57. Ibid.

3. Surveillance Nation

1. Javier C. Hernández, "Vote Endorses Muslim Center Near Ground Zero," *New York Times*, May 26, 2010, http://www.nytimes.com/2010/05/26/nyregion/26muslim.html.

2. Clyde Haberman, "Near Ground Zero, the Sacred and the Profane," *New York Times*, May 27, 2010, http://www.nytimes.com/2010/05/28/nyregion/28nyc.html.

3. Quinnipiac University, "Muslims Have Right to Build Mosque Near Ground Zero, New York Voters Tell Quinnipiac University Poll; But They Should Agree to Move It Somewhere Else," news release, September 24, 2010, http://www.scribd.com/doc/38069186/Q-poll-092410-Ny-Mosque-Bp.

4. Anti-Defamation League, "Statement on Islamic Community Center Near Ground Zero," news release, July 28, 2010, http://www.adl.org/press-center/press-releases/civil-rights/statement-on-islamic.html.

5. Erica Rakow, "New York City Islamic Center Debate Heats Up Locally," WJHG.com, August 19, 2010, http://www.wjhg.com/home/headlines/101026874.html.

6. South Asian Americans Leading Together, *From Macacas to Turban Toppers: The Rise in Xenophobic and Racist Rhetoric in American Political Discourse*, October 2010, http://saalt.org/wp-content/uploads/2012/09/From-Macacas-to-Turban-Toppers-Report.small_.pdf.

7. Frank Lombardi, "Ahmed Sharif, Muslim Cab Driver Stabbed by Bigot, Says He Was Targeted Because of His Religion," *New York Daily News*, August 26, 2010, http://www.nydailynews.com/new-york/ahmed-sharif-muslim-cab-driver-stabbed-bigot-targeted-religion-article-1.204616.

8. "Sikh Store Clerk Attacked, Called Al-Qaida," UPI, August 31, 2010, http://www.upi.com/Top_News/US/2010/08/31/Sikh-store-clerk-attacked-called-al-Qaida/UPI-83121283303910/.

9. Stephanie Snyder, "Phoenix Mosque Vandalism Being Investigated by FBI," *Arizona Republic*, September 8, 2010, http://www.azcentral.com/news/articles/2010/09/08/20100908phoenix-mosque-vandalized-abrk.html; Dave Lucas, "Arrests Made in Vandalism at Hudson NY Mosque," WAMC Northeast Public Radio, September 10, 2010, http://wamc.org/post/arrests-made-vandalism-hudson-ny-mosque; Diane Macedo, "Ground Zero Controversy Fueled Attacks on Texas Mosque, Islamic Center President Says," FoxNews.com, August 9, 2010, http://www.foxnews.com/us/2010/08/09/texas-islamic-center-president-says-vandals-targeting-mosque-ground-zero/; Eddie Jimenez, "California Mosque Vandalized, Ground Zero Mentioned," *Fresno Bee*, August 25, 2010, http://www.mcclatchydc.com/2010/08/25/99652/california-mosque-vandalized-ground.html.

10. "Burnt Copy of Quran Found Outside Muslim Community Center," *Chicago Tribune*, September 14, 2010, http://articles.chicagotribune.com/2010-09-14/news/ct-met-burnt-quran-0915-20100914_1_quran-muslim-community-center-copy; Brent Begin, "Burnt Quran Found Outside Tenderloin Mosque," *San Francisco Examiner*, September 18, 2010, http://www.sfexaminer.com/sanfrancisco/burnt-quran-found-outside-tenderloin-mosque/Content?oid=2160528; Sherene Tagharobi, "Quran Burning in East Lansing," WILX.com, September 12, 2010, http://www.wilx.com/home/headlines/102737644.html.

11. "Bloomingdale Man Is Fired from NJ Transit Job for Burning Quran Near Ground Zero," *Star-Ledger* (Newark, NJ), September 15, 2010, http://www.nj.com/news/index.ssf/2010/09/bloomingdale_man_fired_by_nj_t.html.

12. White House, "Remarks by the President at Iftar Dinner," news release, August 13, 2010, http://www.whitehouse.gov/the-press-office/2010/08/13/remarks-president-iftar-dinner-0.

13. "Under Fire, Obama Clarifies Support for Ground Zero Mosque," Fox News.com, August 14, 2010, http://www.foxnews.com/politics/2010/08/14/obamas-support-ground-zero-mosque-draws/.

14. Javier C. Hernández, "Mosque Near Ground Zero Clears Key Hurdle," City Room (blog), New York Times, August 3, 2010, http://cityroom.blogs.nytimes.com/2010/08/03/mosque-near-ground-zero-clears-key-hurdle/.

15. Patrick McGeehan, "Con Ed Sells Building Near Ground Zero Where Plans for Mosque Caused Uproar," New York Times, August 20, 2014, http://www.nytimes.com/2014/08/21/nyregion/con-edison-sells-lot-near-ground-zero-where-plans-for-mosque-caused-uproar.html.

16. Mitchell D. Silber and Arvin Bhatt, Radicalization in the West: The Homegrown Terror Threat (New York: NYPD Intelligence Division, 2007), http://www.nyc.gov/html/nypd/downloads/pdf/public_information/NYPD_Report-Radicalization_in_the_West.pdf.

17. Ibid.

18. Matt Apuzzo and Adam Goldman, "With CIA Help, NYPD Moves Covertly in Muslim Areas," Associated Press, August 23, 2011, http://www.ap.org/Content/AP-in-the-News/2011/With-CIA-help-NYPD-moves-covertly-in-Muslim-areas; Matt Apuzzo and Adam Goldman, "Inside the Spy Unit That NYPD Says Doesn't Exist," Associated Press, August 31, 2011, http://www.ap.org/Content/AP-in-the-News/2011/Inside-the-spy-unit-that-NYPD-says-doesnt-exist.

19. Raza v. New York, No. 13 Civ. 3448, complaint at 6 (E.D.N.Y June 18, 2013), http://www.nyclu.org/files/releases/Raza_Complaint_FINAL_6.18.13.pdf; Apuzzo and Goldman, "Inside the Spy Unit That NYPD Says Doesn't Exist."

20. Apuzzo and Goldman, "With CIA Help, NYPD Moves Covertly in Muslim Areas."

21. Chris Hawley "NYPD Monitored Muslim Students All Over Northeast," Associated Press, February 18, 2012, http://www.ap.org/Content/AP-in-the-News/2012/NYPD-monitored-Muslim-students-all-over-Northeast.

22. Matt Apuzzo and Adam Goldman, Enemies Within: Inside the NYPD's Secret Spying Unit and bin Laden's Final Plot Against America (New York: Touchstone, 2013).

23. NYPD Intelligence Division, Demographics Unit, "Sports Venue Report," 16, 29, accessed December 6, 2014, available at http://enemieswithinbook.com/documents/Demographics_Sports%20Venues.pdf.

24. Hassan v. City of New York, amended complaint available at http://ccrjustice.org/files/10_First%20Amended%20Complaint.10.3.2012.pdf.

25. Hassan v. City of New York, 2014 U.S. Dist. LEXIS 20887 (D.N.J. February 20, 2014).

26. Muslim Advocates, "Hassan v. City of New York," accessed January 25, 2015, http://www.muslimadvocates.org/endspying/.

27. Federal Bureau of Investigation, "Protecting America from Terrorist Attack," accessed December 4, 2014, http://www.fbi.gov/about-us/investigate/terrorism/terrorism_jttfs.

28. U.S. Department of Homeland Security, "State and Major Urban Area Fusion Centers," accessed December 6, 2014, http://www.dhs.gov/state-and-major-urban-area-fusion-centers; U.S. Department of Homeland Security, "If You See Something, Say Something," accessed December 6, 2014, http://www.dhs.gov/if-you-see-something-say-something.

29. Michael German and Jay Stanley, American Civil Liberties Union, "What's Wrong with Fusion Centers?," December 2007, https://www.aclu.org/files/pdfs/privacy/fusioncenter_20071212.pdf.

30. Yaman Salahi, "Islamophobia a Major Force in Suspicious Activity Reporting Program," Asian Americans Advancing Justice–Asian Law Caucus, September 19, 2013, http://www.advancingjustice-alc.org/news-media/blog/national-security-and-civil-rights-nscr/islamophobia-major-force-suspicious-activity.

31. American Civil Liberties Union, "Selected Suspicious Activity Reports from the Central California Intelligence Center and Joint Regional Intelligence Center," accessed April 24, 2015, https://www.aclunc.org/sites/default/files/asset_upload_file470_12586.pdf.

32. "Coalition for a Safe San Francisco Wins Ordinance to Prevent Police-FBI Abuse," Rights Working Group, May 10, 2012, http://rightsworkinggroup.org/content/coalition-a-safe-san-francisco-wins-ordinance-prevent-police-fbi-abuse.

33. S.F. Cal., Ordinance 83-12 (passed May 8, 2012), http://www.sfbos.org/ftp/uploadedfiles/bdsupvrs/ordinances12/o0083-12.pdf; S.F. Cal., Ordinance 83-12 (passed May 8, 2012), http://www.sfbos.org/ftp/uploadedfiles/bdsupvrs/ordinances12/o0083-12.pdf; thegrio.com/2013/08/28/ny-police-designate-mosques-as-terrorism-groups/.

34. Linda Sarsour, "Being Arab or Muslim Is Not Probable Cause for NYPD Spying," MSNBC.com, September 1, 2013, http://www.msnbc.com/melissa-harris-perry/being-arab-or-muslim-not-probable-cause.

35. Michael Cooper, "Officers in Bronx Fire 41 Shots, and an Unarmed Man Is Killed," New York Times, February 5, 1999, http://www.nytimes.com

/1999/02/05/nyregion/officers-in-bronx-fire-41-shots-and-an-unarmed-man
-is-killed.html.

36. Stipulation of Settlement, Daniels v. City of N.Y., (No. 99-1695), 2003,
stipulation of settlement, available at https://ccrjustice.org/files/Daniels_
StipulationOfSettlement_12_03_0.pdf.

37. Floyd v. City of N.Y., 959 F. Supp. 2d 540 (S.D.N.Y. 2013).

38. Communities United for Police Reform, "The Community Safety Act,"
accessed December 6, 2014, http://changethenypd.org/community-safety-act
#CSA_Votes.

39. N.Y., N.Y., L. No. Admin. Code §§ 8-502, 14-151 71 (2013).

40. N.Y., N.Y., L. No. 70 Charter ch. 34, §§ 803–804 (2013).

41. Communities United for Police Reform, "The Community Safety Act."

42. Francis Reynolds, "New York City Council Overrides Bloomberg's Veto
of the Community Safety Act," *The Nation*, August 22, 2013, http://www
.thenation.com/blog/175874/new-york-city-council-overrides-bloombergs
-veto-community-safety-act; Communities United for Police Reform, "Community Safety Act."

43. Communities United for Police Reform, "Community Safety Act."

44. Matt Apuzzo and Joseph Goldstein, "New York Drops Unit That
Spied on Muslims," *New York Times*, April 15, 2014, http://www.nytimes
.com/2014/04/16/nyregion/police-unit-that-spied-on-muslims-is-disbanded
.html.

4. Islamophobia in the Bible Belt

1. Brian Justice, "West: Anti-Muslim Facebook Post 'Humorous,' " *Tulla-
homa News*, April 30, 2013, http://www.tullahomanews.com/?p=14827.

2. Robert Steinback, "The Anti-Muslim Inner Circle," *Intelligence Report*,
Summer 2011, http://www.splcenter.org/get-informed/intelligence-report
/browse-all-issues/2011/summer/the-anti-muslim-inner-circle; "Hate Maps:
New York," Southern Poverty Law Center, accessed April 11, 2015, http://
www.splcenter.org/hate-map#s=NY.

3. "Pamela Geller Speaks at Dept of Justice Meeting in Tennessee," You
Tube video, 1:44, posted by "Linc Austin," June 5, 2013, https://www.youtube
.com/watch?v=zOx69hrxtM4.

4. Immigration Policy Center, "New Americans in Tennessee: The Political and Economic Power of Immigrants, Latinos, and Asians in the Volunteer
State," July 2013, http://www.immigrationpolicy.org/sites/default/files/docs
/new_americans_in_tennessee_2013_3.pdf.

5. Partnership for a New American Economy, "New Americans in Nashville: A Snapshot of the Foreign-Born Population," http://www.nashville.gov

/Portals/0/SiteContent/MayorsOffice/docs/news/140922-MONA-FactSheet
.pdf.

6. "Mayor Launches Office of New Americans," Nashville.gov, September 22, 2014, http://www.nashville.gov/News-Media/News-Article/ID/3277/Mayor-Launches-Office-of-New-Americans.aspx; Joey Garrison, "President Obama to Give Immigration Speech in Nashville," *The Tennessean*, December 4, 2014, http://www.tennessean.com/story/news/politics/2014/12/04/obama-to-give-immigration-speech-in-nashville/19893741/; Nashville.gov, "Mayor's Office of New Americans," accessed December 20, 2014, http://www.nashville.gov/Mayors-Office/Priorities/New-Americans.aspx.

7. Hero Karimi, "The Kurdish Immigrant Experience and a Growing American Community," *Kurdish Herald* 2, no. 1 (February 2010), http://www.kurdishherald.com/issue/v002/001/article04.php; Monica Campbell, "Touring a Kurdish Capital in the US," *BBC News* magazine with Public Radio International's *The World*, August 28, 2014, http://www.bbc.com/news/magazine-28891241.

8. U.S. Department of Justice, "Tennessee Man Sentenced to 183 Months in Prison for Burning Islamic Center," news release, March 25, 2010, http://www.justice.gov/opa/pr/tennessee-man-sentenced-183-months-prison-burning-islamic-center.

9. Jeff Woods, "After Sensationalized TV Report, Vandals Strike Nashville Mosque," *Nashville Scene*, February 10, 2010, http://www.nashvillescene.com/pitw/archives/2010/02/10/after-sensationalized-tv-report-vandals-strike-nashville-mosque.

10. U.S. Census Bureau, "State & County Quick Facts: Murfreesboro (county), Tennessee," accessed December 1, 2014, http://quickfacts.census.gov/qfd/states/47/4751560.html.

11. "Vandals Spray Paint Murfreesboro Islamic Center Sign," WKRN-TV, January 18, 2010, accessed November 30, 2014, http://www.wkrn.com/story/11838718/vandals-spray-paint-murfreesboro-islamic-center-sign.

12. Bradley Blackburn, "Plan for Mosque in Tennessee Town Draws Criticism from Residents," ABC News, June 18, 2010, http://abcnews.go.com/WN/murfreesboro-tennessee-mosque-plan-draws-criticism-residents/story?id=10956381.

13. "County Commission Meeting—June 17, 2010," YouTube video, 1:48:45 and 1:29:17, posted by "Rutherford County Government," June 18, 2010, https://www.youtube.com/watch?v=nWO_9ApSyg8.

14. Ibid., at 1:34:22 and 1:27:35.

15. "Zelenik Issues Statement on Proposed Islamic Center," *Murfrees-boro Post*, June 24, 2010, http://www.murfreesboropost.com/zelenik-issues-statement-on-proposed-islamic-center-cms-23606.

16. "DN! Tennessee GOP Candidate Questions Whether Islam Is a Religion," YouTube video, 0:18, posted by "Start Loving-Wage Love or die," July 27, 2010, http://youtu.be/PSwnd6Px_6k.

17. Wajahat Ali et al., *Fear, Inc.: The Roots of the Islamophobia Network in America*, Center for American Progress, August 2011, http://cdn.american progress.org/wp-content/uploads/issues/2011/08/pdf/islamophobia_intro.pdf.

18. Faiz Shakir, "Report: $42 Million from Seven Foundations Helped Fuel the Rise of Islamophobia in America," *Think Progress*, August 26, 2011, http://thinkprogress.org/politics/2011/08/26/304306/islamophobia-network/.

19. Bob Smietana, "Anti-Islam Group Finds Fertile Ground in Nashville," *The Tennessean*, July 10, 2011, http://archive.tennessean.com/article/20110710/NEWS/307100058/Anti-Islam-group-finds-fertile-ground-Nashville; Bob Smietana, "Anti-Muslim Crusaders Make Millions Spreading Fear," *The Tennessean*, October 24, 2010, http://archive.tennessean.com/article/20101024/NEWS01/10240374/Anti-Muslim-crusaders-make-millions-spreading-fear.

20. Erik Schelzig, "Tenn. Tea Party Won't Drop Speaker for Islam Views," *Huffington Post*, May 21, 2010, http://www.huffingtonpost.com/huff-wires/20100521/us-tenn-tea-party/; Smietana, "Anti-Muslim Crusaders Make Millions Spreading Fear."

21. "Murfreesboro Shows Its Support for Mosque," *The Tennessean*, August 30, 2010, http://www.tennessean.com/article/20100830/NEWS01/100830079/Murfreesboro+shows+its+support+for+mosque.

22. Christian Grantham, "Lawsuit Filed to Stop Mosque as Supporters Speak Up," *Murfreesboro Post*, September 17, 2010, http://www.murfreesboro post.com/lawsuit-filed-to-stop-mosque-as-supporters-speak-up-cms-24454.

23. "Federal Judge Paves Way for Tennessee Mosque to Open for Ramadan," CNN.com, July 18, 2012, http://www.cnn.com/2012/07/18/justice/tennesee-mosque-lawsuit/; Sarah Darer Littman, "Don't Be a Bystander," CT News Junkie, November 21, 2010, http://www.ctnewsjunkie.com/archives/entry/op-ed_dont_be_a_bystander/.

24. U.S. Department of Justice, "Justice Department Files Brief in Support of Continued Construction of Murfreesboro, Tenn., Mosque," news release, October 18, 2010, http://www.justice.gov/opa/pr/justice-department-files-brief-support-continued-construction-murfreesboro-tenn-mosque.

25. U.S. Department of Justice, "Justice Department Files Lawsuit Requiring Rutherford County, Tenn., to Allow Mosque to Open in City of

Murfreesboro," news release, July 18, 2012, http://www.justice.gov/opa/pr/2012/July/12-crt-883.html; United States v. Rutherford County Tenn., 2012 U.S. Dist. LEXIS 122546, 2012 WL 3762442 (M.D. Tenn. August 29, 2012).

26. Center for New Community, *Islamaphobia, the New Nativism*, 2013, http://newcomm.org/wp-content/uploads/2013/05/Islamophobia-the-New-Nativism.pdf.

27. Brian Mosely, "Tyson Defends Hiring Practices, Works with Refugees," *Shelbyville Times Gazette*, March 28, 2008, http://www.t-g.com/story/1321194.html; "Middle Tennessee State University," *Forbes*, accessed December 1, 2014, http://www.forbes.com/colleges/middle-tennessee-state-university/.

28. "Nashville Mayor Vetoes English-Only Bill," *USA Today*, February 12, 2007, http://usatoday30.usatoday.com/news/nation/2007-02-12-nashville_x.htm.

29. Richard Yeakley, "Tennessee Amends Anti-Sharia Bill," *Huffington Post*, March 25, 2011, http://www.huffingtonpost.com/2011/03/25/tennessee-amends-antishar_n_840787.html; Bob Smietana, "Tennessee Bill Would Jail Shariah Followers," *The Tennessean*, February 23, 2011, http://usatoday30.usatoday.com/news/nation/2011-02-23-tennessee-law-shariah_N.htm.

30. H.B. 1326, 108th Gen. Assemb. (Tenn. 2013), http://www.capitol.tn.gov/Bills/108/Bill/hB1326.pdf.

31. Wajahat Ali and Matthew Duss, "Young Muslim American Voices: Understanding Sharia Law," Center for American Progress, March 31, 2011, https://www.americanprogress.org/issues/religion/report/2011/03/31/9175/understanding-sharia-law/.

32. Kimberly Railey, "More States Move to Ban Foreign Law in Courts," *USA Today*, August 4, 2013, http://www.usatoday.com/story/news/nation/2013/08/04/states-ban-foreign-law/2602511/.

33. Asraa Mustufa, "Tennessee's Radical Anti-Shariah Bill Amended, but Still Targeted at Muslims," *Colorlines*, May 13, 2011, http://colorlines.com/archives/2011/05/tennesees_radical_anti-shariah_bill_amended_but_still_targeted_at_muslims.html.

34. Pew Research Center, "Controversies Over Mosques and Islamic Centers Across the U.S.," September 27, 2012, http://www.pewforum.org/files/2012/09/2012Mosque-Map.pdf.

35. Religious Land Use and Institutionalized Persons Act of 2000, Pub. L. No. 106-274, 114 Stat. 803 (2000).

36. Proclaiming Justice to the Nations, "The Work Continues—Present Initiatives," accessed January 3, 2015, http://www.pjtn.org/work-continues-present-initiatives/.

37. Bob Unruh, "Islam, Anti-Semitism Sneak into Tennessee Textbooks," *WND Education*, November 22, 2014, http://www.wnd.com/2014/11/islam-anti-semitism-sneak-into-tennessee-textbooks/.

38. Institute for Social Policy and Understanding, "Manufacturing Bigotry: A State-by-State Legislative Effort to Pushback Against 2050 by Targeting Muslims and Other Minorities," 2014, http://www.ispu.org/pdfs/ISPU_Manufacturing_Bigotry%5B3%5D.pdf.

39. Jamie Page, "Coffee County Commissioner: Muslim Challenger Opposes American Flag, Public Prayer," *The Tennessean*, July 21, 2014, http://www.tennessean.com/story/news/politics/2014/07/20/muslim-candidate-says-commissioners-letter-untrue/12912043/.

40. Paul Galloway, "Open Letter to President Obama on his Speech in Tennessee," MuslimMatters.org, December 9, 2014, http://muslimmatters.org/2014/12/09/open-letter-to-president-obama-on-his-speech-in-tennessee/.

5. Disruptors and Bridge Builders

1. Evan Sernoffsky, "Anti-Islam San Francisco Muni Ads Defaced . . . with Messages of Love," *SFGate* (blog), *San Francisco Chronicle*, January 26, 2015, http://blog.sfgate.com/stew/2015/01/26/anti-islam-san-francisco-muni-ads-defaced-with-messages-of-love/.

2. Carol M. Swain, "Charlie Hebdo Attacks Prove Critics Were Right About Islam," *The Tennessean*, January 15, 2015, http://www.tennessean.com/story/opinion/contributors/2015/01/15/charlie-hebdo-attacks-prove-critics-right-islam/21809599/.

3. Lauren McGaughy, "Texas Muslim Capitol Day Marred by Anti-Islam Protesters," *Houston Chronicle*, January 29, 2015, http://www.chron.com/news/politics/texas/article/Texas-Muslim-Capitol-Day-marred-by-anti-Islam-6048881.php.

4. Emily Bazelon, "Purvi Patel Could Be Just the Beginning," *New York Times Magazine*, April 1, 2015, http://www.nytimes.com/2015/04/01/magazine/purvi-patel-could-be-just-the-beginning.html.

5. Almost Black, "Frequently Asked Questions," accessed April 18, 2015, http://almostblack.com/faq/.

6. South Asian Americans Leading Together and Asian American Federation, *A Demographic Snapshot of South Asians in the United States*, July 2012, http://saalt.electricembers.net/wp-content/uploads/2012/09/Demographic-Snapshot-Asian-American-Foundation-2012.pdf.

7. Vijay Prashad, "Crafting Solidarities," in *A Part, Yet Apart: South Asians in Asian America*, ed. Lavina Dhingra Shankar and Rajini Srikanth (Philadelphia: Temple University Press, 1998), 115.

8. Michael Omi and Howard Winant, *Racial Formations in the United States*, 3rd ed. (New York: Routledge, 2015), 110.

9. Revisions to the Standards for the Classification of Federal Data on Race and Ethnicity, 62 Fed. Reg. 58782 (October 30, 1997).

10. A race category assigned by the federal government, the term *Black, African American, or Negro* includes individuals who identify as African American, Afro-Caribbean (e.g., Haitian or Jamaican), and sub-Saharan African (e.g., Kenyan or Nigerian). As of 2010, 42 million Blacks lived in the United States, representing 14 percent of the total U.S. population. U.S. Census Bureau, *The Black Population: 2010*, September 2011, http://www.census.gov/prod/cen2010/briefs/c2010br-06.pdf.

11. Considered by the federal U.S. government to be a race group, this category includes people who have origins in any of the original peoples of North, Central, or South America and who "maintain tribal affiliation or community attachment." As of 2010, the Census Bureau reported that 5.2 million American Indians and Alaska Natives lived in the United States, equaling 1.7 percent of the total population. U.S. Census Bureau, *American Indian and Alaskan Native Population: 2010*, January 2012, http://www.census.gov/prod/cen2010/briefs/c2010br-10.pdf.

12. A race category assigned by the federal government, it refers to individuals who have origins in the original peoples of Hawaii, Guam, Samoa, or other Pacific Islands and includes people who are Polynesian, Micronesian, or Melanesian. As of 2010, the Census Bureau estimated that 1.2 million Native Hawaiians and Pacific Islanders lived in the U.S., equaling 0.4 percent of the total population. U.S. Census Bureau, *The Native Hawaiian and Other Pacific Islander Population: 2010*, May 2012, http://www.census.gov/prod/cen2010/briefs/c2010br-12.pdf.

13. A race category assigned by the federal government, it refers to individuals who come from the original peoples of Europe (e.g., Ireland, German, Poland), the Middle East (e.g., Lebanon, Palestine), or North Africa (e.g., Algeria, Egypt, Morocco). According to the Census Bureau, in 2010, 231 million Whites lived in the United States, equaling 75 percent of the total U.S. population. U.S. Census Bureau, *The White Population: 2010*, September 2011, http://www.census.gov/prod/cen2010/briefs/c2010br-05.pdf.

14. The Census Bureau defines Hispanics or Latinos as individuals who trace their heritage or nationality to Cuba, Mexico, Puerto Rico, South or Central America, or other Spanish cultures or origins, regardless of their race. On the 2010 Census forms, people answered two questions on ethnicity and race. The first question asked about Hispanic or Latino origin. Individuals self-identifying as Hispanic or Latino could then choose their

race (from the five racial categories of Asian, Black, American Indian or Alaska Native, Native Hawaiian or Pacific Islander, White, or "Some Other Race"). In 2010, 50.5 million Latinos lived in the United States, equaling 16 percent of the total U.S. population. More than half of the growth in the U.S. total population between 2000 and 2010 was the result of the growth of the Hispanic or Latino population. U.S. Census Bureau, *The Hispanic Population: 2010*, May 2011, http://www.census.gov/prod/cen2010/briefs /c2010br-04.pdf.

15. Susan Koshy, "Historicizing Racial Identity and Minority Status for South Asian Americans," Asian Pacific American Collective History Project, http://www.sscnet.ucla.edu/history/faculty/henryyu/APACHP/teacher /research/koshy.htm.

16. A race category assigned by the federal government, the term *Asian American* includes a number of ethnic groups tracing their origins to East Asia, Southeast Asia, or the Indian subcontinent. It includes ethnic groups such as Burmese, Bangladeshis, Chinese, Hmong, Koreans, and Vietnamese. Between 2000 and 2010, Asian Americans became the fastest-growing race group in the country, with a population of 17.3 million, or 5.6 percent of the total U.S. population. U.S. Census Bureau, *The Asian Population: 2010*, March 2012, http://www.census.gov/prod/cen2010/briefs/c2010br -11.pdf.

17. U.S. Census Bureau, "Race," accessed April 18, 2015, http://www.census .gov/topics/population/race/about.html.

18. Arab American Institute Foundation, "Demographics," accessed January 3, 2015, http://b.3cdn.net/aai/44b17815d8b386bf16_v0m6iv4b5.pdf.

19. Andrea Smith, "Heteropatriarchy and the Three Pillars of White Supremacy: Rethinking Women of Color Organizing," in *Color of Violence: The Incite! Anthology*, ed. Incite! Women of Color Against Violence (Boston: South End Press, 2006), 66–67.

20. Toni Morrison, "On the Backs of Blacks," *Time*, December 2, 1993, http:// collectiveliberation.org/wp-content/uploads/2013/01/Morrison-On-the -Backs-of-Blacks.pdf.

21. Lani Guinier and Gerald Torres, *The Miner's Canary: Enlisting Race, Resisting Power, Transforming Democracy* (Cambridge, MA: Harvard University Press, 2002), 225.

22. United States v. Khobragade, No. 1:14-CR-00176 (S.D.N.Y. March 14, 2014), indictment at 2.

23. U.S. Department of Justice, "Manhattan U.S. Attorney Announces Arrest of Indian Consular Officer for Visa Fraud and False Statements in Connection with Household Employee's Visa Application," news release,

December 12, 2013, http://www.justice.gov/usao/nys/pressreleases/Decem ber13/KhobragadeArrestPR.php?print=1.

24. Max Fisher, "Indians Are Calling Indian American U.S. Attorney 'Uncle Tom' for Prosecuting Khobragade," *Washington Post*, December 19, 2013, http://www.washingtonpost.com/blogs/worldviews/wp/2013/12/19/indian -american-district-attorney-is-being-called-uncle-tom-in-india-for-prosecuting -khobragade/.

25. PJ Crowley, "Devyani Khobragade: Bureaucratic and Diplomatic Neg-ligence," BBC News, December 18, 2013, http://www.bbc.com/news/world -us-canada-25440252.

26. Affan Chowdhury, "Six Reasons Why Indians Are Outraged over U.S. Treatment of Diplomat," *Globe and Mail*, December 18, 2013, http:// www.theglobeandmail.com/news/world/six-reasons-why-indians-are-upset -over-us-treatment-of-diplomat/article16025722/.

27. U.S. Attorney's Office, Southern District of New York, "Statement of Manhattan U.S. Attorney Preet Bharara on U.S. v. Devyani Khobragade," news release, December 18, 2013, http://www.justice.gov/usao/nys/press releases/December13/KhobragadeStatement.php.

28. American Civil Liberties Union, "ACLU Reveals Proof of Racial Tar-geting in Major Meth Investigation," news release, April 5, 2006, https://www .aclu.org/news/aclu-reveals-proof-racial-targeting-major-meth-investigation.

29. Liam Stack, "Indian Guest Workers Awarded $14 Million," *New York Times*, February 18, 2015, http://www.nytimes.com/2015/02/19/us/indian -guest-workers-awarded-14-million.html.

30. South Asian Americans Leading Together and Asian American Feder-ation, *Demographic Snapshot of South Asians in the United States*.

6. Undocumented Youth Rise Up

1. Memorandum from Wesley Lee, Acting Director, Immigration and Customs Enforcement, to Field Office Directors, "Eligibility Criteria for En-rollment into the Intensive Supervision Appearance Program (ISAP) and the Electronic Monitoring Device (EMD) Program," U.S. Immigration and Cus-toms Enforcement, U.S. Department of Homeland Security, May 11, 2005, http://www.ice.gov/doclib/foia/dro_policy_memos/dropolicymemoeligibility fordroisapandemdprograms.pdf.

2. An article from the American Immigration Council notes that the "use of electronic ankle monitors imposes a physical toll, as the devices can make it difficult to walk and often require wearers to station themselves near electrical outlets for hours at a time to allow charging." Ben Winograd, "For Immigrants, Alternatives to Detention Not All They're Cracked Up to Be," American

Immigration Council, Immigration Impact, July 11, 2012, http://immigration impact.com/2012/07/11/for-immigrants-alternatives-to-detention -not-all-theyre-cracked-up-to-be/#sthash.Em48Ymtn.dpuf.

3. Bryan Baker and Nancy Rytina, *Population Estimates: Estimates of the Unauthorized Immigrant Population Residing in the United States: January 2012*, Office of Immigration Statistics, U.S. Department of Homeland Security, March 2013, http://www.dhs.gov/sites/default/files/publications/ois _ill_pe_2012_2.pdf.

4. Pew Research Center, "Unauthorized Immigrants: Who They Are and What the Public Thinks," January 15, 2015, http://www.pewresearch.org /key-data-points/immigration/.

5. Real ID Act of 2005, Pub. L. No. 109-13, § 202, 119 119 Stat. 302 (2005).

6. Affordable Care Act, 42 U.S.C. § 18081.

7. National Employment Law Project, *Broken Laws, Unprotected Workers: Violations of Employment and Labor Laws in America's Cities*, 2009, http:// www.nelp.org/page/-/brokenlaws/BrokenLawsReport2009.pdf.

8. S.B. 1070, 49th Leg., 2nd Gen. Sess. (Arizona 2010).

9. 2013 Legis. Bill Hist. MD H.B. 739.

10. Nick Anderson and Luz Lazo, "Md. Voters Approve 'Dream Act' Law," *Washington Post*, November 7, 2012, http://www.washingtonpost.com/local /md-politics/md-voters-deciding-on-dream-act-law/2012/11/06/d539fe66 -282f-11e2-bab2-eda299503684_story.html.

11. Immigration and Customs Enforcement, "Ice Total Removals," U.S. Department of Homeland Security, accessed December 24, 2014, http://www.ice .gov/doclib/about/offices/cro/pdf/ero-removals1.pdf; Immigration and Customs Enforcement, "FY 2014 ICE Immigration Removals," U.S. Department of Homeland Security, accessed December 24, 2014, http://www.ice.gov/removal -statistics.

12. Immigration Policy Center, "Misplaced Priorities: Most Immigrants Deported by ICE in 2013 Were a Threat to No One," March 28, 2014, http://www.immigrationpolicy.org/just-facts/misplaced-priorities-most -immigrants-deported-ice-2013-were-threat-no-one.

13. Powers of Immigration Officers and Employees, 8 U.S.C. § 1357(g).

14. Immigration Policy Center, "Local Enforcement of Immigration Laws Through the 287(g) Program," April 122, 2010, http://www.immigrationpolicy .org/just-facts/local-enforcement-immigration-laws-through-287g-program.

15. "Valle del Sol v. Whiting et al.," American Civil Liberties Union, May 20, 2014, https://www.aclu.org/cases/valle-del-sol-v-whiting-et-al; "Lowcountry Immigration Coalition, et al. v. Nikki Haley," American Civil Liberties

Union, February 10, 2015, https://www.aclu.org/cases/immigrants-rights/lowcountry-immigration-coalition-et-al-v-nikki-haley; "Buquer, et al. v. City of Indianapolis," American Civil Liberties Union, February 10, 2015, https://www.aclu.org/cases/immigrants-rights/buquer-et-al-v-city-indianapolis; "Crisis in Alabama: Immigration Law Causes Chaos," American Civil Liberties Union, accessed April 27, 2015, https://www.aclu.org/feature/crisis-alabama; "Utah Coalition of La Raza v. Herbert," American Civil Liberties Union, June 18, 2014, https://www.aclu.org/cases/immigrants-rights/utah-coalition-la-raza-v-herbert; "Georgia Latino Alliance for Human Rights, et al. v. Deal," American Civil Liberties Union, March 20, 2015, https://www.aclu.org/cases/georgia-latino-alliance-human-rights-et-al-v-deal.

16. "What the World Is Doing: A Record of Current Events," *Collier's: The National Weekly*, March 26, 1910, 15.

17. Emergency Quota Act of 1921, Pub. L. No. 67-5, 42 42 Stat. 5 (1921); Immigration Act of 1924, Pub. L. No. 68-139, 43 Stat. 153 (1924).

18. Marian L. Smith, "Race, Nationality, and Reality: INS Administration of Racial Provisions in U.S. Immigration and Nationality Law Since 1898, Part 2," *Prologue Magazine* 34, no. 2 (Summer 2002), http://www.archives.gov/publications/prologue/2002/summer/immigration-law-2.html.

19. United States v. Bhagat Singh Thind, 261 U.S. 204 (1923).

20. "About Dr. Thind: His Life Work," accessed December 24, 2014, http://www.bhagatsinghthind.com/about_thind.php; "About Dr. Thind: Life at Hindoo Alley (Astoria, Oregon)," accessed December 24, 2014, http://www.bhagatsinghthind.com/hindooalley.php.

21. *United States v. Bhagat Singh Thind*.

22. "About Dr. Thind: His Life Work."

23. Immigration and Nationality Act of 1965, Pub. L. No. 89-236, 79 Stat. 911 (1965).

24. Ellen D. Wu, *The Color of Success: Asian Americans and the Origins of the Model Minority* (Princeton, NJ: Princeton University Press, 2013).

25. Illegal Immigrant Reform and Responsibility Act of 1996, Pub. L. No. 104-208, 110 Stat. 3009 (1996).

26. White House, "Remarks by the President on Immigration," news release, June 15, 2012, http://www.whitehouse.gov/the-press-office/2012/06/15/remarks-president-immigration.

27. Memorandum from Janet Napolitano, Secretary, U.S. Department of Homeland Security, to David V. Aguilar, Acting Commissioner, U.S. Customs and Border Protection; Alejandro Mayorkas, Director, U.S. Citizenship and Immigration Services; and John Morton, Director, U.S. Immigration and Customs Enforcement, et al., "Exercising Prosecutorial Discretion with Respect

to Individuals Who Came to the United States as Children," June 15, 2012, http://www.dhs.gov/xlibrary/assets/s1-exercising-prosecutorial-discretion -individuals-who-came-to-us-as-children.pdf.

28. Pew Research Center "The Rise of Asian Americans," June 19, 2012, http://www.pewsocialtrends.org/2012/06/19/the-rise-of-asian -americans/.

29. U.S. Department of State, "Visa Bulletin for November 2012," October 9, 2012, http://travel.state.gov/content/visas/english/law-and-policy /bulletin/2013/visa-bulletin-for-november-2012.html; National Council of Asian Pacific Americans, "Immigration Factsheet," accessed April 16, 2015, http://ncapaonline.org/wp-content/uploads/2014/09/NCAPA-Immigration -Fact-Sheet.pdf.

30. Marcos Breton, "Immigrant Confronted Obama from the Heart," *Sacramento Bee*, December 1, 2013, http://www.sacbee.com/news/local/news -columns-blogs/marcos-breton/article2584494.html.

31. U.S. Department of Homeland Security, "Fixing Our Broken Immigration System Through Executive Action — Key Facts," accessed December 24, 2014, http://www.dhs.gov/immigration-action.

32. White House, "Fact Sheet: Immigration Accountability Executive Action," November 20, 2014, https://www.whitehouse.gov/the-press-office/2014/11/20 /fact-sheet-immigration-accountability-executive-action.

33. Molly Hennessy-Fiske and Cindy Carcamo, "Obama Immigration Overhaul and 'Dreamers' Handed Another Legal Setback," *Los Angeles Times*, May 23, 2015, http://www.latimes.com/nation/la-na-obama-immigration -executive-action-20150526-story.html.

7. Ferguson Is Everywhere

1. Ryan Gabrielson, Ryann Grochowski Jones, and Eric Sagara, "Deadly Force, in Black and White," ProPublica, October 10, 2014, http://www.pro publica.org/article/deadly-force-in-black-and-white.

2. Brad Heath, "Racial Gap in U.S. Arrest Rates: 'Staggering Disparity,' " *USA Today*, November 19, 2014, http://www.usatoday.com/story/news /nation/2014/11/18/ferguson-black-arrest-rates/19043207/.

3. Alicia Garza, "A Herstory of the #BlackLivesMatter Movement," *Feminist Wire*, October 7, 2014, http://thefeministwire.com/2014/10/blacklives matter-2/.

4. Zak Cheney-Rice, "The Police Are Killing One Group at a Staggering Rate, and Nobody Is Talking About It," *Mic*, February 5, 2015, http://mic .com/articles/109894/the-police-are-killing-one-group-at-a-staggering-rate -and-nobody-is-talking-about-it.

5. Center for Constitutional Rights, "NYPD's Stop and Frisk Practice: Unfair and Unjust," accessed January 2, 2015, http://ccrjustice.org/racial -disparity-nypd-stops-and-frisks.

6. Amanda Peterson Beadle, "Counties Limit ICE Detainers as DHS Secretary Says He's Taking a 'Fresh Look,' " American Immigration Council, Immigration Impact, May 16, 2014, http://immigrationimpact.com/2014/05/16 /counties-limit-ice-detainers-as-dhs-secretary-says-hes-taking-a-fresh-look/.

7. National Immigration Law Center, "Civil Rights Leaders, Plaintiffs, and Litigators Decry Arizona's Racial Profiling Law," news release, April 23, 2011, http://nilc.org/nr042312.html.

8. Challen Stephens, "Alabama Police Fire, Arrest the Officer Who Badly Injured Indian Grandfather During Sidewalk Stop," AL.com, February 12, 2015, http://www.al.com/news/index.ssf/2015/02/madison_police_fire_and _arrest.html.

9. U.S. Department of Justice, "Former Madison Police Officer Indicted on Use of Unreasonable Force Against a Man He Was Questioning," news release, March 27, 2015, http://www.justice.gov/opa/pr/former-madison-police -officer-indicted-use-unreasonable-force-against-man-he-was-questioning.

10. Lee Fang, "Why Was an FBI Joint Terrorism Task Force Tracking a Black Lives Matter Protest?," The Intercept, March 12, 2015, https:// firstlook.org/theintercept/2015/03/12/fbi-appeared-use-informant-track -black-lives-matter-protest/.

11. Queer South Asian National Network, "It Starts at Home: Confronting Anti-Blackness in South Asian Communities," December 19, 2014, https:// queersouthasian.wordpress.com/?hc_location=ufi.

12. Sections of the narrative on Ferguson immigrant businesses owners were previously published in Colorlines: Deepa Iyer, "Dispatch from Ferguson: Convenience Store Owners Talk Race," Colorlines, October 14, 2014, http://www.colorlines.com/articles/dispatch-ferguson-convenience-store -owners-talk-race.

8. We Too Sing America

1. U.S. Census Bureau, "U.S. Census Bureau Projections Show a Slower Growing, Older, More Diverse Nation a Half Century from Now," news release, December 12, 2012, https://www.census.gov/newsroom/releases/archives /population/cb12-243.html.

2. Ibid.

3. Anna Brown, "U.S. Hispanic and Asian Populations Growing, but for Different Reasons," Pew Research Center, June 26, 2014, http://www.pew

research.org/fact-tank/2014/06/26/u-s-hispanic-and-asian-populations-growing-but-for-different-reasons/.

4. Jens Manuel Krogstad and Richard Fry, "Dept. of Ed. Projects Public Schools Will Be 'Majority-Minority' This Fall," Pew Research Center, August 18, 2014, http://www.pewresearch.org/fact-tank/2014/08/18/u-s-public-schools-expected-to-be-majority-minority-starting-this-fall/; U.S. Department of Education, National Center for Education Statistics, *Projections of Education Statistics to 2022*, February 2014, http://nces.ed.gov/pubs2014/2014051.pdf.

5. Jill H. Wilson and Nicole Prchal Svajlenka, "Immigrants Continue to Disperse, with Fastest Growth in the Suburbs," Brookings Institute, October 29, 2014, http://www.brookings.edu/research/papers/2014/10/29-immigrants-disperse-suburbs-wilson-svajlenka.

6. Elizabeth Grieco et al., "The Size, Place of Birth, and Geographic Distribution of the Foreign-Born Population in the United States: 1960 to 2010," Population Division Working Paper No. 96, U.S. Census Bureau, October 2012, http://www.census.gov/population/foreign/files/WorkingPaper 96.pdf.

7. Daniel C. Martin and James E. Yankay, "Annual Flow Report: Refugees and Asylees 2013," August 2014, Office of Immigration Statistics, U.S. Department of Homeland Security, http://www.dhs.gov/sites/default/files/publications/ois_rfa_fr_2013.pdf.

8. Maureen A. Craig and Jennifer A. Richeson, "On the Precipice of a 'Majority-Minority' America: Perceived Status Threat from the Racial Demographic Shift Affects White Americans' Political Ideology," April 3, 2014, *Psychological Science*, http://groups.psych.northwestern.edu/spcl/documents/Craig%20&%20Richeson%202014%20PS.pdf.

9. Rakesh Kochhar and Richard Fry, "Wealth Inequality Has Widened Along Racial, Ethnic Lines Since End of Great Recession," Pew Research Center, December 12, 2014, http://www.pewresearch.org/fact-tank/2014/12/12/racial-wealth-gaps-great-recession/.

10. National Education Policy Center, "School Discipline: What the Research Tells Us: Myths and Facts," accessed January 3, 2015, http://www.dignityinschools.org/sites/default/files/School%20Discipline%20Myths%20and%20Facts.pdf.

11. Local and Regional Government Alliance on Race & Equity website, accessed April 16, 2015, http://racialequityalliance.org/.

12. Michele Richinick, "DA Seeks Death Penalty in Chapel Hill Shooting of Muslim Students," MSNBC.com, March 2, 2015, http://www.msnbc.com/msnbc/death-penalty-chapel-hill-shooting-muslim-students.

13. Allan Turner, "Interfaith Ministries President Solicits Donations to Rebuild Burned Islamic Facility," *Houston Chronicle*, March 19, 2015, http://www.houstonchronicle.com/news/houston-texas/houston/article/Interfaith-Ministries-president-solicits-6145851.php.

14. "FBI Probing Offensive Graffiti at Islamic School in Rhode Island," CBS News, February 17, 2015, http://www.cbsnews.com/news/fbi-investigates-offensive-graffiti-at-islamic-school/.

15. Council on American-Islamic Relations, "Faith Leaders to Seek Federal Hate Crime Investigation of Vandalism Targeting School, Hindu Temple," news release, February 25, 2015, http://www.cair.com/press-center/press-releases/12874-faith-leaders-to-seek-hate-crime-investigation-of-vandalism-at-school-hindu-temple.html.

16. Sarah Eisenmenger and Natalia Martinez, "Attorney Identifies Driver Shot, Killed on I-71," Wave3 News, March 4, 2015, http://www.wave3.com/story/28205015/attorney-identifies-driver-shot-killed-on-i-71.

17. Dean Obeidallah, "Another Muslim Is Killed in America. Anyone Care?," *Daily Beast*, March 11, 2015, http://www.thedailybeast.com/articles/2015/03/11/another-muslim-is-killed-in-america-anyone-care.html.

Index

Celebrating 25 Years of Independent Publishing

Thank you for reading this book published by The New Press. The New Press is a nonprofit, public interest publisher celebrating its twenty-fifth anniversary in 2017. New Press books and authors play a crucial role in sparking conversations about the key political and social issues of our day.

We hope you enjoyed this book and that you will stay in touch with The New Press. Here are a few ways to stay up to date with our books, events, and the issues we cover:

- Sign up at www.thenewpress.com/subscribe to receive updates on New Press authors and issues and to be notified about local events
- Like us on Facebook: www.facebook.com/newpressbooks
- Follow us on Twitter: www.twitter.com/thenewpress
- Please consider buying New Press books for yourself; for friends and family; or to donate to schools, libraries, community centers, prison libraries, and other organizations involved with the issues our authors write about.

The New Press is a 501(c)(3) nonprofit organization. You can also support our work with a tax-deductible gift by visiting www.thenew press.com/donate.

CPSIA information can be obtained
at www.ICGtesting.com
Printed in the USA
LVOW03s2343080318
569211LV00001B/1/P